MW01639914

PLAZA
NEW YORK

INVESTING IN RESIDENTIAL REAL ESTATE

PAUL J. LYONS

INVESTING IN RESIDENTIAL REAL ESTATE

A GUIDE TO INCREASING YOUR INCOME & PROFIT

RESTON PUBLISHING COMPANY, INC.
A Prentice-Hall Company
Reston, Virginia

Library of Congress Cataloging in Publication Data

Lyons, Paul J
Investing in residential real estate.

Includes index.
1. Real estate investment. 2. Rental housing.
I. Title.
HD1382.5.L96 332.63'243 80-27390
ISBN 0-8359-3304-0

Editorial/production supervision and interior design by Norma M. Karlin
Manufacturing buyer: Ron Chapman

10 9 8 7 6 5 4 3 2 1

PRINTED IN THE UNITED STATES OF AMERICA

To
Michael, Samantha, Doc,
& Ben

CONTENTS

INTRODUCTION

YOUR INVESTMENT IN THIS BOOK

By buying this book, you commit a certain amount of money—the price of the book. If you actually read it in whole or in part—which is the only clear way to earn any return on your investment—you commit some of your time as well as money. Yet books abound, some of them quite well done, on how to cash in fast on real estate, using the leverage of "OPM" (other people's money). Creative financing, tax angles, and pyramiding techniques are also standard fare. This book covers those topics too, and it propounds no new theories.

So why read it if you've read another?

The answer is simple: This book provides the student or professional in real estate, as well as the investor, with practical tools to make sound and profitable investment decisions. Several developments in recent years require us to weigh investment assumptions that were often taken for granted in the past. Inflation, transitional energy usage patterns, erratic money markets, shifting national roles in the international economy, and competing new theories for interpreting the trends all figure in each investment. This book takes such developments into account.

For example, one important, yet often overlooked development is the effect of handheld calculators and computers. With them, you can easily quantify investment alternatives. Although such methods seem complicated to newcomers, they actually simplify analysis and allow overall reviews in a fraction of the time needed for traditional pencil work and tables. Most important, they give a big competitive advantage to anyone who has learned them. This book emphasizes those methods, providing all the basic analytical tools needed by a reader who is new to the field or who is limited in math skills.

Beyond this sort of immediately useful and practical material, other sections of the book enable readers to weigh the effects of larger events on their investment decisions. Keeping one eye on these larger events is very important these days, because real estate investment today takes place amid greater economic uncertainty than in the past. During the New Deal era, FHA and other federal government financing programs revitalized a depressed housing market and made home ownership available to expanded numbers of people. In the decades following World War II several trends in the US economy helped real estate to become a popular vehicle for investors, small and large. The demand that had pent up during the war broke loose afterwards in a housing boom, fueled in large part by GIs returning to start families, spurred on by VA loan rights. The subsequent baby boom of the 1950s helped create the need for more and larger homes into which people could "move up." Therefore, because housing was not built in pace with this expanding demand, the scarcity of homes assured higher and higher prices in a growing economy, even before high inflation rates became one of its central features.

Besides a favorable supply-and-demand situation in the past, public policy encouraged home ownership by all, and tax incentives consistently favored home ownership over most other forms of investment. For instance, owner-occupants of income property could take deductions for their interest payments on large mortgage loans. Upon resale, the capital gains from an appreciated market value—which many consider more certain than the continued value of money—is taxed at a lower rate than "ordinary" income, if at all. Thus their projected future earnings are sheltered against heavy taxation. In addition, currently taxable income can be reduced substantially through hefty deductions for depreciation each year if an investor rents the property to someone else. As owners increase their tax brackets, these annual tax benefits become worth more and more.

The investment decision today—where should I put my money?—is more complicated than ever. The interrelated forces of inflation, high energy costs, and interest rates all have dramatic impacts on the profitability of all investments. As long as savings accounts' interest rates were higher than the inflation rate, your deposits produced real growth in your assets. At other times, the interest on money market funds, certificates of deposit, or other vehicles may be the only way to stay ahead of inflation. Other investors may not be interested in earnings that are taxable as ordinary income, such as dividend income from stocks. They might be more interested in tax-free income from municipal bonds, with their reduced yields. The potential yield from such investments can be further increased by not taking current income right away, thus putting off tax payments as well, and by speculating on future capital gains. Yet that approach introduces additional risks and/or costs, including those related to liquidity.

In the 1980s, however, real estate still holds many advantages over other investments, and it helps to resolve many problems that investors associate with an uncertain economy. You can receive returns (or realize losses) on any investment in three ways:

1. as a source of income,
2. as a capital gain, and
3. as a tax benefit.

If you can purchase an investment with borrowed money, you can enhance those returns by leverage. On each point, income-producing real estate is expected to compare favorably, in the future, with such investments as common stocks, bonds, commodities, and collectibles.

What kind of future makes real estate investment so attractive? Even though this book is not a work on futurology and the projections are therefore only general in nature, a few simple assumptions can tell us much about what's going to happen. For one thing, higher inflation rates will be a feature of the US economy throughout the 1980s, in spite of deflationary forces and government actions. The world's supplies of crude oil will continue to go down, and extraction costs for the remainder will continue to go up. These two trends will force us to look for new energy sources, compel real economic growth to decline, and reduce our standards of living during the transitional period. In the long term, interest rates must remain higher than inflation rates—barring an economic depression on a scale possibly great enough to trigger a terminal world war—to provide any incentive for lending money. All these forces are likely to make housing construction costs increase at a greater rate than that of general inflation, as measured by the Consumer Price Index.

For investors in residential income property—the main focus of this book—the implications of these assumptions reach far. In the world of real estate, the effect of these economic pressures is quite predictable: As they drive housing prices up, fewer and fewer would-be buyers are able to make a purchase; as a result, the demand for rental units increases without an immediate increase in supply. So if the first edition of this book does indeed circulate in a period of inflationary pressures and of general belt-tightening, then that sort of economic uncertainty alone will cause the construction of rental property to lag behind demand. The resulting scarcity in rental housing would then clearly favor increases in the market values of existing units.

The effect of such pressures on income from other investment vehicles, such as stock dividends, is considerably harder to predict. In fact, it is not at all clear, or even likely, that these forces will cause increases in the market value of stocks or bonds.

Yet what about other investment products and services, such as commodities? Do they entail any tax benefits and incentives? Corn, copper, wheat futures, and even gold generate no current income. Ordinarily, the only tax attraction to commodities is that the returns—based entirely on buying and selling with limited leverage—are taxed as capital gains rather than as ordinary income. They offer no depreciation deductions.

Do collections of art, antiques, coins, stamps, or other collectibles give you the same benefits as real estate? Collectibles suffer not only from the same limitations as commodities, but their "liquidity risk" is also higher; that is, they're harder to sell quickly. Also, it usually takes time for a Queen Anne table, a Florence Nightingale commemorative stamp, a Rockwell print, or a family heirloom to appreciate enough to make a sale profitable. In the meantime, unless placed for viewing in a museum, they produce neither income nor a tax shelter. They can only be worn on the person, looked at by few, eaten or stared at, cleaned and shined, or just saved for the rainy day that you hope never comes.

Even the long-term effects of our "assumed" economic conditions will not necessarily favor commodities and collectibles. If supply and demand still influence prices and values, despite economic manipulation by government and by other special interests, some commodities will continue to perform better than others on the basis of short-term shortages, shifting demand, and speculative buy/hold/sell patterns. Collectibles may also gain and lose, probably in temporary ups and downs, in step with fickle investor *expectations* concerning inflation and with the collecting activity of other investors. As in the past, but even more so, experts working for their own accounts will do better than the amateurs in commodity and collectible markets.

Is residential income property a viable option for the small investor in the 1980s and beyond? If the decade proceeds as it began, several generalizations will probably hold true:

- Large detached houses in the higher price ranges will cease to appreciate in market value as rapidly as in the past. The reasons are that smaller families will bring about reduced demand and that increased interest rates and energy costs will widen the gap between such houses and potential buyers. Sluggish recoveries from cyclical downturns in that market will discourage the former common practice of buying your residence at the highest price for which financing can be secured.

- Townhouses and condominium units will become increasingly popular among both owner-occupants and investors. Duplexes and quadraplexes will become a greater part of the national housing inventory, as associated zoning patterns change to accommodate the need for more economical use of available land. Demand for such housing will be driven up continuously, both by buyers who are no longer able to afford detached houses and by new people who are coming into the market from the post-World War II baby boom population. Yet a scarcity of appropriate building sites, the need for large capital expenditures on larger projects, and the bearishness of a troubled housing construction industry will keep supply lagging. The result will be even higher price inflation/appreciation than in the past for this type of housing.
- Passive solar features will be incorporated into all types of building construction. Double-shell construction, along with other rediscoveries and innovations that eliminate expensive central heating and cooling systems and ductwork, will make such features cost competitive with the "conventional" building techniques of almost one hundred years of cheap fossil fuel energy. New building materials and methods will be introduced to minimize dependence on products of the petrochemical industry. Weight and distance will become key factors, because of transportation costs. Use of modular building techniques will expand, as will emphasis on use of local building materials (such as earth, stone, concrete, steel) for the heavier portions of a building.
- Great pressures will exist for rents to increase at rates greater than general inflation. Scarcity of units and escalated operating costs, even with much separate metering of energy usage, will be the driving forces. Yet rent controls will have a braking effect in many areas. Shared housing and roommating will become more common, as the cost of privacy becomes prohibitive for those on the lower rungs of the economic ladder. Apartment-style rooming houses—previously associated mainly with student housing and homes for the aged—may appear more generally, with passive solar and other modern features.
- Pre-inflation mortgage financing tools—forged in the 1930s to combat depression and refined through the 1970s—will be largely replaced. Lenders and their institutions will become even more reluctant to make loans at competitive interest rates with long, fixed payback periods. Loans in the new era will include variable principal and interest payments, interest rates, and/or amortization periods (number of fixed payments). Government-sponsored incentive and guarantee programs—inaugurated in a spirit of fiscal conservatism—may hasten that development. Real estate investment trusts will re-

emerge as an important vehicle for small investor activity in the housing market, along with old and new investment syndication forms.

- Tax laws should remain favorable for small investor activity in the residential real estate market. Scarcity of rental housing will require tax incentives to provide it. Since the greatest lags in residential construction to meet demand will come in the multi-unit projects needing large amounts of capital, new incentives will be needed to direct private investor funds to them. Capital-raising fees in creating syndications, for example, may be made deductible or depreciable. Tax exemption of interest income to lenders, as with industrial revenue bonds used in small business expansions, could similarly promote such residential construction projects. Tax incentives of various types would also be most likely to thrive if the need to encourage employment in the housing industry were added to scarcity of its products.

These generalizations, whether or not correct in the final analysis, highlight the underlying considerations in the writing of this book. Although the real estate investor observes optimistically that, "Everyone has to live somewhere," you have to ask some realistic questions. Specifically:

- how many people will pay
- how much rent
- to cover which portion of an investor's carrying costs
- on a property that is likely to yield what after-tax return upon disposition,
- netting how many dollars,
- which are worth how much at the time after the inflation "bite"?

Each reader has to make his or her own projection, by some formal measuring device or just instinct, of the economic climate that will affect a potential investment. This book gives you the practical tools that enable you to evaluate alternatives in that climate and to make sound and profitable decisions.

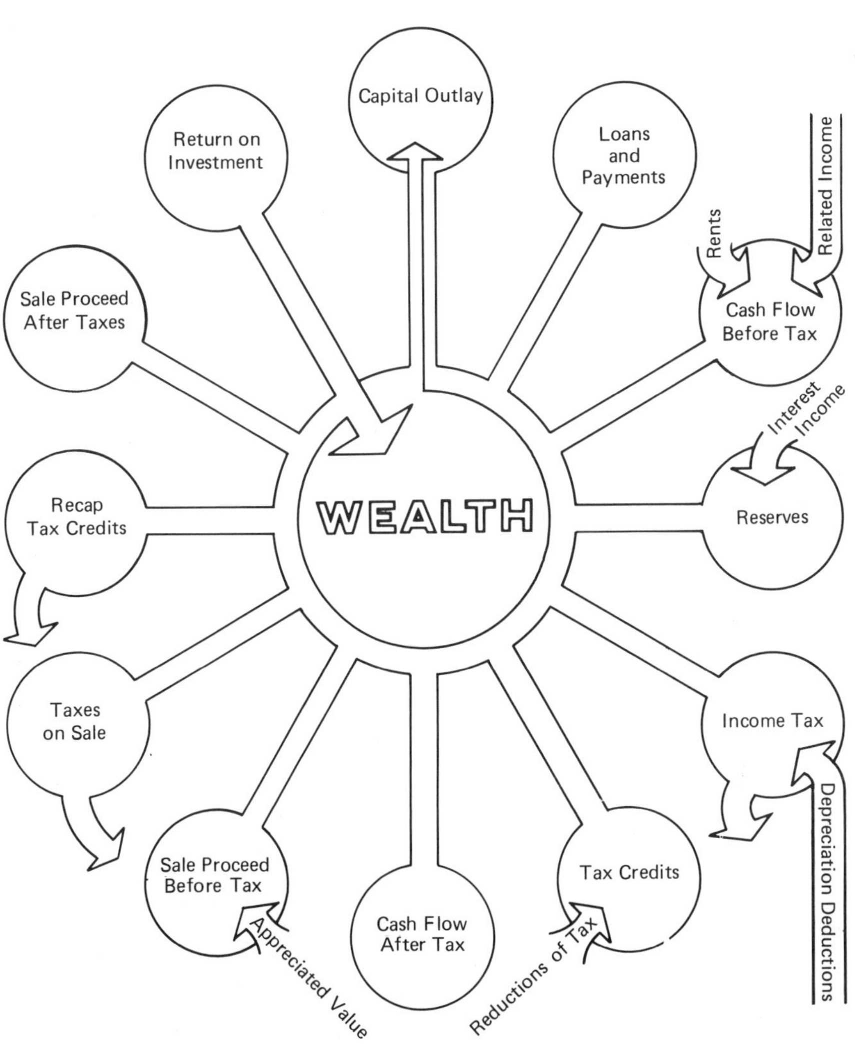
WEALTH
Capital Outlay
Return on Investment
Loans and Payments
Sale Proceed After Taxes
Cash Flow Before Tax
Rents
Related Income
Interest Income
Reserves
Recap Tax Credits
Taxes on Sale
Income Tax
Depreciation Deductions
Sale Proceed Before Tax
Appreciated Value
Cash Flow After Tax
Tax Credits
Reductions of Tax

1

OPPORTUNITIES FOR THE SMALL INVESTOR

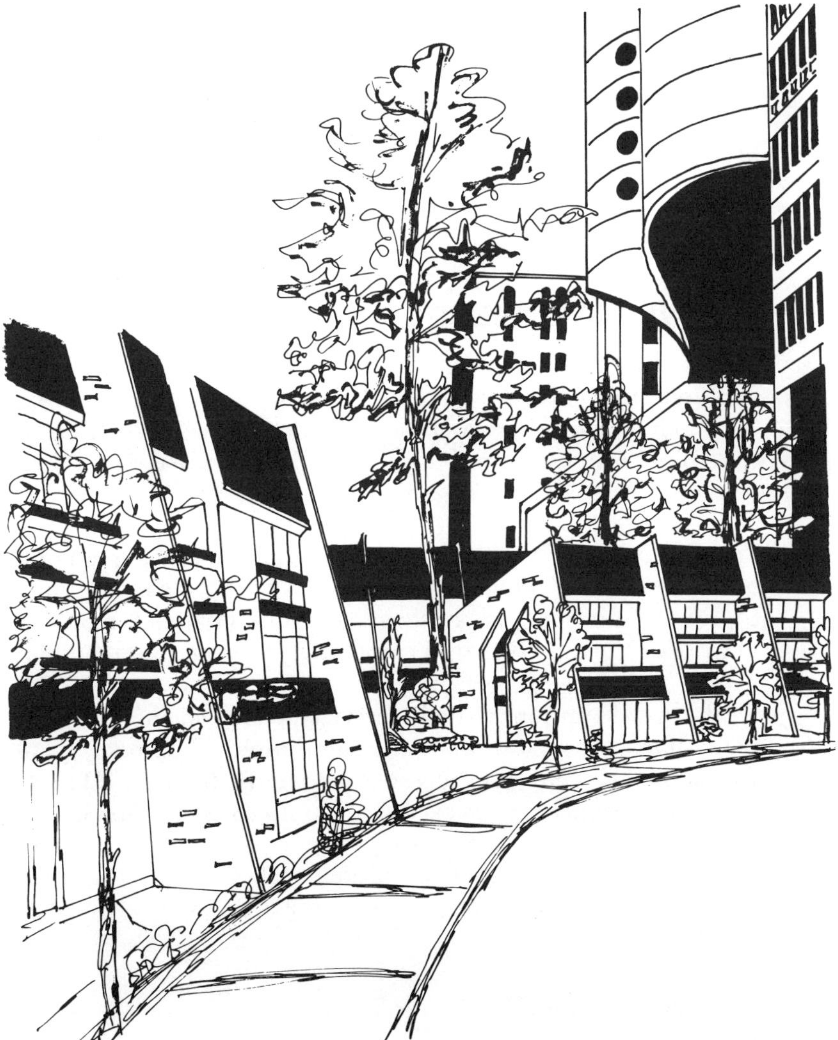

SMALL INVESTOR NEEDS

Who are "small investors" in residential real estate? No definition other than a relatively arbitrary one can be made. Since, however, a definition is merely a resolution to use a word in a certain way, we will define a "small investor" as follows:

> A person or a group of persons (a) who acquires the legal rights to the equity and other benefits of one or more dwelling units, (b) whose purpose is at least partially financial gain, and (c) whose total holdings aren't more than one apartment building.

Within that definition, virtually every type of residential real estate investment, short of large-scale planned community development, can and does take place. The definition includes the family that buys a home as their principal residence, but it excludes investment syndicates or other entities in which other investment groups participate in whole or in part.

What do small investors seek in real estate? They seek pretty much the same benefits that the large investor does, which is cash flow from:

- income,
- market appreciation,

- value gain, and
- combinations of these three elements.

BASIC INVESTMENT DYNAMICS

Investors use the same basic methods to compare real estate investments with each other as they do to compare other investments with each other—or with real estate. They make capital outlays, which generate positive and/or negative cash flows during the holding period through income, operating expenses, and/or tax effects. At the end of that period, they receive a positive or negative net proceed after disposition costs and taxes. On the basis of all those projected cash flows, they compute an internal rate of return (IRR) or some such variation by which they can compare an investments's overall performance with that of others.

Example A: Cash

You can analyze even *cash* with these methods. Assume that you sew $5,000 into a mattress for 5 years during a period in which general inflation runs a constant 10 percent per year, and then you remove the $5,000 at the end of the period. Your initial capital outlay in this "investment" is $5,000. It produces no positive or negative cash flows from income or from operating expenses during the holding period. At the end of the period the disposition proceed is $5,000, reduced by inflation at 10 percent per year. The rate of return is shown in Figure 1-1.

With no income, market appreciation, or value gain—and with theoretically *no risk* other than that inflation might be higher than anticipated—this sort of treatment of your funds cannot be considered an investment in any dynamic sense of the word. The only investment criterion it meets is safety of the capital investment.

Initial cash flow – $5,000	Year				
	1	2	3	4	5
Income	0	0	0	0	0
Disposition proceed	4,500	4,050	3,645	3,281	2,952
IRR[1]	–10.0%	–10.0%	–10.0%	–10.0%	–10.0%

[1] Internal rate of return.

Figure 1-1. Example A—Cash.

Example B: Income Investments

Some investments—such as savings accounts, various kinds of corporate and government bonds, and Treasury bills—are held simply because they produce a fixed income stream. The amount of income generally depends on the degree of risk. Yet, since the backer of these securities (which is often the federal government) guarantees the income, the risk is limited to the backer's ability to meet its obligations. In the case of municipal bonds, for example, the rate of income return (or the "yield") tends to be less than that from bonds of similar risk, because municipals' tax-exempt status produces additional income. Income-producing securities in general are also highly liquid—almost instantly convertible into cash. For those securities whose liquidity is limited by a time requirement, such as certificates of deposit and other time deposits, the cost of early withdrawal or liquidation is merely a reduction in yield.

With the same 10 percent inflation rate as in example A, let's assume a corporate bond has a face value of $5,000 and an annual yield of 11 percent. It is redeemed for its face value of $5,000 at the end of a 5-year period, after earning, in effect, a slightly negative return per year because of the 10 percent inflation rate, and because the passage of time itself reduces the value of money received. For purposes of simplification, no penalty is added here for early redemption.

Many investors use these securities as a low-risk way of providing a fixed income while partially offsetting the effects of inflation. Let's assume, for example, that a corporate bond has a face value of $5,000 and an annual yield of 11 percent. Your capital outlay is $5,000. Over, say, a 5-year period, that inflation cuts into both the bond's income stream and its redemption value. If inflation averages 10 percent a year (as it did in example A), then the bond earns, in effect, only 1 percent a year (11 percent annual yield minus 10 percent inflation rate). In dollar figures, that 1 percent comes out to $50 a year ($550–$500). Inflation also undercuts the value of the bond—your capital outlay. If the buying power of that $5,000 decreases by 10 percent every year, then after 5 years its *true* redemption value is only $2,952—not $5,000. (See Figure 1–2.)

Initial cash flow – $5,000	Year				
	1	2	3	4	5
Income	495	446	401	361	325
Redemption value[1]	4,500	4,050	3,645	3,281	2,953
IRR	–0.1%	–0.09%	–0.1%	–0.09%	–0.09%

[1]Reduced by inflation at 10% per year.

Figure 1–2. Example B—Corporate Bond.

Initial cash flow – $5,000	Year				
	1	2	3	4	5
Income	0	0	0	0	0
Value of proceed	5,500	6,050	6,655	7,321	8,053
IRR	10.0%	10.0%	10.0%	10.0%	10.0%

Figure 1-3. Example C—Rare Coin Collection.

Example C: Appreciation Investments

There is another way to hedge against inflation, while speculating on the possibility of higher gains through increased scarcity and price inflation. You could put money into an investment that earns no income during the holding period, but that promises to gain in value through appreciation alone, with no improvement made on them during the holding period. Raw land held without development, gold, precious gems, antiques, fine carpets, works of art, stamps, and rare coins are among the investments of this type. Since they carry no guaranteed return, their risk is higher. Liquidity is also less certain. Accordingly, investors expect a greater projected return than for cash or guaranteed yield investments.

Let's assume that you come across a collection of rare coins available for purchase at $5,000. Your study of the market leads to the conclusion that the collection will appreciate at a rate of 20 percent per year. The same 10-percent inflation rate reduces the effective value increase to 10 percent per year. Figure 1–3 displays the analytical data.

In this example, you manage to earn a return significantly greater than needed to compensate for the effects of inflation, but the cost is a greater risk than that incurred through an investment in bonds. Further, the investment promises to generate no income, during the holding period. If your circumstances are such that you need and desire current income, security of principal and income, and/or an overall return on your investment, you must consider still other types of investment.

Example D: Value Gain Investments

Another possibility is to invest for *value gain* through improvements made by the investor, as distinct from "passive" investment for simple price inflation or appreciation. In this category of investment we find such things as:

1. raw land developed for profit;
2. an apartment building or other business (such as a restaurant, motel, an older office building, or small shopping center) developed from scratch or remodeled and reorganized in the hope of doing better than the previous (or present) owner, and reselling at a profit;
3. a "do-it-yourself special" (or a whole stairwell or street full of them), bought cheap after the last tenant (or owner) trashed it, spruced up (or "restored") with a carefully designed budget, and resold for early turnover and capital gain;
4. a portfolio of common stocks carefully selected for quality of management and substantive growth potential, with an eye to profitable resale with minimum dependence on current market conditions.

For example, you are considering the purchase of an older townhouse in an area in which comparable structures in good condition have been bringing $70,000 to $75,000 in recent months. Since it is in an area of the city undergoing urban renewal, the risk of loss is considered minimal. The damaged and dirty doors and walls, the worn floors and wall-to-wall carpeting, and the other cosmetic shortcomings require about $4,000 to make the property attractive for the resale market. It can be bought for $55,000 under financing arrangements permitting a down payment of $4,000 and closing costs of $1,000 (for a capital outlay of $5,000). The monthly interest-only payments are 1 percent ($500) on loans totaling $50,000.

You allow 2 months for the renovation to take place, during which time the house is not rented. During the same period $2,000 is spent each month on the renovation work. Taxes and utilities run $100 per month. You allow 3 months for the property to sell, during which time it easily rents for $600 a month on a short-term basis with furniture leased at $100 per month.

At the end of the 5 months the townhouse sells for $80,000. Loan payoffs are $55,000, and sale costs and commission amount to $5,000. The net proceed is $20,000. Figure 1–4 shows how this investment for value gain would look.

You have projected a relatively high return of over 21 percent over 5 months, which would work out to an almost tenfold increase annually of capital invested, if the process were to be carried on consistently from one year to the next. However, you earn the high return at the cost of increased risk over that incurred in the other types of investments. More detailed planning is involved. More people have to be relied on directly. More things can go wrong. So the higher return is necessary to attract investors.

Initial cash flow − $5,000	Month				
	1	2	3	4	5
Income	−2,100	−2,100	400	400	400
Disposition proceed	—	—	—	—	20,000
IRR	—	—	—	—	21.36%[1]

[1] **Monthly** rate of return, weighing "time value of money." Another approach would be to divide the total of positive cash flows ($21,200) by the total of negative cash flows ($9,200) to arrive at an overall rate of return of 230%.

Figure 1-4. Example D—House Renovation and Resale.

Example E: Balanced Return Investment

Besides making investments for income, appreciation, or value gain only, the small or large investor can invest for any combination of these returns—for what is called a "balanced return." For example, you are considering the purchase of a stairwell of 6 condominium units at the beginning of a larger conversion. The building is 7 years old. The project is selling well at $35,000 per unit, which includes a new paint job. The buyer is given a decorator allowance averaging $1,200 for carpeting, kitchen and bathroom floors and countertops, and several other cosmetic touches; or the buyer can elect to take it off the sale price. Investor financing has been lined up at half a percentage point below the going rate.

You reach an informal meeting of the minds with the developer that your offer of $32,000 for each of the 6 units will be accepted; that offer includes selected renovations averaging $600 per unit value. You lay out another $400 per unit, or $2,400, during the first year. Three of the units will be rented unfurnished at $350 per month. Three will be rented fully furnished at $500 per month, provision for which will add $3,000 per unit, or $9,000, to the initial investment outlay. Gross income will increase at 10 percent per year. The package of 6 units is to be financed with loans totaling $153,600 (80 percent of the $192,000 sale price). The down payment (20 percent) will be $38,400. Settlement costs are $2,000. With an interest rate of 11 percent per year on a 25-year loan, your monthly principal and interest payments will be $1,505, or $18,065 per year. The projected vacancy rate is 8.33 percent (one month per year). Operating expenses are $2,000 per unit and they will increase at 7 percent per year, based on comparable condominium fee and property tax performance.

The price will appreciate because you bought at a per-unit price over 9 percent below the current market value and because scarcity and inflation are projected. You also derive value gain from scheduled improvements, decorating, and furnishing, as well as from renting the units up and developing a record of income, both of which reduce risk for a potential buyer. The investor projects a market value increase at 20 percent per year. Real estate commissions and other disposition costs will be 7 percent of the market value.

Figure 1–5 demonstrates how that investment would look on a before-tax basis.

These figures would change somewhat for most people if computed on an after-tax basis, as is customary in real estate investment analysis. For instance, interest and depreciation deductions during the holding period are more favorable to investors in the higher brackets, but depreciation recapture and capital gain taxes upon sale cost those same investors more than those in lower brackets. In any event, the investment for income, appreciation, and value gain shows an attractive return. Because there is more risk, planning, and active involvement in the investment, its return is higher than the others except for the renovation.

In these examples, you have examined the dynamics involved in investment choices: the "noninvestment" in cash, the "safe" investment for income only, the "speculation" investment for appreciation only, the "development" investment for value gain only, and what we can call a

Initial cash flow – $49,400[1]	Year				
	1	2	3	4	5
Gross income	30,600	33,660	37,026	40,729	44,801
– Vacancies	2,549	2,804	3,084	3,393	3,732
– Operating expenses	2,000	2,140	2,290	2,450	2,622
– Improvements	2,400	0	0	0	0
– Loan payments	18,065	18,065	18,065	18,065	18,065
= Net cash flow[1]	5,586	10,651	13,587	16,821	20,382
Market value	230,400	276,480	331,776	398,131	477,757
– Loan balance(s)	152,370	150,497	149,466	147,757	145,851
– Disposition costs	16,128	19,354	23,224	27,869	33,443
= Before-tax disposition proceed[1]	61,902	106,129	159,086	222,505	298,463
IRR	36.62%	59.51%	60.48%	58.22%	55.62%

[1] IRR computed from these cash flows.

Figure 1-5. Example E—Multi-Unit Development for Income and Gain.

"balanced return" investment for all three sources of cash flow. In the search for such cash flows, the investor must scan a wide range of factors affecting various types of investments under each of these broad categories.

THE INVESTMENT RATING ANALYSIS FORM

Which type of investment is going to give you what you need and want from it? The Investment Rating Analysis Form helps you answer this question. Consider it a "measuring device" for alternative investment decisions. Filled-out versions are shown in Figure 1–7 through 1–10, and a blank form is displayed in Figure 1–6. In the left-most column are listed 25 criteria that investors commonly need to consider in alternative investment decisions, and they are grouped according to the three main areas of decision making: Costs, Risks, and Returns. Across the top-most row of headings are listed the general categories of investments: Safe, Speculation, Development, and Balanced Return. Under these heads are more specific types of investments, from Passbook Savings to Income and Growth Real Estate. All the numbers in the main section of this form are nothing more than a simple arithmetic way of stating how well each of these investments meets each criterion. The Investor's Weighted Factor column contains a numbered weighting system that enables the investor to place more emphasis on some criteria than on others.

Sound complicated? It is actually quite simple. Let's examine the form, section by section, and see how easy it is.

The Criteria

The 25 criteria are listed simply to clarify your investment goals and to guide you in ranking the types of investments under consideration. You must realize, however, that these comparative rankings are not absolute, although in some cases they may appear so. If you can, discuss these criteria with people who are fairly well informed on one or more of the investments types in question. You will undoubtedly find that the relationships between criteria and investments vary for a number of reasons: an investor's background and point of view; differences in the applicable time, place, and market (particularly money market) conditions; tax laws and zoning changes; housing supply and demand; and other objective factors in the economy. It is simply more realistic for us to recognize that, by trying to capture all these factors on a sheet of paper, we are attempting to make a very dynamic process seem static.

Investor's Weighting Factor

Naturally, investors attach different degrees of importance to each criterion or to each set of criteria. The Investor's Weighting Factor column contains numbers that represent the investor's relative concern for each criterion, on a scale of from 1 to 8. Usually, one ranking number is used for an entire block of criteria. For example, in Figure 1–9, the number 1 is used for Costs, 2 for Risks, and 3 for Returns.

Costs. The person with limited funds to invest might give Costs criteria the highest multiplier or the heaviest "weighting factor" (that is, 8). For someone with excess cash on hand who has become concerned about tax problems, cost may be weighted so low as to be a negative factor (that is, 1 or thereabouts); to a point, high costs fill such an investor's need, as long as the returns compete with those of other investment alternatives.

Risks. The degrees to which investors either accept or avoid risk vary considerably. Their attitudes toward risk can be a function of personal temperaments, the amount of "speculation" money available, their ages or retirement statuses, their overall financial and tax planning requirements, and many other factors. For the highly "risk-aversive" investor, the multiplier for Risks criteria would be a high number (6,7,8), because the criteria are ranked in ascending order (1 to 8) from most risky to least risky. The eager speculator might weight most risk factors with fairly low numbers (which represent high degrees of risk). The compulsive gambler (and they exist in real estate too) could give even a negative weight to Risks criteria, thereby defeating the laws of gravity as well as of economics.

Returns. All investors, we might safely assume, should give great weight to Returns criteria. So why not just give Costs and Risks items a weighting factor of one or less and load up Returns items with a multiplier of double, triple, or more? The sheet doesn't work that way. As you will see, the numbers to the right of the equal signs in the columns, when added up, constitute a ranking of the various investment types according to which criteria are important to the investor filling out the form. Returns might not be the most important in every case. That is how the sheet works.

Types of Investments

The 8 types of investments across the top of the form are grouped according to how they tend to "react" to the 25 criteria. For example, either the Passbook savings or Bonds and time deposits box represents an investment that, under almost any market conditions, requires very little in way of an initial investment. Either investment would therefore be ranked with a high number—say a 6, 7, or 8—because it is highly favorable in terms of that criterion.

How do you go about ranking the other investments and criteria? We have to take the criteria one by one. As we do, follow the rankings in Figure 1–7.

Cost Criteria

Initial Investment Required. Under Costs, you must ask, "How much will it cost to get in on it?" To arrive at an answer, you have to consider the availability of financing, ways of reducing the closing costs, and other factors to bring the initial cash outlay down to a minimum. This question, quite simply, gets at whether you can afford to enter a particular investment. It makes you consider placing the needed capital someplace else. [Leverage, the ratio between equity (cash down) and debt (money borrowed), is a separate question discussed later under return criteria.] Investments that require heavy initial outlays get ranked with low numbers, which represent a lack of desirability; those that need only a small outlay warrant high numbers, which indicate their high degree of desirability in this respect. Compare Passbook savings to Income & growth real estate.

Development Costs. In addition to the initial outlay, several investments require further capital expenditures, or *Development costs,* to create or to improve income production or market value. No such costs, for instance, are involved with Passbook savings, Bonds, or Time deposits, and they are not ordinarily required for Common stocks or Portfolios. On the other hand, such costs are often the key factor in the construction of a Residential subdivision. They are also essential in most Renovations, though usually less so in properties bought with immediate occupancies in mind or with those already in place. They are also a factor in collector items put together *as collections* to enhance their value. Again, high numbers here mean these costs are low or nonexistent. See once again Passbook savings versus Income & growth real estate.

Operating Expenses. The position of Income & growth property is least favorable of all (it gets a 1) because such expenses are an integral part of the business. They generally are less so in Development investments, although they are a factor if such projects (as in example D, Figure 1–4) are rented before sale. In the case of Savings and Bonds, again, the costs are nonexistent or nominal (hence the 5 in either case).

Debt Service Costs. Short-term development loans are relatively risky and expensive, making these costs the highest for any kind of investment that needs them. Such costs are also a major factor for Income & growth real estate, in which the desired leverage causes investors to seek large, long-term loans. Such financing is ordinarily either not available or not practicable for the remaining types of investments.

Income Taxes. The effects of this criteria vary all over the place. For example, Passbook savings offer no meaningful benefits. Tax-free municipal bonds are arguably more desirable from that perspective, but such benefits tend to be offset by reduced yields. Appreciated collector items are subject to capital gain taxes on sale, and they are not ordinarily associated with income tax benefits, except perhaps for the depreciation of antiques used in luxury furnished rentals. Some special tax benefits exist for certain types of investments bought through the purchase of common stock, but they are not generally as good as for real estate. In particular, residential income and growth property is entitled not only to the usual interest deductions for large loans and accelerated depreciation for buildings, but it also is eligible for additional benefits from component depreciation and the depreciation of personal property.

On this point, the ranking is reversed from the previous criteria. The Safe investments score low because they are the least desirable from an income tax point of view. Balanced return investments, at the other end of the spectrum, rate very high with their depreciation deductions.

Required Expertise. For any Development or Balanced return investment, the expertise requirement is high, whether you do the work directly or employ professional services to do some or all of it; these investments therefore rank as 1s. Common stocks outside a planned portfolio and Collector item can usually be acquired and held on a less intense basis, although in some cases a very high degree of expertise and personal involvement is needed. Relatively little is needed to put money in the Safe investments. In Figure 1-7, the relative numerical rankings reflect the increasing desirability of other investments over Balanced return or Development investments.

Management Effort. This criterion ranks highest for a Residential subdivision, because extremely detailed planning, direction of workers, and other activities—all under tight time constraints—are involved. Renovations very often demand the same type of control, but usually on a smaller scale. The effort required for other types of investment are closer questions, but clearly it is least for Savings and Bonds (both rated at 7, highly desirable).

Fees & Other Disposition Costs. These costs are generally highest for Income & growth real estate and Renovations, assuming that the properties are to be sold through real estate brokers whose marketing efforts involve higher fees than those of securities dealers. Real estate brokerage fees in the case of a subdivision are usually lower, because volume comes into play. Although securities brokerage fees (Common stocks or Stock portfolio) tend to be considerably lower than real estate fees across the board, keep in mind that real estate investors can attain direct access to their market more easily than can investors in stocks and bonds. Finally, no direct fees or costs are charged for the disposition of Passbook savings accounts.

Risk Criteria

All the risk criteria are ranked in the same way. First, establish a numerical ranking system based on the number of investments under consideration. For example, if you are comparing eight investments, then the ranking system consists of 8 numbers, 1 through 8. The investment on the sheet that carries the greatest degree of risk receives the lowest number (in all cases 1), because it is the least acceptable from the point of view of risk. The investment that bears the least degree of risk is assigned the highest number (in this case an 8), because it is the most acceptable with regard to risk.

Loss of Investment Outlay. Because the value of Common stocks depends so much on the vagaries of the marketplace, on the psychology of the investing public, and on other factors over which the investor has no control, the risk of loss of investment outlay is greater for such investments than for others. Through Stock portfolio balancing, you can offset that risk to some extent. In a real estate development investment, the risk is somewhat less because more of the value is based on tangibles and because market trends are generally slower-paced and more predictable in real estate. Collectibles tend to be even riskier, since they are generally selected on the basis of long-term trends and built-in scarcity. Bonds, like Passbook savings, have guaranteed returns, which in the latter case are insured by the federal government.

Increase in One or More Costs. This risk is more significant in real estate investments than in others because most cost items tend to play a larger role in a real estate investment than in other types. With Savings and Bonds, the costs associated with the investment are nominal or minimal, except for taxes on the income.

Reduced Income During Holding. For the same reasons that security of capital is lower for Common stocks than for other investments, the risk that income will be reduced during holding is greater for them. Yet keep in mind that income is generally a far more important aspect of real estate investments; that is, you not only cannot afford to lose income, but you must also be sure to make enough to cover costs. Because Collectibles usually produce no income and because the "safe" investments have guaranteed income, this risk is minimal for both of them.

Physical Hazard Loss. Even though you can take out insurance against physical hazards, this risk is greatest in real estate investments because the potential consequent losses of income are not covered by insurance. The damage or destruction of Collectibles does not ordinarily involve a loss of income. With stocks, bonds, and savings accounts, the only physical hazard is to relatively easily replaceable *paper evidences* of indestructible intangible ownership rights.

Adverse Political Developments. Apart from income tax law revisions—which have generally favored real estate investment since the 1930s—perhaps the most common political risks associated with real estate investments are local zoning changes and legislative action, such as rent controls and condominium conversion moratoriums, which affect land use. While some political developments can be profitable as well as costly for real estate investors, the possibility of a favorable outcome is at least matched by the risk of loss. Political risk is greatest for Income & growth real estate, which is a visible target for political action in times of rising housing costs. Such property also tends to be held for periods that reach beyond the point at which political moods can be meaningfully projected. The stock of corporations visibly involved in such industries as the production and distribution of energy and military hardware suffer a degree of such risk, but the consequences are more likely to be transient public relations disruptions than crippling legislation.

Uncertainties from Passage of Time. Here there are arguably only two categories of investment: (1) real estate and (2) everything else. With Development investments in real estate, the time risk is compressed into a short period of tightly scheduled logistics, in which a fumble can make a profitable project just the opposite. Income & growth property involves the longest commitment to a holding over time and therefore to its uncertainties.

Restricted Investment Options. Because income and growth properties involve relatively large amounts of capital tied up over a relatively long period of time, they are the least favorable investment in terms of restricting your investment options. The risk associated with such restrictions is that capital is not available in the event that a more attractive investment opportunity arises. While they do not generate income, Development investments generally tie up more money, but over a shorter time. Collector items usually require the passage of time to work as investments through price appreciation, if it is assumed that both buyer and seller are well informed about the value of an item. Stocks are more liquid. Holding them in a portfolio enables the investor to dispose of them with flexibility to take advantage of more attractive investments. Bonds and time deposits are liquid, but they involve penalties for early disposition. Passbook savings carry no such restrictions.

Loss of Value Gain Potential. Keep in mind that a distinction exists between value gain and price appreciation. Loss of value gain comes about through unforeseen occurrences that prevent or decrease the effect of an investor's actions to enhance the value of an investment through development or improvement. Since improvement is the basic purpose of Development investments, they are the most vulnerable to the risk of loss of value/gain potential. The losses can come through the discovery or development of legal or engineering problems, an increase in material or labor costs, delivery or other time problems, or a range of other events. Common stocks, if selected for long-term growth in value, envisage sound management, favorable economic trends for the goods or services involved, and other value-enhancing factors for which there is a risk of decline—over which the investor has no control. More control exists over such factors for Income & growth real estate and Stock portfolios. Such risks are lower for Collector items simply because value enhancement is a relatively minor source of return from this kind of investment. It is not a factor in the "Safe" investment.

Failure of Appreciation Potential. This risk is the greatest for Collector items, because appreciation is almost the entire basis for returns from that kind of investment. Appreciation is also usually the major return from Common stock bought mainly for that purpose, but the risk for stock investment is lessened through portfolio dynamics. Inflation and, in times of diminished new construction, scarcity tend to lessen that risk still more for Income & growth real estate. It is less of a factor, and therefore less of a risk, for Development investments. One of the definitive characteristics of the Safe investments is that they do not appreciate; so their failure to do so is not a risk. (In only one sense do Safe investments run such a risk—"in reverse", that is, inflation could reduce the value of the initial capital outlay and its earnings.)

Return Criteria

With Return criteria, you must once again use the same number-ranking system. In this case, however, the lowest number indicates the least amount of benefit, and the highest number reflects the greatest desirability. For example, Passbook savings are very liquid, so they rate a 5 in Figure 1-7; but they yield practically no benefits in way of leverage so they rank a 1 by that criterion.

Advantages from Leverage. Often presented as the primary and overriding reason for investment in real estate, leverage is sometimes compared with buying on margin, which was pursued with an almost religious fervor prior to the 1929 stock market crash. That use of margin was, of course, much more risky, because it was much less predictable, than real estate investment in general—which also crumbled along with the economy at large. One of the solutions to the Depression of the early 1930s was to reverse the use of leverage in stock market and real estate transactions. It was discouraged in the stock market and encouraged in real estate. Today that policy and its underlying assumptions remain intact:

1. With many exceptions, the amount of useful real estate is becoming increasingly scarce in a market economy with an expanding population.
2. Most other goods and services that are traded in the competitive sectors of a market economy are characterized by a scarcity that is of a far more speculative and temporary nature.
3. The promotion of healthy economic growth is better served if people are enabled to finance things of more certain and permanent value, rather than things of a less certain and permanent value.

Investors seeking maximum gains in proportion to their costs and risks must constantly ask if these assumptions are still true. At this writing, they probably still are. Yet which properties are most "useful"? Which age groups within the population are expanding in which geographical areas? What are their income patterns? And what kinds of real estate will individuals and businesses want to buy, if they decide to acquire through well-leveraged financing?

Over the years, a combination of market forces and public policy has brought about real estate loan programs that provide up to 100 percent financing for GI owner-occupants, and investors can sometimes assume these loan balances on favorable terms. For new conventional loans, cash down of 20 percent or more has been a common requirement for investment real estate. There are many financing methods between those two. The longer you can earn income and enhance market value through the effects of leverage, the greater the potential return from its operation. Ordinarily, therefore, the greatest return is likely to be realized on Income & growth real estate, over other types of investment.

Direct Income During Holding Period. Income and growth real estate also has the clear edge for direct income, while Collector items have the least potential. Certain Common stocks can be selected for income, which can be further enhanced through Portfolio selection. Development investments can be either used partially for income or converted entirely to that purpose. Ordinarily, collector items have the least potential in this regard.

Spendable Income from Tax Benefits. Tax benefits are generated in two ways:

1. reductions in taxable income through the deduction of the interest portions of loan payments, and
2. reductions in taxable income through subtractions from the investment's cost basis as depreciation allowances.

Although a portion of depreciation may have to be repaid upon disposition of the investment, if an accelerated depreciation method is used, it is still a benefit unique to real estate investments. Other depreciable assets are almost always associated with businesses requiring greater active involvement than real estate investment does. Except for the tax-free status of income from such securities as municipal bonds, the remaining investments in Figure 1–7 are held without income, direct or through savings, from tax benefits.

Benefits of Liquidity. Passbook savings, lowest among the investments by most measures of return, is singularly favorable in its liquidity benefits. Collector items and Income & growth real estate suffer minimum liquidity, in that the disposition of either investment ordinarily requires significant time to locate and to negotiate specific buyers for specific physical assets. Stocks and bonds fall in between.

Opportunity for Investment Variety. Stocks and collector items offer the greatest opportunity for variety in the types of enterprises or assets available for investment. Every real estate transaction is significantly different from all others, of course, but the types of business involved are of a more sharply defined range. Savings and Bonds are really not much more than savings and bonds, whatever entity borrows the money, at whatever rate.

Gains Through Appreciation. In the long run, the appreciation potential is greatest for well selected Collector items. Raw land, not shown in Figure 1–7, may be sufficiently better in some instances to make it more attractive than most other investments. Income & growth real estate, like collector items, is selected with prospective scarcity over time in mind. Unlike the most promising Collector items, however, such real estate must be considered as subject to additional supply in the future—limited by the fact that additional land cannot be created in most locations. Development investments can also gain from appreciation, as well as from a gain in real value, but investors usually do not hold them long enough for appreciation to be the primary return. Depending on the current status of the stock market, portfolio development, and other factors, Common stocks can appreciate to levels comparable to real estate, though on a more speculative basis. Remember, all these rankings are necessarily tentative, except for the ranking of Safe investments at the lowest end. Like so many of these criteria, potential gains from appreciation can vary from one time and place to another, as well as with individual investment skill and luck.

Gains Through Value Increase. Safe investments are lowest also in this respect, because their values are set. Development investments are highest, because such gains are their primary purpose. Income & growth property can also be improved for value gain, but less so. In Common stocks, such gains usually come over the long run through careful selection for such qualities as sound management, durability of product demand, and corporate adaptability to changes in the marketplace.

Internal Rate of Return. Now we come to what many consider to be the bottom line in any investment: the projected *internal rate of return* or some such variation. This comprehensive rate of return on an investment considers the flow of all money in and out, and weighs the value of *when* it is received or paid out. The types of investments compared in Figure 1–7 vary all the way from 1 to 8, in a manner that you are invited to examine closely and critically. Passbook savings (1) leave little room for disagreement, since they generally bring the lowest return. Bonds and time deposits (2) are fixed a shade higher. Collector items (3) are ranked next on the premise that, although they can earn substantial appreciation, they ordinarily earn no income during their long holding periods, and they enjoy no tax benefits. Common stocks are ranked next (4) because they earn some income, followed by stock portfolios (5) because a portfolio's careful dispersion of risks and potential returns can enhance performance. (If nothing else, it simply requires you to think through a step beyond whatever basic strategy you apply.) Income & growth real estate comes next (6) because it has all the previous sources of return (sometimes even guaranteed fixed income), plus tax benefits. At (7), House renovation is ranked next not only because it has potentially the same sources of income as the preceding investments, but also because it adds a substantial return from value gain (although at a higher level of active involvement in the investment and greater risk). The Residential subdivision is ranked highest (8) because it has by far the potential for the greatest predictable return, although it also has by far the greatest risk and, except for limited partners or stockholders, the greatest degree of direct involvement in running investment.

Filling Out the Sheet

To make the comparison sheet work only four steps are involved:

1. Go down the column for each investment type and rank it for each criterion from least favorable (1) to most favorable (8). Place your ranking numbers to the left of the equal signs. For this step, use the completed versions of the comparison sheets in Figures 1–7 through 1–11 as guides or construct an alternative version using the blank sheet in Figure 1–6.
2. Add a weighting factor for each criterion, according to your investment preferences.
3. Multiply each number left of an equal sign by the applicable weighting factor, and enter the result to the right of the equal sign.
4. Under each investment type heading, add up all the numbers to the right of the equal sign in each column then compare the totals. The highest total indicates the greatest suitability to your wants and needs.

SAMPLE RATING ANALYSIS

Figures 1–7 through 1–11 demonstrate various applications of the Investment Rating Analysis Form. These figures present five distinct investor postures but retain the same basic rankings of investment criteria throughout. Figure 1–6 is blank. You are invited to reproduce that form, rearrange the rankings of criteria as you wish, and experiment with various investor weighting factors. In addition to its uses in comparing real estate

	Investor's Weighting Factor								
COSTS									
Initial investment required	×	=	=	=	=	=	=	=	=
Development costs	×	=	=	=	=	=	=	=	=
Operating expenses	×	=	=	=	=	=	=	=	=
Debt service costs	×	=	=	=	=	=	=	=	=
Income taxes	×	=	=	=	=	=	=	=	=
Required expertise	×	=	=	=	=	=	=	=	=
Management effort	×	=	=	=	=	=	=	=	=
Fees and other disposition costs	×	=	=	=	=	=	=	=	=
RISKS	Subtotals								
Loss of investment outlay	×	=	=	=	=	=	=	=	=
Increase in one or more costs	×	=	=	=	=	=	=	=	=
Reduced income during holding	×	=	=	=	=	=	=	=	=
Physical hazard loss	×	=	=	=	=	=	=	=	=
Adverse political developments	×	=	=	=	=	=	=	=	=
Uncertainties from passage of time	×	=	=	=	=	=	=	=	=
Restricted investment options	×	=	=	=	=	=	=	=	=
Loss of value gain potential	×	=	=	=	=	=	=	=	=
Failure of appreciation potential	×	=	=	=	=	=	=	=	=
RETURNS	Subtotals								
Advantages from leverage	×	=	=	=	=	=	=	=	=
Direct income during holding	×	=	=	=	=	=	=	=	=
Spendable income from tax benefits	×	=	=	=	=	=	=	=	=
Benefits of liquidity	×	=	=	=	=	=	=	=	=
Opportunity for investment variety	×	=	=	=	=	=	=	=	=
Gains through appreciation	×	=	=	=	=	=	=	=	=
Gains through value increase	×	=	=	=	=	=	=	=	=
Internal rate of return	×	=	=	=	=	=	=	=	=
	Subtotals								
TOTALS									

Figure 1–6. Investment Rating Analysis Form: Sample Worksheet. This worksheet may be freely reproduced, with attribution to Reston Publishing Company, Inc., a Prentice-Hall Company, and to Paul J. Lyons.

investments with "non-real eatate" investments, the blank rating analysis matrix can be used either to compare real estate investments with each other (Figures 1–12 through 1–14) or to compare real estate with other investments (Figures 1–7 through 1–11), by various kinds of investor posture.

Keep in mind, however, that the numbers in the Totals line have meanings that are only relative to each other. They do not reflect any ranking on an absolute scale, and they change from one set of weighting factors to another. For example, you may not believe that Stock portfolios are generally 9 points "better" than random Common stock purchases (99 versus 91 in Figure 1–8). In that case, you should go back to the weighting factors and/or to the ranking of criteria, make the appropriate adjustments, and thus produce a result in keeping with your assessment of the investment opportunities at a given time and place. Until you do so, you are, by definition, unsure of your own assessments.

If You Are Trying to Avoid Both Cost and Risk . . .

If an investor gives the eight Returns criteria the same weight as the seventeen Costs and Risks criteria, the bottom-line results favor Safe investments. The reason is that there are slightly more than twice as many Costs and Risks as Returns criteria. In Figure 1–7, Savings and Bonds (at 94 and 93) rate about 45 percent higher than the more expensive and risky Development investments, with the other types falling in between.

If You Want to Balance Risks and Costs . . .

In Figure 1–8, by giving the Returns criteria a weighting factor of 2, the investor essentially balances Costs and Risks against Returns, which now have a "weight" of 16 while Costs and Risks add up to 17. One result is that Passbook savings work out to the same score as Income & growth real estate—107. All the other investments are in the 90s, showing fairly even comparisons. (Again, remember that they are *not* absolute.)

If You Can Accept Risk . . .

Figure 1–9 shows that, as you give greater weight to Returns than to Costs and Risks, which are weighted evenly, the Safe investments begin to fall behind the others in their scores. In this example, Speculation investments are on a par with Safe investments (the four averaging 165).

	Investor's Weighting Factor	Safe Investment		Speculation Investment		Development Investment		Balanced Return Investment	
		Passbook Savings	Bonds and Time Deposits	Common Stocks	Collector Items	Residential Subdivision	House Renovation	Stock Portfolio	Income and Growth Real Estate
COSTS									
Initial investment required	1 x	6 = 6	5 = 5	4 = 4	3 = 3	1 = 1	2 = 2	3 = 3	3 = 3
Development costs	1 x	5 = 5	5 = 5	4 = 4	3 = 3	1 = 1	2 = 2	4 = 4	3 = 3
Operating expenses	1 x	5 = 5	5 = 5	4 = 4	3 = 3	2 = 2	2 = 2	3 = 3	1 = 1
Debt service costs	1 x	3 = 3	3 = 3	3 = 3	3 = 3	1 = 1	1 = 1	3 = 3	2 = 2
Income taxes	1 x	1 = 1	2 = 2	3 = 3	2 = 2	4 = 4	4 = 4	3 = 3	5 = 5
Required expertise	1 x	3 = 3	3 = 3	2 = 2	2 = 2	1 = 1	1 = 1	1 = 1	1 = 1
Management effort	1 x	7 = 7	7 = 7	5 = 5	6 = 6	1 = 1	2 = 2	4 = 4	3 = 3
Fees and other disposition costs	1 x	5 = 5	4 = 4	3 = 3	3 = 3	2 = 2	1 = 1	3 = 3	1 = 1
RISKS	Subtotals	35	34	28	25	13	15	24	19
Loss of investment outlay	1 x	8 = 8	7 = 7	1 = 1	6 = 6	3 = 3	4 = 4	2 = 2	5 = 5
Increase in one or more costs	1 x	6 = 6	6 = 6	5 = 5	4 = 4	1 = 1	2 = 2	4 = 4	3 = 3
Reduced income during holding	1 x	5 = 5	5 = 5	3 = 3	5 = 5	2 = 2	2 = 2	4 = 4	1 = 1
Physical hazard loss	1 x	3 = 3	3 = 3	3 = 3	2 = 2	1 = 1	1 = 1	3 = 3	2 = 2
Adverse political developments	1 x	3 = 3	3 = 3	2 = 2	3 = 3	3 = 3	3 = 3	2 = 2	1 = 1
Uncertainties from passage of time	1 x	2 = 2	2 = 2	2 = 2	2 = 2	1 = 1	1 = 1	2 = 2	1 = 1
Restricted investment options	1 x	8 = 8	7 = 7	5 = 5	4 = 4	3 = 3	2 = 2	6 = 6	1 = 1
Loss of value gain potential	1 x	5 = 5	5 = 5	2 = 2	4 = 4	1 = 1	1 = 1	3 = 3	4 = 4
Failure of appreciation potential	1 x	6 = 6	6 = 6	2 = 2	1 = 1	5 = 5	5 = 5	3 = 3	4 = 4
RETURNS	Subtotals	46	44	25	31	20	21	29	22
Advantages from leverage	1 x	1 = 1	1 = 1	1 = 1	2 = 2	3 = 3	3 = 3	1 = 1	4 = 4
Direct income during holding	1 x	2 = 2	3 = 3	2 = 2	1 = 1	4 = 4	4 = 4	3 = 3	7 = 7
Spendable income from tax benefits	1 x	1 = 1	2 = 2	1 = 1	1 = 1	4 = 4	3 = 3	1 = 1	5 = 5
Benefits of liquidity	1 x	5 = 5	4 = 4	3 = 3	1 = 1	2 = 2	2 = 2	3 = 3	1 = 1
Opportunity for investment variety	1 x	1 = 1	1 = 1	3 = 3	3 = 3	2 = 2	2 = 2	3 = 3	2 = 2
Gains through appreciation	1 x	1 = 1	1 = 1	3 = 3	5 = 5	3 = 3	3 = 3	4 = 4	4 = 4
Gains through value increase	1 x	1 = 1	1 = 1	2 = 2	2 = 2	5 = 5	5 = 5	3 = 3	4 = 4
Internal rate of return	1 x	1 = 1	2 = 2	4 = 4	3 = 3	8 = 8	7 = 7	5 = 5	6 = 6
	Subtotals	13	15	19	18	31	29	23	33
TOTALS		94	93	72	74	64	65	76	74

Figure 1-7. Investment Rating Analysis Form: Even Weighting—Cost/Risk Aversive Investor.

	Investor's Weighting Factor	Safe Investment		Speculation Investment		Development Investment		Balance Return Investment	
		Passbook Savings	Bonds And Time Deposits	Common Stocks	Collector Items	Residential Subdivision	House Renovation	Stock Portfolio	Income and Growth Real Estate
COSTS									
Initial investment required	1 x	6 = 6	5 = 5	4 = 4	3 = 3	1 = 1	2 = 2	3 = 3	3 = 3
Development costs	1 x	5 = 5	5 = 5	4 = 4	3 = 3	1 = 1	2 = 2	4 = 4	3 = 3
Operating expenses	1 x	5 = 5	5 = 5	4 = 4	3 = 3	2 = 2	2 = 2	3 = 3	1 = 1
Debt service costs	1 x	3 = 3	3 = 3	3 = 3	3 = 3	1 = 1	1 = 1	3 = 3	2 = 2
Income taxes	1 x	1 = 1	2 = 2	3 = 3	2 = 2	4 = 4	4 = 4	3 = 3	5 = 5
Required expertise	1 x	3 = 3	3 = 3	2 = 2	2 = 2	1 = 1	1 = 1	1 = 1	1 = 1
Management effort	1 x	7 = 7	7 = 7	5 = 5	6 = 6	1 = 1	2 = 2	4 = 4	3 = 3
Fees and other disposition costs	1 x	5 = 5	4 = 4	3 = 3	3 = 3	2 = 2	1 = 1	3 = 3	1 = 1
RISKS	Subtotals	35	34	28	25	13	15	24	19
Loss of investment outlay	1 x	8 = 8	7 = 7	1 = 1	6 = 6	3 = 3	4 = 4	2 = 2	5 = 5
Increase in one or more costs	1 x	6 = 6	6 = 6	5 = 5	4 = 4	1 = 1	2 = 2	4 = 4	3 = 3
Reduced income during holding	1 x	5 = 5	5 = 5	3 = 3	5 = 5	2 = 2	2 = 2	4 = 4	1 = 1
Physical hazard loss	1 x	3 = 3	3 = 3	3 = 3	2 = 2	1 = 1	1 = 1	3 = 3	2 = 2
Adverse political developments	1 x	3 = 3	3 = 3	2 = 2	3 = 3	3 = 3	3 = 3	2 = 2	1 = 1
Uncertainties from passage of time	1 x	2 = 2	2 = 2	2 = 2	2 = 2	1 = 1	1 = 1	2 = 2	1 = 1
Restricted investment options	1 x	8 = 8	7 = 7	5 = 5	4 = 4	3 = 3	2 = 2	6 = 6	1 = 1
Loss of value gain potential	1 x	5 = 5	5 = 5	2 = 2	4 = 4	1 = 1	1 = 1	3 = 3	4 = 4
Failure of appreciation potential	1 x	6 = 6	6 = 6	2 = 2	1 = 1	5 = 5	5 = 5	3 = 3	4 = 4
RETURNS	Subtotals	46	44	25	31	20	21	29	22
Advantages from leverage	2 x	1 = 2	1 = 2	1 = 2	2 = 4	3 = 6	3 = 6	1 = 2	4 = 8
Direct income during holding	2 x	2 = 4	3 = 6	2 = 4	1 = 2	4 = 8	4 = 8	3 = 6	7 = 14
Spendable income from tax benefits	2 x	1 = 2	2 = 4	1 = 2	1 = 2	4 = 8	3 = 6	1 = 2	5 = 10
Benefits of liquidity	2 x	5 = 10	4 = 8	3 = 6	1 = 2	2 = 4	2 = 4	3 = 6	1 = 2
Opportunity for investment variety	2 x	1 = 2	1 = 2	3 = 6	3 = 6	2 = 4	2 = 4	3 = 6	2 = 4
Gains through appreciation	2 x	1 = 2	1 = 2	3 = 6	5 = 10	3 = 6	3 = 6	4 = 8	4 = 8
Gains through value increase	2 x	1 = 2	1 = 2	2 = 4	2 = 4	5 = 10	5 = 10	3 = 6	4 = 8
Internal rate of return	2 x	1 = 2	2 = 4	4 = 8	3 = 6	8 = 16	7 = 14	5 = 10	6 = 12
	Subtotals	26	30	38	36	62	58	46	66
TOTALS		107	108	91	92	95	94	99	107

Figure 1-8. Investment Rating Analysis Form: Returns Weighted to Costs and Risks—Balanced Cost/Risk Position.

	Investor's Weighting Factor	Safe Investment		Speculation Investment		Development Investment		Balance Return Investment	
		Passbook Savings	Bonds And Time Deposits	Common Stocks	Collector Items	Residential Subdivision	House Renovation	Stock Portfolio	Income and Growth Real Estate
COSTS									
Initial investment required	1 x	6 = 6	5 = 5	4 = 4	3 = 3	1 = 1	2 = 2	3 = 3	3 = 3
Development costs	1 x	5 = 5	5 = 5	4 = 4	3 = 3	1 = 1	2 = 2	4 = 4	3 = 3
Operating expenses	1 x	5 = 5	5 = 5	4 = 4	3 = 3	2 = 2	2 = 2	3 = 3	1 = 1
Debt service costs	1 x	3 = 3	3 = 3	3 = 3	3 = 3	1 = 1	1 = 1	3 = 3	2 = 2
Income taxes	1 x	1 = 1	2 = 2	3 = 3	2 = 2	4 = 4	4 = 4	3 = 3	5 = 5
Required expertise	1 x	3 = 3	3 = 3	2 = 2	2 = 2	1 = 1	1 = 1	1 = 1	1 = 1
Management effort	1 x	7 = 7	7 = 7	5 = 5	6 = 6	1 = 1	2 = 2	4 = 4	3 = 3
Fees and other disposition costs	1 x	5 = 5	4 = 4	3 = 3	3 = 3	2 = 2	1 = 1	3 = 3	1 = 1
RISKS	Subtotals	35	34	28	25	13	15	24	19
Loss of investment outlay	1 x	8 = 8	7 = 7	1 = 1	6 = 6	3 = 3	4 = 4	2 = 2	5 = 5
Increase in one or more costs	1 x	6 = 6	6 = 6	5 = 5	4 = 4	1 = 1	2 = 2	4 = 4	3 = 3
Reduced income during holding	1 x	5 = 5	5 = 5	3 = 3	5 = 5	2 = 2	2 = 2	4 = 4	1 = 1
Physical hazard loss	1 x	3 = 3	3 = 3	3 = 3	2 = 2	1 = 1	1 = 1	3 = 3	2 = 2
Adverse political developments	1 x	3 = 3	3 = 3	2 = 2	3 = 3	3 = 3	3 = 3	2 = 2	1 = 1
Uncertainties from passage of time	1 x	2 = 2	2 = 2	2 = 2	2 = 2	1 = 1	1 = 1	2 = 2	1 = 1
Restricted investment options	1 x	8 = 8	7 = 7	5 = 5	4 = 4	3 = 3	2 = 2	6 = 6	1 = 1
Loss of value gain potential	1 x	5 = 5	5 = 5	2 = 2	4 = 4	1 = 1	1 = 1	3 = 3	4 = 4
Failure of appreciation potential	1 x	6 = 6	6 = 6	2 = 2	1 = 1	5 = 5	5 = 5	3 = 3	4 = 4
RETURNS	Subtotals	46	44	25	31	20	21	29	22
Advantages from leverage	6 x	1 = 6	1 = 6	1 = 6	2 = 12	3 = 18	3 = 18	1 = 6	4 = 24
Direct income during holding	6 x	2 = 12	3 = 18	2 = 12	1 = 6	4 = 24	4 = 24	3 = 18	7 = 42
Spendable income from tax benefits	6 x	1 = 6	2 = 12	1 = 6	1 = 6	4 = 24	3 = 18	1 = 6	5 = 30
Benefits of liquidity	6 x	5 = 30	4 = 24	3 = 18	1 = 6	2 = 12	2 = 12	3 = 18	1 = 6
Opportunity for investment variety	6 x	1 = 6	1 = 6	3 = 18	3 = 18	2 = 12	2 = 12	3 = 18	2 = 12
Gains through appreciation	6 x	1 = 6	1 = 6	3 = 18	5 = 30	3 = 18	3 = 18	4 = 24	4 = 24
Gains through value increase	6 x	1 = 6	1 = 6	2 = 12	2 = 12	5 = 30	5 = 30	3 = 18	4 = 24
Internal rate of return	6 x	1 = 6	2 = 12	4 = 24	3 = 18	8 = 48	7 = 42	5 = 30	6 = 36
	Subtotals	78	90	114	108	186	174	138	198
TOTALS		159	118	167	164	219	210	191	239

Figure 1-9. Investment Rating Analysis Form: Costs and Risks Weighted Even on Return-Oriented Scale—Risk Accepting.

The others range upward from Stock portfolios at 191, House renovations at 210, Subdivisions at 219, and Income & growth real estate at 239, the last being about 45 percent higher than the safe investments.

If You Want to Take a Risk . . .

In Figure 1–10, the 3-to-1 ratio in weighting between Returns (9) and Costs and Risks combined (3) remains unchanged. Avoidance or control of risk is less of a factor in the investor's decision-making process, because it is weighted at only 1. The result is that all investments now outrank Savings and Bonds, especially the Development and Balanced return investments, which stand out even more than they did in Figure 1–9.

If You Want to Avoid Risk . . .

The investor who filled out Figure 1–11 weighted Risks as a 2—more than Costs but less than Returns. The result is that Safe investments come out only slightly more favorable for this investor than the other investments. An interesting note if that Income & growth real estate ranks as a very close second-best.

Try It Yourself . . .

Reproduce the form in Figure 1–6, and experiment with variations in the ranking and weighting processes. Compare some or all of the investment types covered in Figures 1–7 through 1–11, and go on to others, if you wish (the number system, for example, need not be eight). Use the same blank also to compare various types of real estate investments with each other, as in Figures 1–13 through 1–15.

REAL ESTATE INVESTMENT ALTERNATIVES

Everyone who decides to establish a fixed residence must eventually make a real estate investment decision: to rent or to buy? Figure 1–12 addresses this question by comparing total housing costs over a 5-year period. In this figure, the owner-occupant of a $70,000 house fares $14,773 better than the

	Investor's Weighting Factor	Safe Investment		Speculation Investment		Development Investment		Balance Return Investment	
		Passbook Savings	Bonds And Time Deposits	Common Stocks	Collector Items	Residential Subdivision	House Renovation	Stock Portfolio	Income and Growth Real Estate
COSTS									
Initial investment required	2 x	6 = 12	5 = 10	4 = 8	3 = 6	1 = 2	2 = 4	3 = 6	3 = 6
Development costs	2 x	5 = 10	5 = 10	4 = 8	3 = 6	1 = 2	2 = 4	4 = 8	3 = 6
Operating expenses	2 x	5 = 10	5 = 10	4 = 8	3 = 6	2 = 4	2 = 4	3 = 6	1 = 2
Debt service costs	2 x	3 = 6	3 = 6	3 = 6	3 = 6	1 = 2	1 = 2	3 = 6	2 = 4
Income taxes	2 x	1 = 2	2 = 4	3 = 6	2 = 4	4 = 8	4 = 8	3 = 6	5 = 10
Required expertise	2 x	3 = 6	3 = 6	2 = 4	2 = 4	1 = 2	1 = 2	1 = 2	1 = 2
Management effort	2 x	7 = 14	7 = 14	5 = 10	6 = 12	1 = 2	2 = 4	4 = 8	3 = 6
Fees and other disposition costs	2 x	5 = 10	4 = 8	3 = 6	3 = 6	2 = 4	1 = 2	3 = 6	1 = 2
RISKS	Subtotals	70	68	56	50	26	30	48	38
Loss of investment outlay	1 x	8 = 8	7 = 7	1 = 1	6 = 6	3 = 3	4 = 4	2 = 2	5 = 5
Increase in one or more costs	1 x	6 = 6	6 = 6	5 = 5	4 = 4	1 = 1	2 = 2	4 = 4	3 = 3
Reduced income during holding	1 x	5 = 5	5 = 5	3 = 3	5 = 5	2 = 2	2 = 2	4 = 4	1 = 1
Physical hazard loss	1 x	3 = 3	3 = 3	3 = 3	2 = 2	1 = 1	1 = 1	3 = 3	2 = 2
Adverse political developments	1 x	3 = 3	3 = 3	2 = 2	3 = 3	3 = 3	3 = 3	2 = 2	1 = 1
Uncertainties from passage of time	1 x	2 = 2	2 = 2	2 = 2	2 = 2	1 = 1	1 = 1	2 = 2	1 = 1
Restricted investment options	1 x	8 = 8	7 = 7	5 = 5	4 = 4	3 = 3	2 = 2	6 = 6	1 = 1
Loss of value gain potential	1 x	5 = 5	5 = 5	2 = 2	4 = 4	1 = 1	1 = 1	3 = 3	4 = 4
Failure of appreciation potential	1 x	6 = 6	6 = 6	2 = 2	1 = 1	5 = 5	5 = 5	3 = 3	4 = 4
RETURNS	Subtotals	46	44	25	31	20	21	29	22
Advantages from leverage	9 x	1 = 9	1 = 9	1 = 9	2 = 18	3 = 27	3 = 27	1 = 9	4 = 36
Direct income during holding	9 x	2 = 18	3 = 27	2 = 18	1 = 9	4 = 36	4 = 36	3 = 27	7 = 63
Spendable income from tax benefits	9 x	1 = 9	2 = 18	1 = 9	1 = 9	4 = 36	3 = 27	1 = 9	5 = 45
Benefits of liquidity	9 x	5 = 45	4 = 36	3 = 27	1 = 9	2 = 18	2 = 18	3 = 27	1 = 9
Opportunity for investment variety	9 x	1 = 9	1 = 9	3 = 27	3 = 27	2 = 18	2 = 18	3 = 27	2 = 18
Gains through appreciation	9 x	1 = 9	1 = 9	3 = 27	5 = 45	3 = 27	3 = 27	4 = 36	4 = 36
Gains through value increase	9 x	1 = 9	1 = 9	2 = 18	2 = 18	5 = 45	5 = 45	3 = 27	4 = 36
Internal rate of return	9 x	1 = 9	2 = 18	4 = 36	3 = 27	8 = 72	7 = 63	5 = 45	6 = 54
	Subtotals	117	135	171	162	279	261	207	297
TOTALS		233	247	252	243	325	312	284	357

Figure 1-10. Investment Rating Analysis Form: Risks Weighted Minimum on Return-Oriented Scale—Risk-Taking.

	Investor's Weighting Factor	Safe Investment		Speculation Investment		Development Investment		Balance Return Investment	
		Passbook Savings	Bonds and Time Deposits	Common Stocks	Collector Items	Residential Subdivision	House Renovation	Stock Portfolio	Income and Growth Real Estate
COSTS									
Initial investment required	1 x	6 = 6	5 = 5	4 = 4	3 = 3	1 = 1	2 = 2	3 = 3	3 = 3
Development costs	1 x	5 = 5	5 = 5	4 = 4	3 = 3	1 = 1	2 = 2	4 = 4	3 = 3
Operating expenses	1 x	5 = 5	5 = 5	4 = 4	3 = 3	2 = 2	2 = 2	3 = 3	1 = 1
Debt service costs	1 x	3 = 3	3 = 3	3 = 3	3 = 3	1 = 1	1 = 1	3 = 3	2 = 2
Income taxes	1 x	1 = 1	2 = 2	3 = 3	2 = 2	4 = 4	4 = 4	3 = 3	5 = 5
Required expertise	1 x	3 = 3	3 = 3	2 = 2	2 = 2	1 = 1	1 = 1	1 = 1	1 = 1
Management effort	1 x	7 = 7	7 = 7	5 = 5	6 = 6	1 = 1	2 = 2	4 = 4	3 = 3
Fees and other disposition costs	1 x	5 = 5	4 = 4	3 = 3	3 = 3	2 = 2	1 = 1	3 = 3	1 = 1
RISKS	Subtotals	35	34	28	25	13	15	24	19
Loss of investment outlay	2 x	8 = 16	7 = 14	1 = 2	6 = 12	3 = 6	4 = 8	2 = 4	5 = 10
Increase in one or more costs	2 x	6 = 12	6 = 12	5 = 10	4 = 8	1 = 2	2 = 4	4 = 8	3 = 6
Reduced income during holding	2 x	5 = 10	5 = 10	3 = 6	5 = 10	2 = 4	2 = 4	4 = 8	1 = 2
Physical hazard loss	2 x	3 = 6	3 = 6	3 = 6	2 = 4	1 = 2	1 = 2	3 = 6	2 = 4
Adverse political developments	2 x	3 = 6	3 = 6	2 = 4	3 = 6	3 = 6	3 = 6	2 = 4	1 = 2
Uncertainties from passage of time	2 x	2 = 4	2 = 4	2 = 4	2 = 4	1 = 2	1 = 2	2 = 4	1 = 2
Restricted investment options	2 x	8 = 16	7 = 14	5 = 10	4 = 8	3 = 6	2 = 4	6 = 12	1 = 2
Loss of value gain potential	2 x	5 = 10	5 = 10	2 = 4	4 = 8	1 = 2	1 = 2	3 = 6	4 = 8
Failure of appreciation potential	2 x	6 = 12	6 = 12	2 = 4	1 = 2	5 = 10	5 = 10	3 = 6	4 = 8
RETURNS	Subtotals	92	88	50	62	40	42	58	44
Advantages from leverage	3 x	1 = 3	1 = 3	1 = 3	2 = 6	3 = 9	3 = 9	1 = 3	4 = 12
Direct income during holding	3 x	2 = 6	3 = 9	2 = 6	1 = 3	4 = 12	4 = 12	3 = 9	7 = 21
Spendable income from tax benefits	3 x	1 = 3	2 = 6	1 = 3	1 = 3	4 = 12	3 = 9	1 = 3	5 = 15
Benefits of liquidity	3 x	5 = 15	4 = 12	3 = 9	1 = 3	2 = 6	2 = 6	3 = 9	1 = 3
Opportunity for investment variety	3 x	1 = 3	1 = 3	3 = 9	3 = 9	2 = 6	2 = 6	3 = 9	2 = 6
Gains through appreciation	3 x	1 = 3	1 = 3	3 = 9	5 = 15	3 = 9	3 = 9	4 = 12	4 = 12
Gains through value increase	3 x	1 = 3	1 = 3	2 = 6	2 = 6	5 = 15	5 = 15	3 = 9	4 = 12
Internal rate of return	3 x	1 = 3	2 = 6	4 = 12	3 = 9	8 = 24	7 = 21	5 = 15	6 = 18
	Subtotals	39	45	57	54	93	87	69	99
TOTALS		166	167	135	141	146	144	151	162

Figure 1-11. Investment Rating Analysis Form: Risks Weighted Above Costs at Balanced Position—Risk-Aversive.

renter of a $350 per month apartment, after all costs. The final figure results from:

1. selling the house after 5 years of appreciation at 8.5 percent per year,
2. reducing the 5-year cost of house ownership ($39,612) by the amount of the net sale proceed ($29,498), and
3. deducting the difference ($10,114, the actual cost of 5-year ownership) from the 5-year cost of renting, with 8.5 percent per year rent increases ($24,887).

From the standpoint of money saved in housing costs, the owner–occupant who started with no down payment fairly clearly winds up with a lot more house for a lot less money. The main risks taken by those choosing to buy rather than to rent are that the house might fail to appreciate, that it might actually decrease in value, or that rents might go down over the period, making rental the better option. These possibilities ordinarily occur—as long as the inflationary trend does not reverse itself—as a result of decline in the neighborhood or in the building rented, a reversal of inflationary trends.

The decision to rent or to buy is equivalent to the decision to invest or to save your "extra" money. As the save/invest alternatives were evaluated in Figures 1–7 through 1–11, the rent/buy options are weighed in Figures 1–12 through 1–14. In these figures, *Primary residence,* equivalent to Safe investments, is compared with 8 other types of residential real estate investments. Beyond Primary residence, we consider:

1. Raw land held either for Long-term appreciation or Development (surveying, engineering, or rezoning—not construction) and early resale;
2. New residential construction built for immediate sale or held over time for income and growth, and
3. Used rental property bought in the resale market, rented unfurnished or furnished, and held over time for income and growth.

By changing the across-the-board weighting factors assigned to Costs, Risks, and Returns, or by changing the factors with regard to specific criteria, you can effect differing relative scores for these types of investments.

Primary Residence

For Risk-Aversive Investors. With little surprise to most, the primary residence that you rent or own scores highest among real estate investments for the risk-aversive investor portrayed in Figure 1–10. In Figure 1–13—

	Year				
	1	2	3	4	5
Sales price	6,387	13,323	20,855	29,035	37,918
– Loan balance	75,950	82,406	89,411	97,011	105,257
= Equity[1]	69,563	69,083	68,556	67,976	67,339
ANNUAL					
Paid on loan	437	480	527	580	637
+ Property tax	1,200	1,302	1,413	1,533	1,663
+ Interest paid	6,631	6,588	6,541	6,488	6,431
+ Hazard insurance	152	165	179	194	211
+ Utilities and maintenance	1,048	1,137	1,234	1,339	1,452
= Cash outlay[2]	9,468	9,672	9,894	10,134	10,394
– Tax savings[3]	1,958	1,973	1,989	2,006	2,024
= Actual cost	7,510	7,699	7,905	8,128	8,370
MONTHLY					
Average PIT payments	689	698	707	717	728
Average utilities, maintenance, and insurance	100	109	118	128	139
After-tax cost to own $70,000 residence[4]	626	642	659	677	698
After-tax cost to rent at $350, including utilities[5]	350	380	412	447	485
CUMULATIVE					
Tax savings	1,958	3,930	5,919	7,925	9,949
After-tax cost to own $70,000 residence	7,510	15,209	23,114	31,242	39,612
After-tax cost to rent at $350, including utilities	4,200	8,757	13,701	19,066	24,887

SALE AT 5 YEARS

In this computation, the net proceed from sale after the typical holding period of 5 years is deducted from the cumulative after-tax cost of owning over that period, to show real housing costs.

Disposition costs[6]	8,420
Net sale proceed[7]	29,498
Total housing cost: 5-year ownership of $70,000 residence	24,887 (169 per mo.)
Total housing cost: 5-year renting at initial $350 per month	10,114
Total gain from owning, versus renting	14,773

Notes: [1]Most of the equity growth here is due to an 8.5% appreciation rate, which is also applied as an inflation rate to utilities, maintenance, and rent.

[2]PITI, plus utilities and maintenance. Latter two items assumed here to be equivalent to property taxes.

[3]Tax savings here are interest and property tax deductions for single or couple in 25% income tax bracket.

[4]PITI plus utilities and maintenance, minus 1/12 of annual tax savings.

[5]No tax gains from renting.

[6]Future sales commission and settlement costs included.

[7]Any capital gain tax, excluded here, normally deferred.

Figure 1-12. Owning a $70,000 House Versus Renting a $350 Apartment. Terms: House purchased VA, 9½% interest, no down payment, 30-year loan.

	Investor's Weighting Factor	Primary Residence		Raw Land		New Residential Construction		Used Rental Property	
		Rent	Own	Long-Term Appre-ciation	Develop-ment and Resale	Immediate Sale	Income and Growth	Unfurn-ished	Furnished
COSTS									
Initial investment required	1 x	7 = 7	6 = 6	3 = 3	2 = 2	1 = 1	1 = 1	5 = 5	4 = 4
Development costs	1 x	8 = 8	6 = 6	7 = 7	3 = 3	2 = 2	1 = 1	5 = 5	4 = 4
Operating expenses	1 x	6 = 6	4 = 4	7 = 7	5 = 5	5 = 5	3 = 3	2 = 2	1 = 1
Debt service costs	1 x	5 = 5	3 = 3	4 = 4	4 = 4	2 = 2	2 = 2	1 = 1	1 = 1
Income taxes	1 x	2 = 2	3 = 3	1 = 1	1 = 1	4 = 4	6 = 6	5 = 5	7 = 7
Required expertise	1 x	8 = 8	7 = 7	6 = 6	3 = 3	2 = 2	1 = 1	5 = 5	4 = 4
Management effort	1 x	4 = 4	4 = 4	4 = 4	3 = 3	3 = 3	1 = 1	2 = 2	1 = 1
Fees and other disposition costs	1 x	5 = 5	3 = 3	3 = 3	1 = 1	4 = 4	2 = 2	3 = 3	3 = 3
RISKS	Subtotals	45	36	35	22	23	17	28	25
Loss of investment outlay	2 x	8 = 16	6 = 12	7 = 14	1 = 2	2 = 4	3 = 6	4 = 8	5 = 10
Increase in one or more costs	2 x	6 = 12	3 = 6	7 = 14	2 = 4	1 = 2	5 = 10	3 = 6	4 = 8
Reduced income during holding	2 x	5 = 10	5 = 10	6 = 12	6 = 12	4 = 8	3 = 6	1 = 2	2 = 4
Physical hazard loss	2 x	4 = 8	3 = 6	5 = 10	6 = 12	2 = 4	2 = 4	1 = 2	1 = 2
Adverse political developments	2 x	5 = 10	3 = 6	3 = 6	1 = 2	4 = 8	3 = 6	2 = 4	3 = 6
Uncertainties from passage of time	2 x	5 = 10	3 = 6	1 = 2	4 = 8	4 = 8	3 = 6	2 = 4	2 = 4
Restricted investment options	2 x	4 = 8	3 = 6	1 = 2	1 = 2	1 = 2	1 = 2	2 = 4	3 = 6
Loss of value gain potential	2 x	6 = 12	5 = 10	5 = 10	1 = 2	2 = 4	3 = 6	4 = 8	4 = 8
Failure of appreciation potential	2 x	5 = 10	3 = 6	1 = 2	4 = 8	4 = 8	3 = 6	2 = 4	3 = 6
RETURNS	Subtotals	96	68	72	52	48	52	42	54
Advantages from leverage	1 x	1 = 1	6 = 6	2 = 2	3 = 3	4 = 4	5 = 5	5 = 5	5 = 5
Direct income during holding	1 x	2 = 2	3 = 3	1 = 1	1 = 1	3 = 3	5 = 5	4 = 4	5 = 5
Spendable income from tax benefits	1 x	2 = 2	4 = 4	1 = 1	1 = 1	3 = 3	6 = 6	5 = 5	6 = 6
Benefits of liquidity	1 x	6 = 6	5 = 5	1 = 1	2 = 2	2 = 2	3 = 3	4 = 4	4 = 4
Opportunity for investment variety	1 x	2 = 2	7 = 7	2 = 2	1 = 1	4 = 4	3 = 3	6 = 6	5 = 5
Gains through appreciation	1 x	1 = 1	4 = 4	5 = 5	2 = 2	2 = 2	3 = 3	3 = 3	3 = 3
Gains through value increase	1 x	1 = 1	3 = 3	2 = 2	7 = 7	6 = 6	8 = 8	4 = 4	5 = 5
Internal rate of return	1 x	1 = 1	2 = 2	3 = 3	6 = 6	7 = 7	8 = 8	4 = 4	5 = 5
	Subtotals	16	34	17	23	31	41	35	38
TOTALS		157	138	124	97	102	110	105	117

Figure 1-13. Investment Rating Analysis Form: Risk-Aversive Small Investor.

assuming that the rankings of criteria are essentially correct—the Risks factor is given a weight equal to that of Costs and Returns combined. If the person viewing the situation from that perspective had only one real estate investment decision to make, it would probably be to rent a place to live. Even buying a home (138) falls 12 percent below renting (157).

The least attractive investment for the risk-aversive investor is Raw land bought for quick Development and resale (as finished building lots, for example), which scores 97 with the given weighting factors. If the risk-aversive investor were to make a second investment decision after renting a place to live, it would probably be to buy Raw land and hold it for Long-term appreciation, which scores 124, or only 10 percent below Owning a home.

For Risk-Accepting Investors. In a general "risk-accepting" posture, the investor is willing to take some degree of risk in the hope of increasing returns. The investor characterized as "risk-accepting" in Figure 1–9 now evaluates the rent/buy options in Figure 1–14. This investor scores ownership of a residence 9 percent higher than renting (206 versus 189). New construction of residential Income and growth property and Furnished rentals also come out 2 to 3 percentage points above Renting. The lowest score, 143 or 24 percent below, goes to raw land for quick Development and resale.

For Risk-Taking Investors. In the general "risk-taking" posture, the investor is likely to take greater risks to earn greater returns. In Figure 1–15, Returns are given a weight that is double (6) that of Costs and Risks combined (3). Only Raw land investments score lower—by about 11 percent—than Renting a Primary residence. In the case of land held Long-term, the Costs position is not favorable enough to overcome Risks. Land for quick Development and resale, on the other hand, suffers a risk ranking too high to be overcome by a more favorable Costs position.

The Alternative "Mix." Clearly, the decision to rent or buy a place to live bears no meaningful comparability with a large institution's decision as to whether to buy a motel, shopping mall, or office building. For the small individual investor, however, the choice of living arrangements may be the first in a series of interrelated investment decisions. For example, in buying the $70,000 townhouse, represented in Figure 1–12, rather than renting the $350 apartment, the buyer gains $14,773 over a 5-year period upon sale. On an annual after-tax basis, however, someone wishing to begin an investment program would have $6,482 available to do so at the end of 2 years if he or she had decided to rent instead. At the end of 4 years, an additional $5,694 would become available. Still another housing

	Investor's Weighting Factor	Primary Residence		Raw Land		New Residential Construction		Used Rental Property	
		Rent	Own	Long-Term Appreciation	Development and Resale	Immediate Sale	Income and Growth	Unfurnished	Furnished
COSTS									
Initial investment required	1 x	7 = 7	6 = 6	3 = 3	2 = 2	1 = 1	1 = 1	5 = 5	4 = 4
Development costs	1 x	8 = 8	6 = 6	7 = 7	3 = 3	2 = 2	1 = 1	5 = 5	4 = 4
Operating expenses	1 x	6 = 6	4 = 4	7 = 7	5 = 5	5 = 5	3 = 3	2 = 2	1 = 1
Debt service costs	1 x	5 = 5	3 = 3	4 = 4	4 = 4	2 = 2	2 = 2	1 = 1	1 = 1
Income taxes	1 x	2 = 2	3 = 3	1 = 1	1 = 1	4 = 4	6 = 6	5 = 5	7 = 7
Required expertise	1 x	8 = 8	7 = 7	6 = 6	3 = 3	2 = 2	1 = 1	5 = 5	4 = 4
Management effort	1 x	4 = 4	4 = 4	4 = 4	3 = 3	3 = 3	1 = 1	2 = 2	1 = 1
Fees and other disposition costs	1 x	5 = 5	3 = 3	3 = 3	1 = 1	4 = 4	2 = 2	3 = 3	3 = 3
RISKS	Subtotals	45	36	35	22	23	17	28	25
Loss of investment outlay	2 x	8 = 16	6 = 12	7 = 14	1 = 2	2 = 4	3 = 6	4 = 8	5 = 10
Increase in one or more costs	2 x	6 = 12	3 = 6	7 = 14	2 = 4	1 = 2	5 = 10	3 = 6	4 = 8
Reduced income during holding	2 x	5 = 10	5 = 10	6 = 12	6 = 12	4 = 8	3 = 6	1 = 2	2 = 4
Physical hazard loss	2 x	4 = 8	3 = 6	5 = 10	6 = 12	2 = 4	2 = 4	1 = 2	1 = 2
Adverse political developments	2 x	5 = 10	3 = 6	3 = 6	1 = 2	4 = 8	3 = 6	2 = 4	3 = 6
Uncertainties from passage of time	2 x	5 = 10	3 = 6	1 = 2	4 = 8	4 = 8	3 = 6	2 = 4	2 = 4
Restricted investment options	2 x	4 = 8	3 = 6	1 = 2	1 = 2	1 = 2	1 = 2	2 = 4	3 = 6
Loss of value gain potential	2 x	6 = 12	5 = 10	5 = 10	1 = 2	2 = 4	3 = 6	4 = 8	4 = 8
Failure of appreciation potential	2 x	5 = 10	3 = 6	1 = 2	4 = 8	4 = 8	3 = 6	2 = 4	3 = 6
RETURNS	Subtotals	96	68	72	52	48	52	42	54
Advantages from leverage	3 x	1 = 3	6 = 18	2 = 6	3 = 9	4 = 12	5 = 15	5 = 15	5 = 15
Direct income during holding	3 x	2 = 6	3 = 9	1 = 3	1 = 3	3 = 9	5 = 15	4 = 12	5 = 15
Spendable income from tax benefits	3 x	2 = 6	4 = 12	1 = 3	1 = 3	3 = 9	6 = 18	5 = 15	6 = 18
Benefits of liquidity	3 x	6 = 18	5 = 15	1 = 3	2 = 6	2 = 6	3 = 9	4 = 12	4 = 12
Opportunity for investment variety	3 x	2 = 6	7 = 21	2 = 6	1 = 3	4 = 12	3 = 9	6 = 18	5 = 15
Gains through appreciation	3 x	1 = 3	4 = 12	5 = 15	2 = 6	2 = 6	3 = 9	3 = 9	3 = 9
Gains through value increase	3 x	1 = 3	3 = 9	2 = 6	7 = 21	6 = 18	8 = 24	4 = 12	5 = 15
Internal rate of return	3x	1 = 3	2 = 6	3 = 9	6 = 18	7 = 21	8 = 24	4 = 12	5 = 15
	Subtotals	48	102	51	69	93	123	105	114
TOTALS		189	206	158	143	164	192	175	193

Figure 1–14. Investment Rating Analysis Form: Risk-Accepting Small Investor.

	Investor's Weighting Factor	Primary Residence		Raw Land		New Residential Construction		Used Rental Property	
		Rent	Own	Long-Term Appre-ciation	Develop-ment and Resale	Immediate Sale	Income and Growth	Unfurn-ished	Furnished
COSTS									
Initial investment required	2 x	7 = 14	6 = 12	3 = 6	2 = 4	1 = 2	1 = 2	5 = 10	4 = 8
Development costs	2 x	8 = 16	6 = 12	7 = 14	3 = 6	2 = 4	1 = 2	5 = 10	4 = 8
Operating expenses	2 x	6 = 12	4 = 8	7 = 14	5 = 10	5 = 10	3 = 6	2 = 4	1 = 2
Debt service costs	2 x	5 = 10	3 = 6	4 = 8	4 = 8	2 = 4	2 = 4	1 = 2	1 = 2
Income taxes	2 x	2 = 4	3 = 6	1 = 2	1 = 2	4 = 8	6 = 12	5 = 10	7 = 14
Required expertise	2 x	8 = 16	7 = 14	6 = 12	3 = 6	2 = 4	1 = 2	5 = 10	4 = 8
Management effort	2 x	4 = 8	4 = 8	4 = 8	3 = 6	3 = 6	1 = 2	2 = 4	1 = 2
Fees and other disposition costs	2 x	5 = 10	3 = 6	3 = 6	1 = 2	4 = 8	2 = 4	3 = 6	3 = 6
RISKS	Subtotals	90	72	70	44	46	34	56	50
Loss of investment outlay	1 x	8 = 8	6 = 6	7 = 7	1 = 1	2 = 2	3 = 3	4 = 4	5 = 5
Increase in one or more costs	1 x	6 = 6	3 = 3	7 = 7	2 = 2	1 = 1	5 = 5	3 = 3	4 = 4
Reduced income during holding	1 x	5 = 5	5 = 5	6 = 6	6 = 6	4 = 4	3 = 3	1 = 1	2 = 2
Physical hazard loss	1 x	4 = 4	3 = 3	5 = 5	6 = 6	2 = 2	2 = 2	1 = 1	1 = 1
Adverse political developments	1 x	5 = 5	3 = 3	3 = 3	1 = 1	4 = 4	3 = 3	1 = 1	3 = 3
Uncertainties from passage of time	1 x	5 = 5	3 = 3	1 = 1	4 = 4	4 = 4	3 = 3	2 = 2	2 = 2
Restricted investment options	1 x	4 = 4	3 = 3	1 = 1	1 = 1	1 = 1	1 = 1	2 = 2	3 = 3
Loss of value gain potential	1 x	6 = 6	5 = 5	5 = 5	1 = 1	2 = 2	3 = 3	4 = 4	4 = 4
Failure of appreciation potential	1 x	5 = 5	3 = 3	1 = 1	4 = 4	4 = 4	3 = 3	2 = 2	3 = 3
RETURNS	Subtotals	48	34	37	26	24	26	20	27
Advantages from leverage	6 x	1 = 6	6 = 36	2 = 12	3 = 18	4 = 24	5 = 30	5 = 30	5 = 30
Direct income during holding	6 x	2 = 12	3 = 18	1 = 6	1 = 6	3 = 18	5 = 30	4 = 24	5 = 30
Spendable income from tax benefits	6 x	2 = 12	4 = 24	1 = 6	1 = 6	3 = 18	6 = 36	5 = 30	6 = 36
Benefits of liquidity	6 x	6 = 36	5 = 30	1 = 6	2 = 12	2 = 12	3 = 18	4 = 24	4 = 24
Opportunity for investment variety	6 x	2 = 12	7 = 42	2 = 12	1 = 6	4 = 24	3 = 18	6 = 36	5 = 30
Gains through appreciation	6 x	1 = 6	4 = 24	5 = 30	2 = 12	2 = 12	3 = 18	3 = 18	3 = 18
Gains through value increase	6 x	1 = 6	3 = 18	2 = 12	7 = 42	6 = 36	8 = 48	4 = 24	5 = 30
Internal rate of return	6 x	1 = 6	2 = 12	3 = 18	6 = 36	7 = 42	8 = 48	4 = 24	5 = 30
	Subtotals	96	204	102	138	186	246	210	228
TOTALS		234	310	209	208	256	306	286	305

Figure 1-15. Investment Rating Analysis Form: Risk-Taking Small Investor.

arrangement might be to buy two $35,000 condominium units, rather than the $70,000 townhouse, and rent one of them out.

In Figures 1–13 through 1–15 owning a Primary residence scores higher than all the other types of real estate investment, except Renting (Figure 1–13). This uniformity in the outcomes does not detract from the validity of the comparisons. Home ownership is in fact an excellent real estate investment by the measures investors actually use. Costs are relatively low, partly because of government programs and lender attitudes favoring such ownership, and partly because the relatively low risk involved justifies lower financing costs. A key factor minimizing risk is that the owner is presumed to reside at the property. That fact gives the property a high likelihood of being occupied and well maintained over a relatively long period of time. Returns are relatively high for reasons paralleling the favorable cost and risk positions.

Raw Land

In Figures 1–13 through 1–15, the two basic types of investment in raw land are very different in relative Costs and Risks, but both are generally higher than for most real estate investments. Raw land is difficult to finance, so it usually does not involve large loans that make for good interest deductions from income taxes; and it has no improvements from which income and depreciation deductions can be derived. Property taxes, though lower than on improved land, must still be paid, but the land earns no income to pay them. So the cash flow is always negative during the holding period.

Another potential drawback is that almost all the Returns from land held for Long-term gain come from price appreciation; upon its sale, you must pay disposition costs and capital gains taxes. Since the appreciation rate needs to be relatively high for such an investment to bring significant returns, these taxes can be high also.

> Example: Assume that $5,000 is invested in raw land by a person in the 40-percent income tax bracket, that it appreciates in price at a rate of 15 percent per year, and that property taxes are a flat $50 per year during a five-year holding period. The analysis of this investment is shown in Figure 1–16.
>
> With a 15-percent annual appreciation rate needed to bring a return approaching 10 percent (per year upon sale) by the fifth year, the type of investment reflected in this example can be viewed as similar to a savings bond in performance. How specific parcels of land will appreciate, of course, depends on such factors as development patterns, zoning, transportation, demo-

Initial cash flow – $5,000[1]	Year				
	1	2	3	4	5
Income[1]	– 50	– 50	– 50	– 50	– 50
Sale price	5,750	6,613	7,604	8,745	10,057
Disposition costs (2%)	115	132	152	175	201
Capital gain tax[2]	920	1,058	1,217	1,399	1,609
Net sale proceed[1]	4,715	5,423	6,235	7,171	8,247
IRR	– 6.7%	– 3.16%	6.71%	8.56%	9.7%

[1] IRR computed from these cash flows.
[2] Before-tax capital gain reduced 60% (per 1978 tax law), resulting amount taxed at 40% rate (bracket in this example).

Figure 1-16. Example "F".

graphics, and many others. If the trends are clearly very favorable, then the prices will be proportionately high. To the extent that the trends are not clear, the investment is speculative, only negative cash flows are certain, and you need a lot of study and expertise to make a purchase work for you.

Raw land purchased for quick Development and resale suffers not only from all the basic infirmities of land held for the long term, but from others as well. Instead of requiring less active involvement than other types of real estate investment, however, it requires much more than most. Instead of requiring relatively little expertise, it requires very much. If an attractive property with development potential becomes available, you must search through the public records (otherwise, you have to make risky decisions about engineering and zoning problems), and then you must take action often within limited time constraints.

The "Raw Land" Investor. Raw land investments are not for everyone. Even though Raw land Returns are higher than for most real estate investments, the prospect for additional gain is not enough to attract most investors. The risk-aversive investor in Figure 1-13 ranks it at 97 points, compared with 124 points for land held Long term, and gives between 102 and 119 points to investments other than in a Primary residence. Only the risk-taking investor, depicted in Figure 1-15, considers Raw land held short term (208 points) as a match for that held for Long-term appreciation (209). At that point, however, the potentials for higher returns from other kinds of investments produce higher overall scores. These results do not mean that raw land investments are necessarily inferior to the alternatives. Changes in the weighting factors or in the rankings of investment criteria could change the score in many sets of circumstances, but investments of this kind are of a specialized nature and the number of investors involved in them tends to be small.

New Residential Construction

Timing and Turnover. The two types of new residential construction compared in Figures 1–13 through 1–15 are very general in definition:

1. anything from one, two, or a subdivision of detached houses to a rental or condominium apartment building put up for immediate sale, and
2. the same range of properties built with the idea of acquiring (through construction rather than resale) below market prices, developing for value gain, operating for income and tax benefits, holding for appreciation, and selling or trading for maximum returns.

These two distinct investment strategies are simple enough to identify. Those seeking immediate resale base their gains, if they "survive" in the entrepreneurial sense, on careful land purchases (usually finished lots at prices they consider good for the finished lot market), on tightly scheduled cash flows and construction activity, and on a well planned marketing program that includes competitive financing for the final product. Timing and turnover are the keys to success, because capital is tied up, and short-term loans are running. The cash flows projected from sales cannot begin until work has progressed sufficiently.

The Right Investor(?) As scored in Figures 1–13 through 1–15, both types of new construction rank substantially below Renting or Owning a residence for the risk-aversive investor. Construction for Immediate resale (102) ranks only slightly above Raw land bought for Development and resale (97), the least desirable investment for the risk-aversive investor. For the risk-accepting investor, home ownership (206) still slightly outranks construction for Income and growth (192), which slightly outranks Renting a residence (189). Construction for Immediate resale comes out at 164, which is now above both kinds of Raw land investment (158 long term, and 143 for quick turnover). For the risk-accepting or the risk-taking investor, the New construction investments rank similarly to used rental properties. For the risk-taker, the main change in relative rankings is that New construction becomes more favorable in comparison with raw land investments.

The Right Investment(?) Throughout these same figures, the two types of New construction are close in Costs and Risks, with a slight edge on risk for that held for Income and growth, which has higher Costs but also a greater edge on Returns. In overall scoring, the Income and Growth investment is 7.8 percent more favorable than immediate resale for the risk-accepter and it is 19.5 percent greater for the risk-taking investor. The general reason for this edge is that its Costs are reduced, if it is viewed as income property, by acquiring it through construction. Risks are also reduced, if it is viewed as a construction project, because it is located and designed to produce income, as well as to be resold at some later date. Returns are higher because they come not only from building for quick value gain, but also from the value gain through development as an income property, from the income itself, and from price appreciation.

So why don't all investors put their money into the construction and development of Income and growth properties? One answer is that construction and management are two different businesses requiring separate sets of skills and modes of operation. Another is that the types of property that can be held most profitably for income are more limited than those that can be built for immediate resale, an activity in which small firms building one or several detached houses abound. Relatively speaking, detached houses are not usually favorable for income production although they remain popular among small investors. Properties developed for economies of scale—multi-unit dwellings—require scarcer types of land, more detailed planning and organizing, and a larger scale of operation than attracts most small investors.

Used Rental Property

Used rental property can come in many forms: detached houses, townhouses, individual apartment units (condominium or co-op), or multi-unit buildings, such as duplexes, quadraplexes, or apartment buildings. Excluding temporary "house-sitting" or trading situations, the comparisons made in Figures 1–13 through 1–15 are between furnished and unfurnished properties, without distinguishing among the types or sizes of the units. As a practical matter, such a comparison ordinarily is taken to mean condominium apartment units or multi-unit buildings in most areas, or townhouses in some. There are exceptions, of course, in which detached houses would be the preferred alternative.

Study the rent levels in an area before deciding. As you know, rents do **not** increase proportionately as the price level of units under consideration increases. In most places where a significant market exists for furnished rentals—such as urban areas and those with more seasonal activities (college towns, recreational spots, and the like)—such units tend to draw significantly greater rents than unfurnished ones. If properties and furnishings are selected carefully for high quality, the gains can more than offset the risk to furnishings and accessories. [Furniture can be either rented from leasing companies or purchased outright. If it is rented, the costs are deducted from taxable income as operating expenses; if it is purchased, you can take more substantial tax benefits through depreciation deductions (as discussed more thoroughly in Chapter 2 and elsewhere in this book).]

Furnished Rentals

How Risky Are They? Although furnished rentals are commonly regarded by small investors as more risky than unfurnished, that assessment may be less real than perceived. In many areas, the supply lags behind demand, because small investors shy away from additional capital expenditures for furnishings, from several turnovers a year, and from real and imagined physical hazards to the property. Large institutional investors, on the other hand, tend to put money into such projects as motels rather than into furnished rental units. In many areas the short supply, caused by the operation of these factors, gives rise to higher rents than would result from a market organized in some other way. In many urban areas, the rental of furniture itself has become an important business; you should study its impact when deciding whether, where, and how to invest in a furnished rental unit.

In the weighted rankings of Figures 1-13 through 1-15, unfurnished rentals show better on Costs and furnished better on Risks. How can furnished rentals be *less* risky than unfurnished? Here are the main assumptions leading to that result:

1. Furnished rentals are less vulnerable to operating cost increases because their rents vary more and because the leases are usually shorter-term.
2. The same factors offset the risk of reduced income during the holding period.
3. Furnished rentals can become "unfurnished," should rental market conditions change.
4. That flexibility also reduces the risk associated with restricted investment options.
5. Failure of appreciation potential becomes less of a risk factor because you earn additional income from furnishing.

For risk-aversive, risk-accepting, and risk-taking investors, the scores for used rental property track pretty closely to those for new residential construction. For the risk-accepting investor, rental properties of both kinds outdo both kinds of raw land investment. For the risk-taker, the appeal of rental property, as well as that of Construction for Income and growth, approaches ownership of a primary residence as an attractive investment.

THE IDEAL INVESTMENT?

If all these figures and observations suggest an "ideal investment," it would seem to consist of buying raw land, zoning and engineering it for a multi-unit furnished rental complex, building the complex, operating it and developing its rental base, and buying one or more of the units to live in. Yet no type of investment is the right one in every place and every time. So the search goes on.

THE REAL DECISIONS IN RESIDENTIAL INCOME PROPERTY

SIXTEEN TYPES OF RENTAL PROPERTY

Once you make the general decision to invest in residential income-producing property, whether in addition to or instead of other types of investment, you have to make at least three other decisions before establishing a final list of specific alternatives. The decisions center around three questions:

1. Should the property or properties consist of detached houses, townhouses, individual condominium units, or multi-unit dwellings such as duplexes, quadraplexes, portions of condo projects, or entire apartment buildings?
2. Should they be purchased new or in the resale or conversion market?
3. Should they be rented furnished or unfurnished?

These three questions give rise to 16 alternatives, which are shown in Figure 2–1, with additional variations on each. Let's try to answer these questions one at a time.

Detached				Townhouse				Condo Unit				Multi-Unit			
New		Used		New		Used		New		Used		New		Used	
F	UF	F	UF	F	UF	F	UF	F	UF	F	UF	F	UF	F	UF
1	2	3	4	5	6	7	8	9	10	11	12	13	14	15	16

Figure 2-1.

DETACHED, TOWNHOUSE, CONDO, OR MULTI-UNIT?

The Dubious OPM Miracle

Until recently the term "single family dwelling unit" meant a detached house in the United States. As government programs, population increases, and general economic prosperity spurred on the post-Depression and World War II housing boom, the detached house came to be of interest to the small investor. Even when the stock market performed poorly, housing prices continued to climb, both in sales and rents. Tax benefits were, and are, attractive. Rental markets have tended to hold up overall, outside areas in economic decline.

"Miracle books" were, and are, written on the subject of how you can get rich in a few years by using leverage ("OPM" or Other People's Money) to pyramid a modest initial investment into a real estate empire. The basic idea is that the small investor first borrows money with as little down as possible (such as through a VA or FHA assumption, semifancy financing, or some other more or less obvious scheme) and buys into a single-unit rental property. That property is then rented out for an amount that covers loan payments, taxes, and other costs as closely as possible. It is held for a period of time to gain in market price through appreciation and then disposed of at a profit.

See? Just like the big holding companies . . . lots of money out, with little or no money in.

The next step is to take the profits from the sale of the initial investment and acquire two or more others on a similarly leveraged basis. With little or nothing laid out, you get it to operate on a profitable or at least a break-even basis, and then you sell it at a profit to buy a small apartment building—and so on. The detached house gained much from the beliefs that developed around such a theme: "Everybody has to live somewhere, and they ain't making any more land."

The basic idea is not completely crazy, as long as two conditions are present:

1. Income from the investment must be sufficient to make operating and debt service costs manageable.
2. Market value changes during the holding period must be great enough to enable investors to dispose of their investments at a greater overall rate of return, on an after-tax and after-inflation basis, than they would likely derive from less risky investments.

Negative Cash Flows: More Going Out Than Coming In

In practice, it is difficult, with an initial single-unit investment, to both buy a property with maximum leverage and cover the carrying costs with rental income, even after annual income tax deductions for interest payments and depreciation. Unless you can make a substantial down payment of 25 percent or more to keep the loan amount and payments low, you usually run up a negative cash flow (that is, more going out than coming in), at least during the first 2 or 3 years of holding, until rents catch up through the effects of inflation and scarcity of comparable housing in the rental market. In effect, such an investment must be subsidized in the beginning by some source of income outside itself, whether from a funded reserve, from a positive cash flow generated by another investment, from a job, or from something else.

This sort of difficulty tends to defeat the purpose of holding detached houses purely as investment property for income, appreciation, and tax benefits. For such an investment to work out, the projected appreciation rate for detached houses has to be substantially higher than for townhouses, condo units, and other alternative investment property types. The reason is that rents do not increase in step with the properties' market value indefinitely. Instead, as the market value reaches the higher ranges, the increases in associated rents fall off disproportionately—they do not keep up. Figure 2–2 illustrates the trends.

Although actual figures vary from one time and place to another, the reason for the *kind* of curves shown in Figure 2–2 is clear enough. It is largely a matter of supply and demand. Individuals renting on the lower end of the price spectrum include those who cannot afford to buy their own residences, as well as those who do not judge the economic incentive great enough to own their own homes. As people move into income ranges that enable them to pay higher rents, they are also more able to buy, and the tax

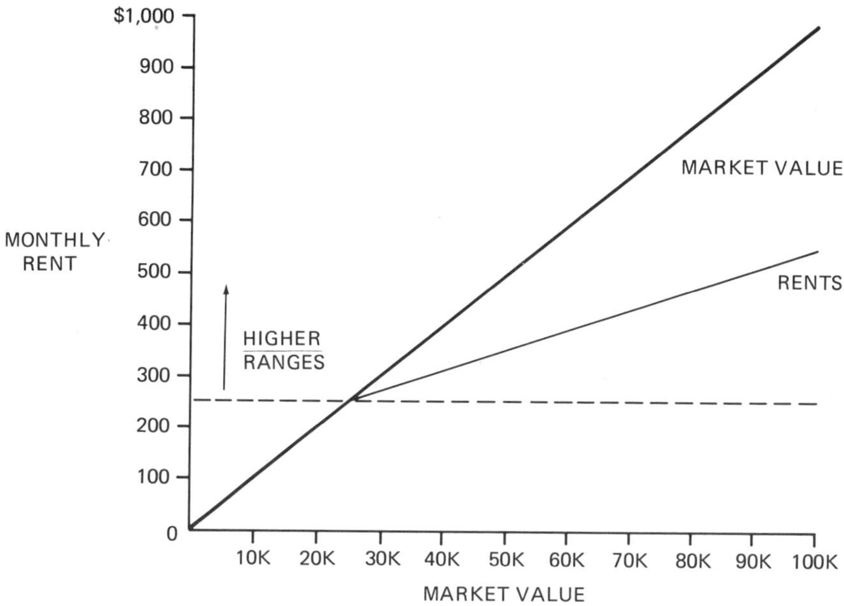

Figure 2-2.

and related incentives for them to do so become greater. Accordingly, demand for rental housing falls off as the rents and market values increase. At the same time (for reasons we shall discuss), higher-cost housing is generally more available than lower-cost housing. The results of all these factors are (a) relatively high rents for lower-cost housing and (b) relatively low rents for higher-cost housing.

Detached Housing Versus Other Types of Property

The round numbers in Figure 2-2 reflect only a general relationship between price and income, with many exceptions and variations. Yet to the extent that they reflect general expectations, they do not favor detached houses, which tend to be at the higher end of the price spectrum where increases in market values are usually expected to outpace increases in rents. As a result, buying detached houses for rental until you can sell for a handsome profit usually creates at least a temporary negative cash flow. Simply stated, you have to make up the difference between the rent you take in and the (higher) expenses you pay out, until you can increase the rent so that it covers your expenses. Other types of rental property—such as townhouses and multi-unit dwellings—do not have the same drawback. In fact the negative cash flow for detached housing tends to be larger than that for other types of investment property generally due to the typically larger initial investment outlays or subsequent payments over time. Several other factors may widen the discrepancies between detached houses and other investments. They are:

1. supply,
2. demographics,
3. lifestyle and family size, and
4. energy costs.

Supply. Over the years, detached houses, favored by zoning, have been built in quicker response to perceived demand than the other types of residential property. Small construction companies, which make up the bulk of the building industry, can put up as few as needed—even one at a time—and turn them over faster than they can other types of housing. These companies generally get favorable front-end financing and a good return in a relatively short time. If they see a short-term decline in demand, they can stop building until there is a turnaround, without the risk of having to complete a large unprofitable project. Such conditions have encouraged the production of much detached housing at the high end of the price spectrum, relative to other types of housing.

Demographics. The basic demand for large detached houses in recent decades has come primarily from the expansion of families begun during the post-World War II baby boom, as well as from their tendency to build up equity and to "buy up" in value. The continuation of this process obviously depends in the long run on having others "in line," waiting to buy properties from people who are buying up. The progeny of the baby boom year of 1950 were 30 years old in 1980.

Lifestyle and Family Size. The life style of 30- to 40-year-olds during the 1950s is somewhat different from those of the 1980s. Increased career-mindedness among women and diminished family sizes have lessened the prospective need for living space and increased the need for convenience and efficiency of maintenance.

Energy Costs. Large houses with central heating . . . unused rooms cooled during the warm season . . . much of America's detached housing inventory came into existence during an era of high-riding energy *un*consciousness. Although stopgap measures abound for cutting down on rising energy costs—less usage, solar heating, more insulation, heat pumps, electric blankets, wood stoves, and so on—they all mean higher costs to acquire and/or to maintain living space.

Detached Housing and the Small Investor

Despite these recent trends, detached houses remain an important part of the small investor's real estate inventory. A partial reason is the American's traditional attachment to land and open space, an emotional factor that has a very real effect on demand. Another consideration is that many small investors in real estate begin their investment program by buying a place as their own residence, living there for several years, and then renting it out. With this course of action, after rents inflate enough after awhile to cover the carrying costs for a house, people do not have to subsidize large negative cash flows. Sometimes they even do better than break even. If you view the investment primarily as a hedge against inflation or bad times and a nest egg, rather than as a vehicle for maximum returns, your approach probably makes sense.

Investment for Maximum Returns

On the other hand, the investor who is interested primarily in maximum returns must give the level of income to be derived from a property greater weight than other benefits. Such an investor must keep in mind that returns from a real estate investment can come only from the following sources:

1. income,
2. tax benefits,
3. value gain, and
4. price appreciation.

Dollar for dollar, returns received from the first two sources are more valuable, in an economy not characterized by deflation, than returns received from the latter two sources. The reason is that you receive returns from income and tax benefits (interest and depreciation deductions) during the holding period when their present value is highest. At the same time, any returns you hope to achieve from value gain require capital outlays in current dollars. Finally, returns from price appreciation are realized only at the end of the holding period, after their value has been progressively diminished by the passage of time and by the effects of inflation.

To overcome the usually unfavorable ratio between income and market value that handicaps detached houses, the investor must be convinced that returns from the other sources, primarily appreciation, will substantially *outweigh the negative cash flows,* which are typically larger than those expected from an investment in a townhouse or condo apartment unit. Such investors thus believe that time will bring the long-term benefits they seek.

An important risk factor must then be weighed: *uncertainties from the passage of time*. Rental income is current and based pretty much on the relatively safe proposition that everyone must live somewhere. Returns from appreciation, no matter how certain you may feel that they will come, are prospective and therefore completely speculative. On that point, you can speculate every bit as easily against detached houses as in favor of them.

Single-Unit or Multi-Unit?

When investors decide to invest in only one unit, they do so usually because they have only so much capital either that is available in liquid assets or that can be borrowed against. Because small investors often prefer to operate individually, or because they lack the information or confidence needed to organize an investment group, they usually invest in one unit at a time. Whatever their motives or reasons, they incur significant costs in the form of lost economies of scale. In the past, small investors stood a fair chance of making such investments work. Buying and renting out one detached house at a time—with an eye to pyramiding investments through the resale of the original property and the purchase of apartment buildings—was the only starting place available to many small investors in real estate. Today, that approach remains popular, partly because of romantic notions about the intrinsic value of land and the home as a "castle." Yet it has become a dubious, if not downright dangerous, practice in an era of transitional energy usage patterns and after years of price inflation in housing on the high end of the price spectrum.

Townhouses. In recent years, greater efficiency in townhouse construction costs, in land usage, and in income production has brought townhouses into competition for the small investor's financial involvement. A very general economy-of-scale rule (with many exceptions) is that two townhouses on the lower end of the price spectrum may be bought for about the same price as a detached house at a mid-range price; for example, you can purchase either two townhouses or one detached house at $100,000. If the ratios between rents and market value shown in Figure 2–2 apply, then Figure 2–3 displays the contrasts in income flows between investments in one detached and two townhouses. The investment in this figure is "multi-unit" only in the simple sense that it consists of two units, not necessarily in the same project, instead of one unit. Figure 2–3 also assumes that the same financing arrangement is available for either investment and that the vacancy rate and operating expenses are the same.

In Figure 2–3, the negative cash flow before taxes for the one-unit investment is $2,200 greater annually (or $183 monthly) than that for two

	Single Unit	Two Units
Market value	$100,000	$100,000
Gross income (first year)	6,000 (500 per month)	8,400 (350 per month each)
– Vacancies (8.33%)	500	700
– Operating expenses	2,500	2,500
= Net operating income	3,000	5,200
– Loan payments (80% loan)	9,777	9,777
= Net cash flow	– 6,777	– 4,577
Capitalization rate	3.0%	5.2%

Figure 2-3.

units. That difference, which represents 2.2 percent of the market value of either investment, has to be made up in greater appreciation by the single unit. The appreciation must be even greater than 2.2 percent to offset the "weathering" effects of inflation on the value of money—since returns from appreciation come only upon disposition, while those from income are current.

Buying two units rather than one also reduces your risk. If one unit goes unrented for a time, the other has a chance to earn income. If one is damaged by fire, by tenants, or by something else, the other may be spared. If one fails to realize its anticipated appreciation, the other is likely to gain in a different area, as long as the general trend remains upward for the type of property in question. Costs of management increase, however, as the number of units in different places goes up.

As you increase the number of units located in one place, you do two things: (a) You decrease your per-unit cost to build or to acquire, thus achieving a greater-than-usual economy of scale, and (b) you increase your risk. However, if the site is located well, if the design and construction are sound and efficient, and if the timing is right, the potential economies of scale in multi-unit investment ordinarily outweigh the risk associated with having too many "eggs in one basket."

Condominiums. Multi-unit investment has become more convenient in recent years with the rise of condominium apartments. The individual units are owned in fee simple, a form of ownership that makes the units financable and that limits the degree to which other owners can restrain investor activity. Depending on the rate of sales and on the overall economics of the project, the developer or owner may be willing to negotiate a favorable price for more than 2 or 3 units at a time. In selecting a condominium project for investment, you must review the applicable declaration of condominium and by-laws to assure that none of their provisions makes the project unprofitable for investors. If you buy units through investor financing lined up by the developer or through other money made available specifically for investors, the lender is likely to have already made a rather thorough review.

Figure 2–4 compares 6 two-bedroom condominium units bought in two different ways: (a) at the going market price per unit at several different places, and (b) at a 10-percent discount for buying a "stairwell" of 6 units at one location. The assumptions in this illustration are: that the going price for each unit, bought individually, is $33,333, rounded to $200,000 for 6 units; and that financing is available on the same terms as in Figure 2–3—80 percent of the sale price at 12-percent annual interest for 30 years. The rents, including utilities, are taken from the curve suggested in Figure 2–2. The result reflects advantages both in investing at the lower end of the price spectrum and in multi-unit investment.

COMPARISON RATING ANALYSIS

Figures 2–6 through 2–10 are sample analyses, using the same rating system as in Chapter 1, for furnished and unfurnished rentals, new and used properties, and single-unit and multi-unit investments. Figure 2–12 is a blank table that you may reproduce and use as a worksheet for additional comparisons, with criteria rankings and weighting factors that are specific to your own real estate investment market.

Figures 2–6, 2–7, and 2–8 cover furnished and unfurnished rental properties that are detached, a townhouse, a condominium apartment, and a multi-unit investment. Here the "multi-unit investment" is taken to

	Six Condominium Apartment Units Separate Purchases, Several Locations	Six Condominium Apartment Units Single Purchase, Same Location
Market value	$200,000	$180,000
Gross income (first year)	25,200	25,200
– Vacancies (8.33%)	2,099	2,099
– Operating expenses (condominium fee and taxes)	10,800	10,800
= Net operating income	12,301	12,301
– Loan payments (80% loans)	24,442	21,998
= Net cash flow	– 12,141	– 9,697
Capitalization rate	6.15%	6.83%

Figure 2–4.

mean a number of apartments sufficiently large to realize economies of scale, ordinarily 6 or more. Investor weighting factors are added, and comparisions are made among risk-aversive, risk-accepting, and risk-taking investors.

Figure 2–11 covers new and used properties acquired for income production and for market value increase. Here "used" means a property bought in the resale market; it has been lived in, and it is old enough that some of its appliances may be due for major repairs or replacement, but it is not old enough to require significant remodeling or to be considered part of the antique market. In this figure, the types of property have been ranked according to the 25 Costs, Risks, and Returns criteria, but no investor weighting factors have been added. You are invited to reproduce the figure and experiment with weighting factors of interest to you.

Figure 2–10, which compares 3 kinds of single-unit investments and 5 kinds of multi-unit investment, is also presented without assignment of investor weighting factors. As a small investor, as a realtor serving the small investor, or as a student of practical real estate investment, you need to go through the weighting process on your own. Here "apartment building" means one that could be acquired by a small investor or by a group of small investors through an active general partnership or a limited partnership promoted through a small-scale private offering. This would generally exclude, for example, a large building of 100 or more units with elevators, recreational facilities, and other such amenities.

NEW, USED, OR CONVERSION?

The second major question, when buying income-producing property, is whether to buy new or used. If used, how old? If condo, should it be a recent conversion? On such points, the balance of pros and cons is usually so close that decisions are bound to vary according to the area, time, investor, and portfolio.

In Favor of Buying New . . .

The main factors favoring new properties are their:

1. presumed ease and economy in maintenance,
2. attractive financing arrangements, and
3. advantageous tax treatment as to depreciation.

Each of these positive considerations, however, must be examined closely in terms of offsetting disadvantages.

Maintenance. Clearly, new appliances, new plumbing, new wiring, new roofs, new paint, and the like all require less immediate care than their older equivalents. Not until 8 or 10 years go by do you face the possibility that appliances with moving parts will have to undergo major repairs or be replaced. On the other hand, brand new properties have not had a chance to be "debugged." As such problems develop, they tend to be large—leaky roofs or basements, settling foundations, creaky floors, peeled siding, initially hidden construction flaws, and so on. Resolving such problems with a developer, as a property stands by producing little or no income, can be costly. An added risk is that the developer will not be able or willing to correct the problem, without costly and time-consuming litigation.

Financing. At some cost to the developer, blocks of mortgage money are lined up at guaranteed interest rates for periods of time coinciding with the duration of the project. To attract buyers, interest rates and down payments are purposely set below the going rates and terms in the general money market. These attractive financing arrangements are often an appeal for new developments, but you must be aware that their costs are generally worked into the price of the property. (Furthermore, many methods of creative financing can be devised just as well for used properties.)

So while the financing terms are appealing, they are actually applied to a higher sales price. To compare the advantages and disadvantages in the trade-off between financing and sales price, you have to work out the numbers for the alternatives—preferably right down to the projected after-tax internal rates of return. (See Chapters 3 and 4 for the applicable investment analysis techniques and for the uses of sensitivity analysis. The methods in those sections make it a fairly simple matter to check the bottom line by holding the sales price constant and changing the loan rates and terms, and *vice versa.*)

Depreciation. A major depreciation angle gives new property an advantage over used—namely, depreciation on an accelerated schedule up to 200 percent on a declining balance or on a straight line basis. Component depreciation enables you to depreciate parts of the property (such as the roof, plumbing, heating and air conditioning plant, siding, hot water equipment, and other items), on a shorter-term schedule than the building itself. The reason is that these "components" are likely to wear out faster than the "shell." Component depreciation schedules can sometimes also be set up for used property, but they are more difficult. In contrast, the depreciation of used residential income property can be accelerated to a maximum of only 125 percent on a declining balance, but it may be done over a shorter period of time, since the life expectancy of the building can be assumed to be shorter.

In weighing the respective advantages of accelerated and component depreciation, you must weigh all the factors, long- and short-term. For example, keep in mind that the amounts deducted during the holding period beyond what could be deducted through straight-line depreciation are subject to tax as "recaptured" depreciation upon the sale of the property. Again, as in comparing financing arrangements and sales price, the only meaningful way to judge the bottom line effects of alternative depreciation methods is to run the respective numbers through a sensitivity analysis (Chapter 4).

Other Factors. In addition to maintenance, financing arrangements, and tax angles, some less tangible factors bear upon the decision between new and used properties. Owners of new properties bought early in the project might have to put up with unsightly construction in the area for a lengthy period. If you plan to live in the dwelling until the area has matured into a community, that sort of intangible can bring an advantage. Early prices are often set lower to attract buyers who make the project "for real." If the project goes well, the likelihood of a good value gain is highly enhanced. Yet there is risk: If you find it necessary to move before planned, the developer's offerings may compete with resale, while the construction activity and uncompleted amenities make rental (with which the developer may also compete) more difficult than in an established community.

Many conditions affect both the resale and the rental markets. For example what about resales and rentals by other owners or, in the case of condominium units, by co-owners? Americans are mobile. Some 20 percent of us change residence every 5 years. Depending on the character of a given local economy, people may be more or less transient than that figure suggests. Generally, in an area of starter homes, people are likely to be more transient than in an area of high-cost, family-oriented housing. Important exceptions to this rule are military or company towns, in which officers and executives are routinely shifted in three to five year cycles. The relevance and proximity of schools, of shopping, and of transportation; the values and trends in nearby properties; the average age and typical lifestyle of the local population; and so forth—all these factors need to be weighed in choosing between new and used investment properties.

How Old, How New?

What is "new"? What is "old"? A "new" income property can be the first built in a development project, or it can be the last one put on sale at the tail end of the project a year or two later. A property can be "used," on the one hand, if its legal or equitable ownership is transferred more than once, or, on the other hand, if it is a dilapidated antique in need of restoration.

A condominium conversion has characteristics of both old and new: Financing arrangements may be comparable to those for new housing, but the building itself is eligible for depreciation accelerated to a maximum of 125 percent on a declining balance. If the buildings are 5 to 10 years old, the conversion is likely to include the replacement of carpeting and appliances, painting and other cosmetic work, and such relatively minor changes as a switchover to the individual metering of utilities. If the buildings are older, check out engineering reports on the plumbing, electrical wiring, heating and air conditioning system (if central), and other aspects of the plant as if you were buying a detached house rather than one or more condo units.

Does this double nature make used condo units more risky than used townhouses or detached houses? Not really. Although the potential costs of system failure are greater in absolute terms, two other elements offset the "damage" they could do. First, they are spread out over a greater number of people, and, second, they are designed with initial economies of scale as a significant goal (if they started out as rental properties). Most states have condominium laws requiring full disclosure of engineering details to prospective buyers, a protection rarely afforded consumers in the resale of detached houses or non-condo townhouses.

FURNISHED OR UNFURNISHED?

The third major investment question is whether to rent furnished or unfurnished. In responding to this question, you must also decide:

1. the extent to which the rented units should be furnished, and
2. whether the furnishings and appointments should be purchased or leased by the investor.

The Market for Furnished Units

Such questions relate closely to the kind of furnished rental market that you can tap in the area under consideration. This market can range widely. It can be a room and board arrangement, or it can be a fine large home, full of antiques and rented on a highly selective basis either temporarily while the owner is away or even permanently for a special kind of clientele. Such extremes represent the fringes of the market. More commonly, furnished units fall into five significant groups, found in most large urban areas:

People Between Their Regular Homes. This category includes:

1. those who have left a previously rented or owned residence and who are waiting for the availability of another through its vacancy or completion of construction;
2. those who are new to an area and who prefer to rent for a time (but not long enough to justify moving in furniture) before choosing a place to buy;
3. those temporarily displaced by fire or other misfortune; and
4. others with temporary housing needs precluding the use of their own furniture and accessories.

Individuals Visiting the Area for Short-Term, Job-Related Purposes. "Visitors" may be persons in a training program whose duration makes staying in a hotel or motel uneconomical or uncomfortable, persons on a temporary assignment of some kind, persons moving into a new area with a company or government employer for whom housing is not yet available, or persons in some other similar situation.

Tourists and Others on Extended Recreational or Family Visits. For this market, keep in mind that most jurisdictions in which the investor might operate have zoning and/or business regulations to distinguish rental property from rooming houses and from hotels and motels. Typically, rooming houses are prohibited from renting to transients for less than a month and from providing such amenities as room service and housekeeping.

Students and Military Personnel. While obviously different in occupation, these two groups have important characteristics in common: They tend to be (with exceptions, of course) young, impecunious, and unsettled. They are also semi-communal—at least partly for economic reasons; more than others in the furnished rental market, they are likely to live together in groups. It is perhaps an understatement to say that informality, large crowds and loud sounds tend to characterize their patterns of entertainment. All those factors should be considered in choosing furniture and accessories, and in establishing both rents and management policies, if you want to operate in that market.

Childless Young Professionals. In recent years the values and lifestyles of many of the nation's World War II "baby boomers" have undergone change and development, reflecting their *phenomenal wealth.* Lately in their twenties and thirties, they are largely college-educated in an economy that is more service-oriented than any other at any time or place—and there are just more of them. If single, which they often are, they tend to have larger incomes than their parents had at the same age (during the post-Depression and wartime eras), and a greater portion of their income is disposable (wisely or not). If married, the wives tend to continue their careers, and if the couple have children—more don't than do—they tend to have fewer children later in their marriages.

In this youthful economy that insists on "more," a sizable industry has emerged to provide instant gratification for this populous subculture. These are people who need to try on different furniture before buying any, to lease furniture to "stay loose" or to avoid the capital commitment, or to maintain flexibility some other way. Furnished rentals and rented furniture are part of that catering industry. The showrooms of the leasing operations reflect the latest in style and the motif: *And you can have it all right now!* In this swinging singles (and doubles) market, apartment complexes and furniture leasing companies often enjoy a very profitable two-way traffic. In this market, more than in the others, the investor in furnished rental property must consider keeping pace with fashion among the advantages and disadvantages of leasing.

Furniture and Accessories: Buy or Lease?

From a purely numerical—and primarily tax—point of view, it makes more sense for the investor to buy furniture than to lease it. For personal property, such as furnishings and accessories, that the investor buys new and rents out as part of a furnished unit, a relatively short-term depreciation schedule can be established (seven years is one possibility) at up to 200 percent on a declining balance. Also, 20 percent of the depreciation amount (the basis) can be taken as "additional first-year depreciation" in the first year, along with any other depreciation deducted on the remainder through the accelerated schedule.

For example, on $3,000 worth of furniture, you are entitled to a first-year "bonus" of $750, plus $643 in depreciation (on a 7-year schedule), for a total of $1,393 in depreciation in the first year. For someone in the 40-percent tax bracket, this amount means a $557 tax gain the first year from depreciation alone.

In the case of leased furniture, the tax benefits are not so dramatic since depreciation is taken by the leasing company rather than by the lessee. However, the amounts spent on leasing furniture can be deducted from taxable income as operating expenses. In deciding whether to buy or lease furniture, you must obviously work out a budget carefully to determine whether the additional income justifies the greater management effort and risk.

In addition to furniture and accessories, your prospective market might require the use of such household items as cooking and eating utensils and bed linens. Young professionals, people between homes, and students and military personnel are likely to have their own. Yet visitors for job-related purposes and those on recreational or family visits are more likely to need them. In determining whether not to include them in the budget, you must decide which market(s) you wish to seek and service.

LONG-TERM OR SHORT-TERM LEASES?

As a general rule the length of the lease's term is inversely proportional to the rent: for shorter-term leases, the rent is higher; for longer-term leases, the rent is lower. The reason is that as you rent the unit more and more frequently (to earn the required income during a given period), you run an ever greater risk of losing a month's rent somewhere along the line. That risk is real, and it must be accounted for, even if the supply of rental units is low and demand high in a given market at a particular time.

Figure 2–5 shows a sample distribution of rent levels across a 12-month range of terms. The specific rents vary depending on such factors

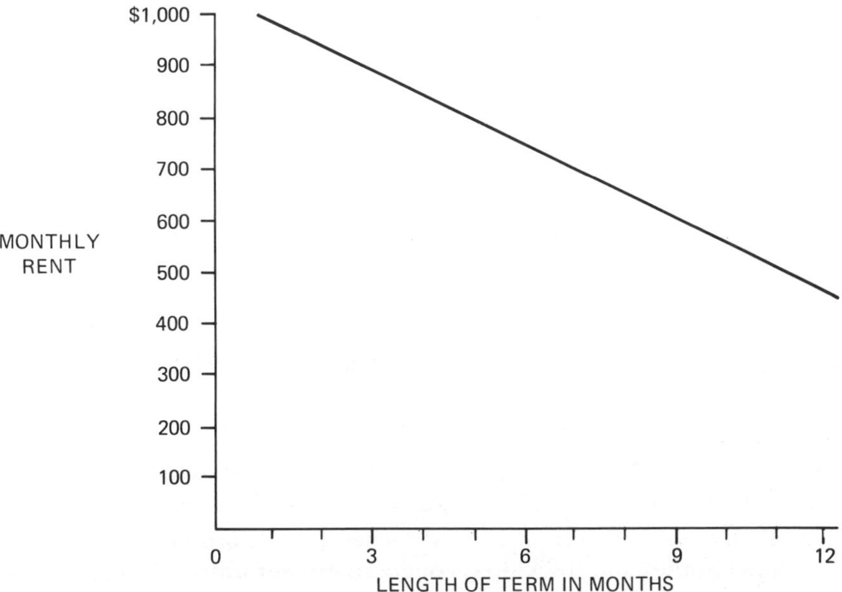

Figure 2–5.

as wear, tear, and seasonality of the market. To the extent that any of those factors adds cost or risk to the business, it should be reflected in additional rent. If the market in question will not bear such adjustments, it may not be the right market for furnished rentals.

CRITERIA RANKINGS

Single- or multi-unit? New or old? Furnished or unfurnished? To make the decisions that best suit your needs and goals, run these questions through the Investment Rating Analysis Form.

Unfurnished and Furnished

For each of our 25 investment criteria, the types of property covered in this chapter may be ranked from least desirable with a 1, to more and most desirable with a 2 or any number up to 8. In ranking property, several broad themes emerge from the way in which the numbers work out:

1. In comparison with the other three basic types of property (detached, townhouse, condo), multi-unit investments rank lowest (the least desirable) on costs, because they involve a greater capital outlay, on an overall project basis.
2. Furnishing one or more units tends to drive up most cost items—*except for income taxes*. By this criterion, furnished properties rank more favorably than unfurnished due to the substantial depreciation benefits in furnished rentals, if the furniture is bought rather than leased. Tax benefits are offset to some extent by the fact that the furniture must be bought and paid for (even if financed) in the first place. Besides using financing, you can add some control to costs in furnished units by mixing bought and leased furniture in the portfolio.
3. Detached houses tend to cost more to acquire, operate, and maintain than do townhouses, which tend to cost more than individual condominium units.
4. Multi-unit investments tend to be more *risky* than the other three types of property, mainly because more money has to be committed to one location.
5. Partly for the same reason, detached houses are more risky than townhouses and individual condo apartment units. With changing energy usage and demographic patterns, the gap could widen. Given

the dwindling supply of and the increasing demand for fossil fuels, energy efficiency is likely to be a key determinant of value in housing of the future.

6. Individual condominium units tend to rank highest (best) by most Risk criteria, because they are on the low end of the price spectrum. Exceptions are increase in one or more costs, uncertainties from passage of time, and adverse political developments. Such exceptions flow from the two facts that boards of directors and other owners control the operating and maintenance budget (as they do partly with townhouses) and that condominiums are affected by more government involvement than townhouses and detached structures.
7. Furnishing one or more units tends to reduce risk by most criteria except loss of investment outlay and physical hazard loss, because furnishing opens the units to the furnished rental markets without necessarily closing them off to the unfurnished market.
8. Multi-unit investments rank highest by every criterion for Returns except benefits of liquidity and opportunity for investment variety, which are the negative trade-offs for the economies of scale which make the returns potentially so favorable for multi-unit investments.
9. Except for benefits of liquidity and opportunity for investment variety, detached houses rank lowest in Returns by each criterion. The liquidity that detached houses are assumed to enjoy results largely from their popularity as primary residences. As we have seen, many assumptions about housing patterns in the past must now be placed under scrutiny.
10. Furnishing increases returns substantially, except in the case of benefits from liquidity, advantages from leverage, and gains through appreciation. Although furniture may have a negative impact on liquidity, because it has to be disposed of if you sell the unit, the generally shorter terms of the leases offset that impact to some extent by making the property available for earlier occupancy by prospective buyers.

Comparative Ratings by Investor Type

Criteria rankings and weighting factors for the *risk-aversive* investor are applied in Figure 2–6. The 8 types of investment property are rated from most to least desirable in the following order:

1. Furnished condo apartment 198
2. Unfurnished condo apartment 190

	Investor's Weighting Factor	Unfurnished				Furnished			
		Detached	Townhouse	Condo-minium Apartment Unit	Multi-Unit	Detached	Townhouse	Condo-minium Apartment Unit	Multi-Unit
COSTS									
Initial investment required	1 x	4 = 4	6 = 6	8 = 8	2 = 2	3 = 3	5 = 5	7 = 7	1 = 1
Development costs	1 x	6 = 6	7 = 7	8 = 8	2 = 2	3 = 3	4 = 4	5 = 5	1 = 1
Operating expenses	1 x	5 = 5	6 = 6	6 = 6	2 = 2	3 = 3	4 = 4	4 = 4	1 = 1
Debt service costs	1 x	3 = 3	3 = 3	2 = 2	1 = 1	3 = 3	3 = 3	2 = 2	1 = 1
Income taxes	1 x	3 = 3	5 = 5	7 = 7	1 = 1	4 = 4	6 = 6	8 = 8	2 = 2
Required expertise	1 x	6 = 6	6 = 6	4 = 4	2 = 2	5 = 5	5 = 5	3 = 3	1 = 1
Management effort	1 x	6 = 6	7 = 7	8 = 8	2 = 2	3 = 3	4 = 4	5 = 5	1 = 1
Fees and other disposition costs	1 x	4 = 4	6 = 6	8 = 8	2 = 2	3 = 3	5 = 5	7 = 7	1 = 1
RISKS	Subtotals	37	46	51	14	27	36	41	9
Loss of investment outlay	2 x	4 = 8	6 = 12	8 = 16	2 = 4	3 = 6	5 = 10	7 = 14	1 = 2
Increase in one or more costs	2 x	7 = 14	5 = 10	3 = 6	1 = 2	8 = 16	6 = 12	4 = 8	2 = 4
Reduced income during holding	2 x	3 = 6	5 = 10	7 = 14	1 = 2	4 = 8	6 = 12	8 = 16	2 = 4
Physical hazard loss	2 x	4 = 8	6 = 12	8 = 16	2 = 4	3 = 6	5 = 10	7 = 14	1 = 2
Adverse political developments	2 x	5 = 10	5 = 10	3 = 6	1 = 2	6 = 12	6 = 12	4 = 8	2 = 4
Uncertainties from passage of time	2 x	6 = 12	5 = 10	3 = 6	1 = 2	6 = 12	5 = 10	4 = 8	2 = 4
Restricted investment options	2 x	3 = 6	5 = 10	7 = 14	1 = 2	4 = 8	6 = 12	8 = 16	2 = 4
Loss of value gain potential	2 x	3 = 6	5 = 10	7 = 14	1 = 2	4 = 8	6 = 12	8 = 16	2 = 4
Failure of appreciation potential	2 x	3 = 6	5 = 10	7 = 14	1 = 2	4 = 8	6 = 12	8 = 16	2 = 4
RETURNS	Subtotals	76	94	106	22	84	102	116	32
Advantages from leverage	1 x	1 = 1	2 = 2	3 = 3	4 = 4	1 = 1	2 = 2	3 = 3	4 = 4
Direct income during holding	1 x	1 = 1	3 = 3	4 = 4	7 = 7	2 = 2	5 = 5	6 = 6	8 = 8
Spendable income from tax benefits	1 x	1 = 1	2 = 2	3 = 3	7 = 7	4 = 4	5 = 5	6 = 6	8 = 8
Benefits of liquidity	1 x	4 = 4	4 = 4	4 = 4	2 = 2	3 = 3	3 = 3	3 = 3	1 = 1
Opportunity for investment variety	1 x	3 = 3	4 = 4	7 = 7	1 = 1	5 = 5	6 = 6	8 = 8	2 = 2
Gains through appreciation	1 x	1 = 1	2 = 2	3 = 3	4 = 4	1 = 1	2 = 2	3 = 3	4 = 4
Gains through value increase	1 x	1 = 1	3 = 3	5 = 5	7 = 7	2 = 2	4 = 4	6 = 6	8 = 8
Internal rate of return	1 x	1 = 1	2 = 2	4 = 4	7 = 7	3 = 3	5 = 5	6 = 6	8 = 8
	Subtotals	13	22	33	39	21	32	41	43
TOTALS		126	162	190	75	132	170	198	84

Figure 2-6. Investment Rating Analysis Form: Furnished and Unfurnished Rental Properties—Risk-Aversive Investor.

3. Furnished townhouse 170
4. Unfurnished townhouse 162
5. Furnished detached 132
6. Unfurnished detached 126
7. Furnished multi-unit 84
8. Unfurnished multi-unit 75

The *risk-accepting* investor in Figure 2–7 weights Returns evenly with Costs and Risks combined. With the same criteria rankings as in Figure 2–11, the ratings work out as follows:

1. Furnished condo apartment 181
2. Unfurnished condo apartment 170
3. Furnished townhouse 151
4. Unfurnished townhouse 137
5. Furnished detached and furnished multi-unit 111
6. Unfurnished multi-unit 103
7. Unfurnished detached 101

The most notable differences between the risk-aversive and risk-accepting investors, as quantified in these figures, are:

1. The multi-unit investment becomes competitive with detached houses for the investor's interest at the bottom ratings. The range between the two ratings shrinks; in Figure 2–6 it is 123 (198 to 75), and in Figure 2–7 it is only 78 (181 to 103).
2. The differences in rating between furnished and unfurnished properties of the same type becomes slightly greater. They run from an 8- to an 11-point spread for condo apartments, 8 to 14 for townhouses, 6 to 10 for detached. For the multi-unit investment, the 9-point spread (84 furnished, 75 unfurnished in Figure 2–6) drops to 8 points (111 and 103) in Figure 2–7.

The *risk-taking* small investor, presented in Figure 2–8 weights Returns 3 times greater than Costs and Risks combined. With unchanged criteria rankings, the ratings work out as follows:

1. Furnished condo apartment 345
2. Unfurnished condo apartment 302
3. Furnished multi-unit 283

	Investor's Weighting Factor	Unfurnished				Furnished			
		Detached	Townhouse	Condominium Apartment Unit	Multi-Unit	Detached	Townhouse	Condominium Apartment Unit	Multi-Unit
COSTS									
Initial investment required	1 x	4 = 4	6 = 6	8 = 8	2 = 2	3 = 3	5 = 5	7 = 7	1 = 1
Development costs	1 x	6 = 6	7 = 7	8 = 8	2 = 2	3 = 3	4 = 4	5 = 5	1 = 1
Operating expenses	1 x	5 = 5	6 = 6	6 = 6	2 = 2	3 = 3	4 = 4	4 = 4	1 = 1
Debt service costs	1 x	3 = 3	3 = 3	2 = 2	1 = 1	3 = 3	3 = 3	2 = 2	1 = 1
Income taxes	1 x	3 = 3	5 = 5	7 = 7	1 = 1	4 = 4	6 = 6	8 = 8	2 = 2
Required expertise	1 x	6 = 6	6 = 6	4 = 4	2 = 2	5 = 5	5 = 5	3 = 3	1 = 1
Management effort	1 x	6 = 6	7 = 7	8 = 8	2 = 2	3 = 3	4 = 4	5 = 5	1 = 1
Fees and other disposition costs	1 x	4 = 4	6 = 6	8 = 8	2 = 2	3 = 3	5 = 5	7 = 7	1 = 1
RISKS	Subtotals	37	46	51	14	27	36	41	9
Loss of investment outlay	1 x	4 = 4	6 = 6	8 = 8	2 = 2	3 = 3	5 = 5	7 = 7	1 = 1
Increase in one or more costs	1 x	7 = 7	5 = 5	3 = 3	1 = 1	8 = 8	6 = 6	4 = 4	2 = 2
Reduced income during holding	1 x	3 = 3	5 = 5	7 = 7	1 = 1	4 = 4	6 = 6	8 = 8	2 = 2
Physical hazard loss	1 x	4 = 4	6 = 6	8 = 8	2 = 2	3 = 3	5 = 5	7 = 7	1 = 1
Adverse political developments	1 x	5 = 5	5 = 5	3 = 3	1 = 1	6 = 6	6 = 6	4 = 4	2 = 2
Uncertainties from passage of time	1 x	6 = 6	5 = 5	3 = 3	1 = 1	6 = 6	5 = 5	4 = 4	2 = 2
Restricted investment options	1 x	3 = 3	5 = 5	7 = 7	1 = 1	4 = 4	6 = 6	8 = 8	2 = 2
Loss of value gain potential	1 x	3 = 3	5 = 5	7 = 7	1 = 1	4 = 4	6 = 6	8 = 8	2 = 2
Failure of appreciation potential	1 x	3 = 3	5 = 5	7 = 7	1 = 1	6 = 6	6 = 6	8 = 8	2 = 2
RETURNS	Subtotals	38	47	53	11	42	51	58	16
Advantages from leverage	2 x	1 = 2	2 = 4	3 = 6	4 = 8	1 = 2	2 = 4	3 = 6	4 = 8
Direct income during holding	2 x	1 = 2	3 = 6	4 = 8	7 = 14	2 = 4	5 = 10	6 = 12	8 = 16
Spendable income from tax benefits	2 x	1 = 2	2 = 4	3 = 6	7 = 14	4 = 8	5 = 10	6 = 12	8 = 16
Benefits of liquidity	2 x	4 = 8	4 = 8	4 = 8	2 = 4	3 = 6	3 = 6	3 = 6	1 = 2
Opportunity for investment variety	2 x	3 = 6	4 = 8	7 = 14	1 = 2	5 = 10	6 = 12	8 = 16	2 = 4
Gains through appreciation	2 x	1 = 2	2 = 4	3 = 6	4 = 8	1 = 2	2 = 4	3 = 6	4 = 8
Gains through value increase	2 x	1 = 2	3 = 6	5 = 10	7 = 14	2 = 4	4 = 8	6 = 12	8 = 16
Internal rate of return	2 x	1 = 2	2 = 4	4 = 8	7 = 14	3 = 6	5 = 10	6 = 12	8 = 16
	Subtotals	26	44	66	78	42	64	82	86
TOTALS		101	137	170	103	111	151	181	111

Figure 2-7. Investment Rating Analysis Form: Furnished and Unfurnished Rental Properties—Risk-Accepting Investor.

4. Furnished townhouse	279
5. Unfurnished multi-unit	259
6. Unfurnished townhouse	225
7. Furnished detached	195
8. Unfurnished detached	153

With the increased weight given to Returns by the risk-taker in this figure, several trends appear:

1. Although furnished and unfurnished individual condo apartments remain at the top of the list, furnished multi-unit investments move up dramatically to third place, while detached houses drop to the bottom rankings.
2. If the investor is looking primarily at the unfurnished market, multi-unit investments become more interesting than townhouses (259 versus 225, or "15 percent" better).
3. Overall, the furnished market is interesting: Three of the top four are furnished properties. Three of the other four are unfurnished. Overall, furnished rentals collect 1,102 points, or 17.4 percent more than the 939 points for unfurnished.

New and Used Property

Disregarding individual investor preferences, how does new property stack up against old? Figure 2–9 summarizes the rankings of each property type, from the standpoints of buying new and used. The following observations can be made:

Cost:

1. Multi-unit investments rank the least desirable with regard to all Cost criteria, with differences by specific criteria between new and used properties.
2. By the Cost criteria, after multi-unit investments, the least to the most desirable investments are detached houses, townhouses, and condo apartments, in that order.
3. With only slight variations, the comparison of new and used properties reveals no significant overall differences.

Risk:

4. Multi-unit investments tend to be more risky than the other types of investment.
5. Detached houses are generally more risky than townhouses and individual condo apartments, in that order.

	Investor's Weighting Factor	Unfurnished				Furnished			
		Detached	Townhouse	Condo-minium Apartment Unit	Multi-Unit	Detached	Townhouse	Condo-minium Apartment Unit	Multi-Unit
COSTS									
Initial investment required	1 x	4 = 4	6 = 6	8 = 8	2 = 2	3 = 3	5 = 5	7 = 7	1 = 1
Development costs	1 x	6 = 6	7 = 7	8 = 8	2 = 2	3 = 3	4 = 4	5 = 5	1 = 1
Operating expenses	1 x	5 = 5	6 = 6	6 = 6	2 = 2	3 = 3	4 = 4	4 = 4	1 = 1
Debt service costs	1 x	3 = 3	3 = 3	2 = 2	1 = 1	3 = 3	3 = 3	2 = 2	1 = 1
Income taxes	1 x	3 = 3	5 = 5	7 = 7	1 = 1	4 = 4	6 = 6	8 = 8	2 = 2
Required expertise	1 x	6 = 6	6 = 6	4 = 4	2 = 2	5 = 5	5 = 5	3 = 3	1 = 1
Management effort	1 x	6 = 6	7 = 7	8 = 8	2 = 2	3 = 3	4 = 4	5 = 5	1 = 1
Fees and other disposition costs	1 x	4 = 4	6 = 6	8 = 8	2 = 2	3 = 3	5 = 5	7 = 7	1 = 1
RISKS	Subtotals	37	46	51	14	27	36	41	9
Loss of investment outlay	1 x	4 = 4	6 = 6	8 = 8	2 = 2	3 = 3	5 = 5	7 = 7	1 = 1
Increase in one or more costs	1 x	7 = 7	5 = 5	3 = 3	1 = 1	8 = 8	6 = 6	4 = 4	2 = 2
Reduced income during holding	1 x	3 = 3	5 = 5	7 = 7	1 = 1	4 = 4	6 = 6	8 = 8	2 = 2
Physical hazard loss	1 x	4 = 4	6 = 6	8 = 8	2 = 2	3 = 3	5 = 5	7 = 7	1 = 1
Adverse political developments	1 x	5 = 5	5 = 5	3 = 3	1 = 1	6 = 6	6 = 6	4 = 4	2 = 2
Uncertainties from passage of time	1 x	6 = 6	5 = 5	3 = 3	1 = 1	6 = 6	5 = 5	4 = 4	2 = 2
Restricted investment options	1 x	3 = 3	5 = 5	7 = 7	1 = 1	4 = 4	6 = 6	8 = 8	2 = 2
Loss of value gain potential	1 x	3 = 3	5 = 5	7 = 7	1 = 1	4 = 4	6 = 6	8 = 8	2 = 2
Failure of appreciation potential	1 x	3 = 3	5 = 5	7 = 7	1 = 1	6 = 6	6 = 6	8 = 8	2 = 2
RETURNS	Subtotals	38	47	53	11	42	51	58	16
Advantages from leverage	6 x	1 = 6	2 = 12	3 = 18	4 = 24	1 = 6	2 = 12	3 = 18	4 = 24
Direct income during holding	6 x	1 = 6	3 = 18	4 = 24	7 = 42	2 = 12	5 = 30	6 = 36	8 = 48
Spendable income from tax benefits	6 x	1 = 6	2 = 12	3 = 18	7 = 42	4 = 24	5 = 30	6 = 36	8 = 48
Benefits of liquidity	6 x	4 = 24	4 = 24	4 = 24	2 = 12	3 = 18	3 = 18	3 = 18	1 = 6
Opportunity for investment variety	6 x	3 = 18	4 = 24	7 = 42	1 = 6	5 = 30	6 = 36	8 = 48	2 = 12
Gains through appreciation	6 x	1 = 6	2 = 12	3 = 18	4 = 24	1 = 6	2 = 12	3 = 18	4 = 24
Gains through value increase	6 x	1 = 6	3 = 18	5 = 30	7 = 42	2 = 12	4 = 24	6 = 36	8 = 48
Internal rate of return	6 x	1 = 6	2 = 12	4 = 24	7 = 42	3 = 18	5 = 30	6 = 36	8 = 48
	Subtotals	78	132	198	234	126	192	246	258
TOTALS		153	225	302	259	195	279	345	283

Figure 2–8. Investment Rating Analysis Form: Furnished and Unfurnished Rental Properties—Risk-Taking Investor.

	Investor's Weighting Factor	New				Used			
		Detached	Townhouse	Condominium Apartment Unit	Multi-Unit	Detached	Townhouse	Condominium Apartment Unit	Multi-Unit
COSTS									
Initial investment required	×	3 =	5 =	7 =	1 =	4 =	6 =	8 =	2 =
Development costs	×	4 =	6 =	8 =	1 =	3 =	5 =	7 =	2 =
Operating expenses	×	4 =	6 =	8 =	2 =	3 =	5 =	7 =	1 =
Debt service costs	×	3 =	5 =	7 =	1 =	4 =	6 =	8 =	2 =
Income taxes	×	4 =	6 =	8 =	2 =	3 =	5 =	7 =	1 =
Required expertise	×	4 =	4 =	6 =	2 =	3 =	3 =	5 =	1 =
Management effort	×	3 =	5 =	7 =	1 =	4 =	6 =	8 =	2 =
Fees and other disposition costs	×	4 =	6 =	8 =	2 =	3 =	5 =	7 =	1 =
RISKS	Subtotals								
Loss of investment outlay	×	3 =	5 =	7 =	1 =	4 =	6 =	8 =	2 =
Increase in one or more costs	×	8 =	5 =	3 =	2 =	7 =	6 =	4 =	1 =
Reduced income during holding	×	3 =	5 =	7 =	1 =	4 =	6 =	8 =	2 =
Physical hazard loss	×	4 =	6 =	8 =	2 =	3 =	5 =	7 =	1 =
Adverse political developments	×	7 =	5 =	3 =	1 =	8 =	6 =	4 =	2 =
Uncertainties from passage of time	×	7 =	5 =	3 =	1 =	8 =	6 =	4 =	2 =
Restricted investment options	×	2 =	3 =	4 =	1 =	2 =	3 =	4 =	1 =
Loss of value gain potential	×	2 =	3 =	4 =	1 =	2 =	3 =	4 =	1 =
Failure of appreciation potential	×	2 =	3 =	4 =	1 =	2 =	3 =	4 =	1 =
RETURNS	Subtotals								
Advantages from leverage	×	1 =	2 =	3 =	4 =	1 =	2 =	3 =	4 =
Direct income during holding	×	2 =	4 =	6 =	8 =	1 =	3 =	5 =	7 =
Spendable income from tax benefits	×	2 =	4 =	6 =	8 =	1 =	3 =	5 =	7 =
Benefits of liquidity	×	3 =	3 =	3 =	1 =	4 =	4 =	4 =	2 =
Opportunity for investment variety	×	3 =	5 =	7 =	1 =	4 =	6 =	8 =	2 =
Gains through appreciation	×	2 =	4 =	6 =	8 =	1 =	3 =	5 =	7 =
Gains through value increase	×	2 =	4 =	6 =	8 =	1 =	3 =	5 =	7 =
Internal rate of return	×	2 =	4 =	6 =	8 =	1 =	3 =	5 =	7 =
	Subtotals								
TOTALS									

Figure 2-9. Investment Rating Analysis Form: New and Used Rental Properties—No Weighting Factors Assigned.

Returns:

6. As a general rule, as you have more and larger units at a given location, you incur higher costs and run greater risks. Consequently, Cost and Risk rankings tend to decrease and, conversely, the rankings for Return criteria tend to increase.

Figure 2–10 compares, among other investments, new with converted condominium units, as six-unit packages. In that comparison, conversions may have advantages in price, in development costs (particularly if the investor is also the developer), and in debt service costs, but new units tend to have the edge by the other Cost criteria. Conversions are also given a slight edge in the Risk criteria, except physical hazard loss (older buildings) and loss of value gain potential, on the ground that conversions allow the buyer more flexibility to make physical improvements to enhance value (which might not be realized). New units, on the other hand, have greater potential for appreciation based on supply and demand, but their unfinished or "untested" character is a negative risk factor. Overall, new units have the edge on Returns.

In the unweighted rankings also in this figure, apartment buildings rank lowest by each Cost and Risk criterion and highest by each Return criterion except benefits of liquidity and opportunity for investment variety. Individual condo apartment units rank highest (most desirable) by all the Cost criteria. Except for the risks of increase in one or more costs (the operating and maintenance budget is under control of others), adverse political developments (such as rent control or other legislation), and uncertainties from passage of time, apartments and condos also rank highest by all Risk factors. Apartment buildings also rank highest by each Return criterion except benefits of liquidity and opportunity for investment variety. Except for these same two criteria, the Return criteria rankings are consistent. The largest single-unit investment (detached house) is least desirable; than the smallest (condo apartment unit), the multi-unit investment with the least number of units (duplex), and the multi-unit investment with the most (apartment building) increase in desirability in that order.

AN "IDEAL" INVESTMENT?

Is there an ideal investment for the small investor in residential income property? If so, what is it? The option to build, for example, is potentially higher on returns than the option to buy from someone else. Likewise,

	Investor's Weighting Factor	Single-Unit			Multi-Unit				
		Detached	Townhouse	Condominium Apartment Unit	Duplex	Quadraplex	6 Condominium Units, New	6 Condominium Units, Conversion	Apartment Building
COSTS									
Initial investment required	×	6 =	7 =	8 =	5 =	4 =	2 =	3 =	1 =
Development costs	×	6 =	7 =	8 =	5 =	4 =	2 =	3 =	1 =
Operating expenses	×	6 =	7 =	8 =	5 =	4 =	3 =	2 =	1 =
Debt service costs	×	6 =	7 =	8 =	5 =	4 =	2 =	3 =	1 =
Income taxes	×	6 =	7 =	8 =	5 =	4 =	3 =	2 =	1 =
Required expertise	×	6 =	7 =	8 =	5 =	4 =	3 =	2 =	1 =
Management effort	×	6 =	7 =	8 =	5 =	4 =	3 =	2 =	1 =
Fees and other disposition costs	×	6 =	7 =	8 =	5 =	4 =	3 =	2 =	1 =
RISKS	Subtotals								
Loss of investment outlay	×	6 =	7 =	8 =	5 =	4 =	2 =	3 =	1 =
Increase in one or more costs	×	6 =	5 =	4 =	8 =	4 =	2 =	3 =	1 =
Reduced income during holding	×	6 =	7 =	8 =	5 =	4 =	2 =	3 =	1 =
Physical hazard loss	×	6 =	7 =	8 =	5 =	4 =	3 =	2 =	1 =
Adverse political developments	×	8 =	5 =	4 =	7 =	6 =	2 =	3 =	1 =
Uncertainties from passage of time	×	8 =	5 =	4 =	7 =	6 =	2 =	3 =	1 =
Restricted investment options	×	6 =	7 =	8 =	5 =	4 =	2 =	3 =	1 =
Loss of value gain potential	×	6 =	7 =	8 =	5 =	4 =	3 =	2 =	1 =
Failure of appreciation potential	×	6 =	7 =	8 =	5 =	4 =	2 =	3 =	1 =
RETURNS	Subtotals								
Advantages from leverage	×	1 =	2 =	3 =	4 =	5 =	7 =	6 =	8 =
Direct income during holding	×	1 =	2 =	3 =	4 =	5 =	7 =	6 =	8 =
Spendable income from tax benefits	×	1 =	2 =	3 =	4 =	5 =	7 =	6 =	8 =
Benefits of liquidity	×	6 =	6 =	6 =	5 =	4 =	3 =	2 =	1 =
Opportunity for investment variety	×	5 =	6 =	7 =	3 =	2 =	4 =	4 =	1 =
Gains through appreciation	×	1 =	2 =	3 =	4 =	5 =	7 =	6 =	8 =
Gains through value increase	×	1 =	2 =	3 =	4 =	5 =	6 =	7 =	8 =
Internal rate of return	×	1 =	2 =	3 =	4 =	5 =	7 =	6 =	8 =
	Subtotals								
TOTALS									

Figure 2-10. Investment Rating Analysis Form: Single- and Multi-Unit Rental Properties—No Weighting Factors Assigned.

	Investor's Weighting Factor								
COSTS									
Initial investment required	x	=	=	=	=	=	=	=	=
Development costs	x	=	=	=	=	=	=	=	=
Operating expenses	x	=	=	=	=	=	=	=	=
Debt service costs	x	=	=	=	=	=	=	=	=
Income taxes	x	=	=	=	=	=	=	=	=
Required expertise	x	=	=	=	=	=	=	=	=
Management effort	x	=	=	=	=	=	=	=	=
Fees and other disposition costs	x	=	=	=	=	=	=	=	=
RISKS	Subtotals								
Loss of investment outlay	x	=	=	=	=	=	=	=	=
Increase in one or more costs	x	=	=	=	=	=	=	=	=
Reduced income during holding	x	=	=	=	=	=	=	=	=
Physical hazard loss	x	=	=	=	=	=	=	=	=
Adverse political developments	x	=	=	=	=	=	=	=	=
Uncertainties from passage of time	x	=	=	=	=	=	=	=	=
Restricted investment options	x	=	=	=	=	=	=	=	=
Loss of value gain potential	x	=	=	=	=	=	=	=	=
Failure of appreciation potential	x	=	=	=	=	=	=	=	=
RETURNS	Subtotals								
Advantages from leverage	x	=	=	=	=	=	=	=	=
Direct income during holding	x	=	=	=	=	=	=	=	=
Spendable income from tax benefits	x	=	=	=	=	=	=	=	=
Benefits of liquidity	x	=	=	=	=	=	=	=	=
Opportunity for investment variety	x	=	=	=	=	=	=	=	=
Gains through appreciation	x	=	=	=	=	=	=	=	=
Gains through value increase	x	=	=	=	=	=	=	=	=
Internal rate of return	x	=	=	=	=	=	=	=	=
	Subtotals								
TOTALS									

Figure 2-11. Investment Rating Analysis Form: Reader's Worksheet.

furnished rentals seems to be more favorable than unfurnished rentals, and new property seems to have the edge over used properties. Condo units seem to be better than townhouses and detached, multi-unit over single-unit rental properties, and so on. So why don't all small investors go out and build new condominium apartment buildings and then rent them furnished? To answer that question, two others have to be asked:

1. How does each property type rank by each investment criterion?
2. What weight does the investor give to each?

Whether you use the ranking and weighting methods suggested in this book or some other method, you must answer those questions before determining any kind of investment to be best for you or for someone else. The possible answers, like the possible investments, vary widely among investors.

FIFTEEN KEYS TO PRACTICAL INVESTMENT ANALYSIS

WHAT IS INVESTMENT ANALYSIS?

A thoughtful investor in real estate, or in anything else, must seek detailed and reliable answers to at least the following five questions:

1. How much cash do I have to invest initially, and how does that amount relate to the market value of the investment?
2. What is the amount of the current (usually monthly) positive or negative cash flows during the holding period?
3. What is the impact of the investment on my financial position annually, after income taxes?
4. What is my cash proceed, before and after taxes, from the sale of the investment at any given time?
5. After consideration of all other relevant factors, what are the key rates of return on my investment during the holding period and upon disposition?

Investment analysis consists of the answers to these five questions, which entail very careful and very specific *projections* into the future. In this respect, investment analysis differs from economic forecasting, which deals in terms of the general population, the money market, and other trends affecting past, present, and future real estate values. Investment analysis is a more specific kind of forecasting that calls for practical answers.

Keep in mind also that investment analysis is a *comparative* process: It compares the projected performances of alternative investments to determine the one that gives the maximum financial gain. There is no such thing as a "good" capitalization rate or a "good" after-tax discounted cash flow. "Good" depends on all the many, many considerations in this chapter.

Investment analysis, by its nature involves a lot of numbers and tables. *Do not be intimidated by them!* Admittedly not self-evident, they require some initial analysis—but you need no special mathematical skills to use them. They are made up from the point of view of those who, after only a little pondering, master the realtor's inventory of guides, tables, and schedules. Anyone who can learn to figure closing costs, PITI, and a seller's "net sheet" can master the paraphernalia of investment analysis.

THE FIFTEEN KEY FACTORS

To conduct a proper and complete investment analysis, you have to weigh the 15 key factors that follow:

1. Purchase price
2. Gross income
3. Vacancy rate
4. Operating expenses
5. Inflation rate
6. Appreciation and inflation rates
7. Down payment
8. Other investment costs
9. Loan amounts
10. Interest rates

11. Loan periods
12. Loan schedules
13. Investor's tax bracket
14. Depreciation factors
    - Initial basis
    - Method
    - Period
15. Future disposition costs
    - Sales commission
    - Other costs

To weigh *all* 15 factors meaningfully, you have to plot the significant interrelationships among them over a period of usually 5 to 10 years. Then you change several factors, one at a time, while holding all the others constant to study the effects of various changes on the bottom line. Finally, you have to reduce everything mathematically to half a dozen or fewer figures, to be used in deciding which investment opportunities are likely to place the most cash in your pocket. On fairly "minor" factors very large amounts can ride.

An Automated "Art"

From the earliest days, investment analysis attempted to convert the raw data from those factors into simple and useful measures of real value among investment property alternatives. Since it all had to be done in the head or by hand in times past, the quest for shortcut methods for making crucial investment decisions was very important. A working knowledge of a few rules of thumb gave someone an advantage, even in fairly sophisticated negotiations.

Today, the pocket financial calculator and the telephone-accessed investment analysis computer program make things much simpler. In recent years, a rapidly developing technology offers meaningful and almost instantaneous computations. In any real estate investment transaction today, therefore, even the neophyte who has learned a few simple lessons with the computer holds a better hand than the oldtimer who has not. In less time than the traditionalist takes to make a "guess-timate" you can make a quick telephone call from a computer terminal and obtain a printout that digests a full range of investment analysis factors and that presents many "hours'" worth of comparison data.

THE VARIOUS METHODS

Yet don't be lulled by the ease of automated analysis. The computer does not replace a knowledge of investment dynamics. Nor is a computer, nor even a sophisticated pocket financial calculator, necessary to conduct a proper analysis. In fact, the knowledgeable analyst sometimes needs to use the calculator to compensate for computer program errors or inadequacies and to work out calculator routines or programs not provided for in the owner's manual. With that said, the computer remains not only a highly efficient tool in investment analysis, but also a highly efficient learning aide.

In this chapter the tables are constructed in a manner compatible with typical computer printout formats. More detail than usual is shown, however, to enable you to go behind the computations and understand their component steps. For the sake of simplicity, each algebraic formula is reduced to a chain calculation occurring just as shown in the sequence and functions (add, subtract, multiply, divide) on the stub (left-hand column) of the table.

Several relatively simple methods have been in use over the years—and still are in some places or for limited purposes—for appraising investment properties, selecting among them, and formulating offers to purchase, to put options, and to perform other actions. Fairly common parlance consists of such terms as "gross rent multiplier . . . net operating income . . . capitalization rate . . . gross and net spendable income . . . discounted cash flows . . . rate of return . . . equity . . . net sale proceed . . . internal rate of return." Although the meanings of some terms vary, and although various terms sometimes describe the same meaning, you can cut through the jargon and take advantage of computer-assisted investment analysis procedures, as long as you have a basic understanding of the calculations underlying the methods. In this chapter, you will work with the most common methods, using data on a hypothetical property, as follows:

1. Purchase price	\$690,000
2. Gross income	\$100,000
3. Vacancy rate	3%
4. Operating expenses	\$ 22,000
5. Inflation rate	8%

6. Appreciation rate	8%
7. Down payment	$ 69,000
8. Other investment costs	$ 23,000
9. Loan amounts	$552.000
Second loan	$69,000
10. Interest rates	
First loan	10%
Second loan	11.5%
11. Loan periods	
First loan	30 years
Second loan	5 years
12. Loan schedules	
First loan	12 payments of $4877 per year, no balloon, 30 years.
Second loan	12 payments of $690 per year, $66,682 balloon at 5 years

GROSS RENT MULTIPLIER (GRM)

With all its variations, the gross rent multiplier (GRM) is the most simple—and the least meaningful—estimator of a property's market value as an investment. The basic formula, from which several broad rules of thumb can be derived is:

$$\text{GRM} = \frac{\text{Sales price}}{\text{Gross income (annual rent)}}$$

What does it mean? And what doesn't it mean? Any investor in income property needs to answer this question: When selecting among several properties, what rental income should I expect to receive relative to a given sales price, or vice versa? The GRMs in Figure 3-1 can be used as a point of departure. The numbers in this figure are only rough approximations. However, they are not just "plucked from the air"; rather, they reflect the somewhat subjective expectations of the author, who formulates them on the basis of his past experience and knowledge of the market. The GRMs represent the ratio of the gross income that you should expect from the property to the sales price that you will have to pay for it. A GRM of 7, for example, means that you must earn enough gross income to equal 1/7, 0.142, or 14.2 percent of the sales price. A property going for, say, $700,000 should earn at least $100,000 a year in gross income. If your estimates and calculations show that you cannot earn that much, then perhaps the property is not worth the investment. (Figure 3–2 demonstrates the GRM role in the purchase decision.)

In effect, then, the GRM formula answers the question, How much gross income must the property generate to make its acquisition feasible? To better suit the question, the formula can be rearranged as follows:

$$\text{Gross income (required)} = \frac{\text{Sales price}}{\text{GRM}}$$

Figure 3–3 shows how an investor can compare four different properties on the basis of this formula. Property 1 is our hypothetical alternative; properties 2, 3, and 4 are made up for this figure only.

	Type of Property	GRM Estimate
A	Apartment building, utilities and heat included in rent	7
B	Condominium unit, fee includes utilities and heat	8
C	Condominium unit, tenant pays own heat and utilities	9
D	Townhouse, tenant pays own heat and utilities	10
E	Detached house, tenant pays own heat and utilities	11

Figure 3–1.

Property Number	GRM	Projected Gross Income		Indicated Market Value	Seller's Offering Price	Percentage Difference
1	7 x	100,000	=	700,000	700,000	0
2	7 x	143,000	=	1,001,000	1,100,000	9.9
3	7 x	215,000	=	1,505,000	1,600,000	6.3
4	7 x	75,000	=	525,000	600,000	14.3

Figure 3–2.

Property Number	Seller's Offering Price	GRM	Required Gross Income	Projected Gross Income	Percentage Difference
1	700,000 ÷	7 =	100,000	100,000	0
2	1,100,000 ÷	7 =	157,143	143,000	– 9.9
3	1,600,000 ÷	7 =	228,571	215,000	– 6.3
4	600,000 ÷	7 =	85,714	75,000	–14.3

Figure 3–3.

Property Number	Seller's Offering Price	Projected Gross Income	GRM	Percentage Difference (From 7)
1	700,000	100,000	7	0
2	1,100,000	143,000	7.69	9.9
3	1,600,000	215,000	7.44	6.3
4	600,000	75,000	8	14.3

Figure 3-4.

Still another way to use the GRM is to divide the offering price by the projected gross income and see how close it comes to the desired GRM. This technique is shown in Figure 3-4, which demonstrates that the *lower* GRMs are the better ones.

An important point to remember with using the GRM (or any other) method is that all other factors must be "equal." In other words, no other purchase criteria should be ignored simply because the GRM method indicates that the property is a "good" investment. However, the GRM formula, in either form, *is* helpful in four respects:

1. deciding whether a property under initial consideration deserves closer examination;
2. arriving at a general idea of the right price range for a particular property;
3. determining what approximate rent should be for a property purchased at a given price; and
4. making rough comparisons among several properties under consideration.

MONTHLY RENT MULTIPLIER

A variation on the GRM is the "1-percent rule," which declares that the monthly rent for a property ought to be about 1 percent of its sales price. The formula looks like this:

$$\text{Approximate market value} = \text{Monthly rent} \times 100$$

Another form is:

$$\text{Approximate monthly rent (required)} = \frac{\text{Sale price}}{100}$$

Type of Property		GRM Estimate	MRM Estimate
B	Condominium unit, fee includes heat and utilities	8	100
C	Condominium unit, tenant pays heat and utilities	9	110
D	Townhouse, tenant pays heat and utilities	10	120
E	Detached, tenant pays heat and utilities	11	130

Figure 3-5.

This kind of quick estimate is more useful for scanning individual living units, whose rents are most commonly stated in monthly terms, than for apartment buildings. Like the GRM, the monthly rent multiplier (MRM) has to be adjusted according to the type of property involved. Actually, the MRM is simply the GRM times 12 and rounded, as shown in Figure 3-5.

CAPITALIZATION RATE

As a tool for investment analysis, the GRM method has a principal and sometimes fatal limitation: It does not weigh the differences among properties in vacancy rates and operating expenses. The capitalization rate method overcomes that problem. The overall formula is as follows:

$$\text{Capitalization rate} = \frac{\text{Gross income} - \text{Vacancies} - \text{Operating expenses}}{\text{Sale Price } \textit{or} \text{ Market value at beginning of year}}$$

Two notes about this formula: First, the Vacancy rate is the amount of income lost through the turnover in occupants. It is sometimes expressed as a percentage, in which case simply multiply the percentage against the Gross income to obtain a dollar figure for Vacancy rate. This rate may be obtained from historical records or estimated on the basis of a projected turnover rate. Second, after the Vacancy rate amount is deducted from Gross income, but before the operating expenses are deducted, the Gross income becomes the Effective gross income. Figure 3-6a demonstrates how the capitalization rates are worked out for each of the four properties carried over from Figure 3-4.

Figures 3-6b and 3-6c, respectively, show computations for Operating ratio and Income ratio. The operating ratio simply states which percentage of income goes into operating expenses—the *lower* the figure, the better. The income ratio states which percentage of gross income

	Property Number			
	1	2	3	4
Gross income	100,000	143,000	215,000	75,000
− Vacancies (vacancy rate)	3,000 (3%)	5,720 (4%)	10,750 (5%)	4,500 (6%)
= Effective gross income	97,000	137,000	204,250	70,500
− Operating expenses	22,000	38,600	68,800	27,800
= Net operating income	75,000	98,680	135,450	42,700
÷ Sale price/market value	700,000	1,100,000	1,600,000	600,000
= Capitalization rate	10.70%	8.97%	8.47%	7.12%

(a)

Operating expenses	22,000	38,600	68,800	27,800
÷ Effective gross income	97,000	137,280	204,250	70,500
= Operating ratio	22.7%	28.2%	33.7%	39.4%

(b)

Net operating income	75,000	98,680	135,450	42,700
÷ Gross income	100,000	143,000	215,000	75,000
= Income ratio	75.8%	69.0%	63.0%	56.9%

(c)

Figure 3–6.

remains after vacancies and operating expenses are deducted—the *higher* that figure, the better. These ratios are not crucial bottom-line figures for every investment analysis, but they do help to focus the meaning of the "cap" rate. Substantial variations in these ratios among alternative properties can be a pretty good clue as to how the remaining numbers are likely to work out.

In general, since vacancy rates and the costs of running income properties vary so widely, the capitalization rate is a much more meaningful indication of likely profitability than is the GRM method.

Cautions About the Cap Rate

Since it is only a simple ratio between net operating income (NOI) and Sales price or Market value in a given year, the capitalization rate is an adequate and useful tool for analysis—for what it measures. Applied in such a way, however, it does not give weight to leverage, as reflected in loan-to-value ratios, to other loan terms, to debt service costs, to tax factors, to inflation and appreciation, or to future disposition costs—in short, to other key factors.

Dated Capitalization Methods

To "capitalize,"as that word is used in real estate investment analysis, is simply to assign a market value to projected net income through the application of a rate designed to measure return on investment from income. In the pre-computer days of investment analysis, when ingenious shortcuts were necessary, many of them took the form of variations on the capitalization rate. As a result, the meaning of the term "capitalization" has been strained by such variations. The main methods are presented in this section primarily to distinguish them from the more limited use of the term.

In addition to the basic capitalization rate, most textbooks mention, and some analysts and appraisers use:

1. the *summation* or *built-up* method,
2. the *band of investment* method, or
3. various *two-step* methods

to arrive at a rate of return from rents and related income received during the holding period. "Income" return is mentioned to emphasize that the capitalization rate does *not* measure gains from the sale of property that has appreciated in value, while income and tax benefits have been enjoyed. The "cap rate" is simply a ratio between income and market value of the property.

Summation Method. Sometimes called the "built-up method," this technique starts with a basic risk or "interest" rate for investment properties, which is normally the "safe" interest rate on a guaranteed-return investment, such as U.S. government bonds. Then you add on points for the greater risk involved in a real estate investment, for the fact that the property cannot be disposed of as quickly as the "safe" investment, and for the greater time and trouble involved in its management as an investment.

Figure 3-7 shows the method in operation. If this were a workable method, and if the percentages assigned to factors B, C, and D were based on reliable data, property 1 needs a capitalization rate of at least 10.0 percent, and property 2 10.7 percent, to be an attractive investment. To derive additional meaning, you have to allow for increases or decreases in market value and in NOI over the holding period. Since this method lacks precision, it is used more properly for arriving at a *rough* idea of which

	Factor	Property 1	Property 2
A	Safe rate	6.0%	6.0%
+ B	Riskiness	2.4%	3.5%
+ C	Illiquidity	1.0%	0.5%
+ D	Time and trouble	0.6%	0.7%
= E	Risk or "interest" rate	10.0%	10.7%

Figure 3–7.

returns should be expected from real estate investments than for analyzing or appraising specific properties.

Band of Investment. This method establishes the capitalization rate by using the loan-to-value ratios (LVRs), which are the percentages that the loans represent of the whole sale price. For example, a loan of $40,000 on a $160,000 purchase has ratio of 25 percent ($40,000 ÷ $160,000). To arrive at the capitalization rate, the LVR of each financing source is weighted in terms of interest rates or the rates of return that investors currently require for each. An allowance for depreciation (or appreciation) in the value of the property can also be added (or subtracted), as in Figure 3–8. In that example 10.85 percent is the return you need from income to justify the investment.

Though more meaningful in results than the summation method, the band of investment approach fails to consider the size of the principal and interest payments, the duration of the loan, and *all* key factors other than loan terms.

Two-Step Methods. Finally, by this method net income is apportioned to land, which does not depreciate, and to improvements, which do. Since improvements have no value without ownership of the real property rights that make them feasible, such methods are more of academic than of practical interest to the investor.

Financing Source	Percentage of Property's Sale Price		Return Currently Required by Lenders/Investors		Weighted Factor
Down payment or equity	10%	x	15%	=	1.5%
Second loan	10%	x	11.5%	=	1.15%
First loan	80%	x	10%	=	8.0%
	Allowance for depreciation				0.2%
	Capitalization rate				10.85%

Figure 3–8.

First Year	25 Units		Per Unit	
	Annual	Monthly	Annual	Monthly
Gross income	100,000	8,333	4,000	333
– Vacancies (3%)	3,000	250	120	10
– Operating expenses	22,000	1,833	880	73
= Net operating income	75,000	6,250	3,000	250
– First loan payments	58,164	4,847	2,327	194
– Second loan payments	8,280	690	331	28
= Gross spendable income	8,556	713	342	28

Figure 3-9.

GROSS SPENDABLE INCOME (CURRENT CASH FLOW)

Gross spendable income is equal to net operating income minus principal and interest payments. Gross spendable income, a crucial figure in even the simplest investment analysis, indicates the amount of positive or negative cash flow that can be projected from an investment on a current (usually monthly) basis. If the current cash flow is *positive,* it is also truly "spendable," since tax benefits increase it still more on an annual basis. If it is *negative,* the investment is both non self-supporting and speculative—even though it might still be profitable. The "returns" from such an investment are spendable only if the cost of financing it is properly budgeted. While the relevant amounts are calculated on an annual basis initially, rents are generally received—and bills paid—monthly.

Figuring them both ways, as in Figure 3-9, is a simple matter. Assume that we have purchased property 1 for $690,000 under loan terms and other conditions reflected in our hypothetical example. The computation of first-year gross spendable income (the positive or negative cash flow before taxes) is presented. (Tax benefits are ignored.)

NET SPENDABLE INCOME

Net spendable income consists of the investor's dollar return after paying income taxes in a given year. All the methods covered up to this point do not permit you to arrive at the net spendable income figure. They do involve the following nine of the 15 key factors:

1. market value,
2. gross income,
3. vacancy rate,
4. operating expenses,
7. down payment,
9. loan payments,
10. interest rate,
11. loan period, and
12. loan payment schedule.

To project net spendable income, you have also to weigh the effects of 3 other factors.

8. other investment costs (needed to compute depreciation),
13. tax bracket, and
14. depreciation factors.

These 3 factors combine to alter the amount of income that the investor has to live on, to position in other investments, just to hold in reserve, or to do something else. "Other investment costs" consist of expenses that the investor must lay out, other than the down payment, to acquire (as distinct from operate) the investment. In the case of real estate, such costs include settlement costs, renovation expenses, if charged to the buyer, and so on. Taxes and depreciation work as opposing forces on the investor's income flow: While income taxation obviously reduces spendable income, depreciation tends to increase it. Deductions from income for depreciation become more and more valuable to investors as their tax brackets become higher and higher; the effect is the same for interest deductions. Figure 3-10 shows the effects of depreciation and interest

First Year	Tax Bracket			
	30%	40%	50%	60%
Gross spendable income	8,556	8,556	8,556	8,556
+ Tax benefit on interest deduction	4,271	5,694	7,117	8,540
+ Tax benefit on depreciation deduction	2,300	3,067	3,834	4,601
= Net spendable income	15,127	17,317	19,507	21,697
(Spendable income from tax benefits)	(6,571)	(8,761)	(10,951)	(13,141)

Figure 3-10.

deductions on the first year's taxable income (from our hypothetical investment) for investors in the 30-, 40-, 50-, and 60-percent tax brackets. For each increase of 10 percent in the tax bracket, the investor saves $2,190 in taxes. Figure 3-11 shows how just the depreciation amount for this investment is computed and Figure 3-12 shows how year 1 figures are then applied to each investor in the 30-, 40-, 50-, or 60-percent bracket.

	Year 1
Purchase price	690,000
x Percentage attributable to improvements	0.95
= Depreciable part of value	655,500
+ Other investment costs	23,000
= Basis	678,500
÷ Depreciation period	25
= Annual depreciation, SL method	27,140
÷ Basis	678,500
= SL depreciation rate	0.04
x Percentage, accelerated method	125%
= Accelerated rate, on declining balance	0.05
x Basis	678,500
= Year-1 depreciation deduction	33,925
Basis	678,500
− Year-1 depreciation deduction	33,925
= First adjusted basis	644,575

	Year 2
First adjusted basis	644,575
x Accelerated rate, on declining balance	0.05
= Year-2 depreciation deduction	32,229

	Year 3
First adjusted basis	644,575
− Year-2 depreciation	32,229
= Second adjusted basis	612,346
x Accelerated rate, on declining balance	0.05
= Year-3 depreciation deduction	30,617

	Year 4
Second adjusted basis	612,346
− Year-3 depreciation	30,617
= Third adjusted basis	581,729
x Accelerated rate, on declining balance	0.05
= Year-4 depreciation deduction	29,086

	Year 5
Third adjusted basis	581,729
− Year-4 depreciation	29,086
= Fourth adjusted basis	552,643
x Accelerated rate, on declining balance	0.05
= Year-5 depreciation deduction	27,632

	Year 6
Fourth adjusted basis	552,643
− Year-5 depreciation	27,632
= Fifth adjusted basis	525,011
x Accelerated rate, on declining balance	0.05
= Year-5 depreciation deduction	26,251

Figure 3–11.

	Year-1 Figures, All Brackets			
Net operating income	75,000			
– Loan interest	62,977			
– Depreciation	33,925			
= Taxable income	– 21,902			
x Percentage attributable to depreciation	35.01%			
= Amount apportioned to depreciation	– 7,668			
x Tax rate	30%	40%	50%	60%
= Tax (benefit) on depreciation deduction	–2,300	–3,067	–3,834	–4,601

Figure 3–12.

One note about depreciation: When you eventually sell the property, you sometimes have to "pay back" some of the depreciation benefits. At the time of sale, the cumulative amount of depreciation allowable under the straight-line method is subtracted from the cumulative amount of depreciation actually taken under the accelerated depreciation method. (The 125 percent on the declining balance method is used in Figure 3–11.) The difference, called "recaptured depreciation," is taxable as ordinary income.

Just as accelerated depreciation methods produce smaller deductions as time goes by, so do interest deductions, as amortization payments include more principal and less interest.

TAX SHELTERING

Our hypothetical investment shows that a real estate investment operating on a marginally profitable basis from month to month can mean substantial cash bonuses for the investor in high tax brackets at the end of the year. From a simple accounting point of view, Figure 3–9 shows the investment to be bringing in a modest positive cash flow (or gross spendable income) of only $8,556. Even this cash flow is a precarious one: An increase in the vacancy rate of only 1 percentage point would reduce the cash flow by $1,000, or a rise in operating expenses of roughly $9,000 would bring it down below zero. Looking at the investment from an annual standpoint, on the other hand, you see that the net spendable income is a little better. For investors in a 50-percent tax bracket, the return from tax benefits from depreciation deductions is $10,951 (see Figure 3–10)—28 percent better than the gross spendable income amount of $8,556. For investors in the 60-percent bracket, the benefit is even higher. Hence an investor in a high bracket can derive spendable income—without making any cash outlay—through depreciation deductions.

Same for all tax brackets:	Year					
	1	2	3	4	5	6
Net operating income	75,000	81,000	87,480	94,478	102,037	110,200
− Loan interest	62,977	62,609	62,201	61,745	61,247	53,057
(Amortization payments)	(3,467)	(3,835)	(4,243)	(4,699)	(71,830)	(5,107)
− Depreciation	33,925	32,229	30,617	29,086	27,632	26,251
= Taxable income	−21,902	−13,838	−5,338	3,647	13,158	30,892
Gross spendable income	8,556	14,556	21,036	28,034	−31,040[1]	52,036

(a)

[1]Payoff of second loan

Depreciation deduction (125% on declining balance)	3,834	2,351	880	−584	−2,045	−5,113
Amortization payments	3,467	3,835	4,243	4,699	71,830	5,107
Amount "sheltered" by depreciation	367	−1,484	−3,363	−5,283	−73,875	−10,220
Spendable income from tax benefits	10,951	6,919	2,669	−1,824	−6,579	−15,446
Net spendable income	19,507	21,475	23,705	26,210	−37,619	36,590
Cumulative net spendable income	19,507	40,982	64,687	90,897	53,278	89,868

(b)

Depreciation deduction (125% on declining balance)	4,601	2,822	1,057	−701	−2,455	−6,135
Amortization payments	3,467	3,835	4,243	4,699	71,830	5,107
Amount "sheltered" by depreciation	1,134	−1,013	−3,186	−5,400	−74,285	−11,242
Spendable income from tax benefits	13,141	8,303	3,203	−2,188	−7,895	−18,535
Net spendable income	21,697	22,859	24,239	25,846	−38,935	33,501
Cumulative net spendable income	21,697	44,556	68,795	94,641	55,706	89,207

(c)

Figure 3-13. (a) All brackets. (b) 50% bracket. (c) 60% bracket.

This example also demonstrates the interplay among the interest portion of the mortgage payment, the principal repayment (amortization), portion of the mortgage payment and depreciation. While interest payments are legitimate deductions for income tax purposes, they nonetheless represent a cash outlay—the mortgage payment. Amortization payments, representing the principal portions of mortgage repayments, are totally nondeductible for tax purposes, and they therefore constitute a cash outlay for which you receive no direct tax benefits. Depreciation deductions, however, represent no cash outlay, and yet they reap cash returns for the investor. To the extent that depreciation is equal to or greater than the amortization payments, the difference between the two is cash that comes back to the investor tax-free. As soon as the amortization payments exceed depreciation, the investor loses the "shelter."

Greater depreciation deductions make greater tax shelters. Accelerated depreciation methods, which compress much of the allowable depreciation into the beginning of the holding period, make better tax shelters at first. As the holding period progresses, however, the amounts of allowable depreciation decrease, and so does the sheltering effect. Finally, upon sale of the property the excess depreciation is subject to "recapture."

THE EFFECTS OF INFLATION

None of the investment analysis methods in this chapter consider the effects of inflation on the value of projected returns. After all other computations are completed, you should apply an average annual inflationary rate that you expect to prevail over the projected holding period. By applying that rate over the holding period, you should have a fairly accurate idea of how much your profit dollars will be worth once you have them in your pocket.

> *Example:* Assume that your investment is expected to return $10,000 in net spendable income each year over the next 5 years. After 5 years, you intend to sell the property for what you believe will be a $50,000 profit, after all expenses.
>
> Since you anticipate an average inflation rate of 10 percent a year, you must assume that your $10,000 in spendable income will be worth $9,000, $8,100, $7,290, $6,561, and $5,905 at the end of years 2, 3, 4, and 5, respectively. Each figure represents a 10-percent decrease in buying power from the previous year's figure. Also, the $50,000 you expect to collect in 5 years has to be reconciled with the effects of inflation. It will be "worth" only $29,525 by the time you get your hands on it.

SUMMARY ANALYSIS

On its face, Figure 3-11 tells us several important things about this investment, its tax implications, and some of the relationships among various investment analysis factors:

1. Net operating income, like gross income, increases at a rate of 8 percent per year, because the same inflation rate is assumed to apply to both income and operating expenses, while the vacancy rate is a constant 3 percent per year.
2. While interest payments *decrease* through the fifth year (when the second loan is paid off) at a rate of less than 1 percent per year, amortization payments *increase* at a rate of about 10.6 percent per year until the large second loan balance is paid off. The depreciation reduction decreases at 5 percent per year.
3. Both taxable income *and* gross spendable income increase annually at increasing rates, except for the fifth-year second loan payoff, because increases in net operating income are greater than taxes paid.
4. The tax shelter effect diminishes. The depreciation-deduction/ amortization-payments relationship favors the investor in the 60-percent bracket during the first 3 years, while it slightly favors the investor in the 50-percent bracket during the second 3 years.
5. For the same general reason—the falloff of depreciation and interest deductions—the investor in the 50-percent bracket has an increasingly more favorable after-tax annual bottom line (net spendable income) than one in the 60-percent bracket from the fourth year on. By the end of the sixth year, the cumulative total net spendable income becomes slightly higher for someone in the 50-percent bracket than for someone in the 60-percent bracket.

With information derivable from Figure 3-11, you can see (1) that tax benefits from a real estate investment diminish with the passage of time and (2) that such benefits vary in significance according to time and tax bracket.

Are all these figures "good" or bad"? If they are, to what extent? Given your initial investment of $92,000, how might you compare the past and/or projected income it generates with that of alternative investment opportunities? An important measuring tool for that purpose is the "internal rate of return," which is the subject of the next chapter.

UNDERSTANDING RATE OF RETURN AND IRR MEASUREMENTS

THE INFLATION FACTOR AND DISCOUNTING

The rate of return on income (excluding sale proceeds) is a simple ratio between cumulative net spendable income and investment outlay. In other words, to figure out the rate of return on your investment, just divide how much you take in each year by how much you laid out initially. For example, if your total investment outlay is $92,000 and your investment earns net spendable income of $19,507 in the first year, then the rate of return is 21.2 percent ($19,507 ÷ $92,000). If it earns another $21,475 in the second year, then the *cumulative* net spendable income becomes $40,982 ($19,507 + $21,475). Divide the cumulative figure by the outlay again, and this time you obtain a rate of return of 44.5 percent. (See the top row of amounts in Figure 4-1a for the rest of this example.)

If inflation were not so much a part of our economy, then those figures would be as reliable as any projection can be. Inflation, however, affects investment considerations in a number of ways. On the upside, it nudges up income and market values. On the downside, it pushes up operating and "other investment costs." For example, acquisition costs, which are normally added to the purchase price for computing depreciation, must also be added to the down payment as part of the initial investment outlay.

The effects of inflation must therefore be reckoned into all your

	Year					
	1	2	3	4	5	6
Net spendable income, 50% bracket	19,507	21,475	23,705	26,210	−37,619	36,590
Present value constant, 8% discount	.925926	.857339	.793833	.735030	.680584	.630170
Present value	18,062	18,411	18,818	19,265	−25,603	23,058
Net present value (cumulative sum)	18,062	36,473	55,291	74,556	48,953	72,011
Investment outlay	92,000	92,000	92,000	92,000	92,000	92,000
Rate of return, 50% tax bracket	19.63%	39.65%	60.10%	81.04%	53.21%	78.27%

(a)

Net spendable income, 60% bracket	21,697	22,859	24,239	25,846	−38,935	33,501
Present value constant, 8% discount	.925926	.857339	.793833	.735030	.680584	.630170
Present value	20,162	19,598	19,242	18,998	−26,499	21,111
Net present value (cumulative sum)	20,162	39,760	59,002	78,000	51,501	72,612
Investment outlay	92,000	92,000	92,000	92,000	92,000	92,000
Rate of return, 60% tax bracket	21.92%	43.22%	64.13%	84.78%	55.98%	78.93%

(b)

Figure 4-1. (a) The 50% bracket. (b) The 60% bracket.

investment projections. Since inflation gnaws at the buying power of dollars received in any year after "year zero" of the holding period, the projected net spendable income dollars have to be "brought back" to the present year's real value. Otherwise you are comparing today's dollar with tomorrow's, and the two simply do not have the same value. If you *discount* the dollar of the future—that is, reduce its present value by the anticipated rate of inflation—then you can compare dollars, then and now, of the same or similar value.

Let's take just one small example of how inflation affects an investment. Assume:

Down payment	$69,000
Other investment costs	23,000
Total investment outlay	92,000
Inflation rate	8%
Tax brackets of two representative investors	50% and 60%

These assumptions form the basis for the calculations in Figure 4-1a, which assume the investor is in the 50-percent tax bracket. The top row of figures represent the investor's annual net spendable income. The present value (PV) constant on the second row is the inflation, or discount, factor. It reflects the cumulative effect of 8-percent inflation over the years: By the end of year 1, the dollar is worth only 0.925926 of what it was worth at the start of the year; by year 2 end, it is worth only 0.857339 of what it was worth at the start of year 1; and so on. Multiplying the PV constant against the net spendable income, you get the discounted or present value of the income for each year—the third row. Adding each year's amount to all preceding years' amounts, you arrive at the cumulative sum for each year, which appears on the fourth row.

At this point, you can see the effect of inflation. The investment outlay, which remains constant for all years at $92,000 (the fifth row figures), is divided into the *discounted* (present) value of net spendable income to arrive at the true rate of return (shown on the last row of the table). Compare 19.63 and 39.65 percent for years 1 and 2 to 21.2 and 44.5 percent, which we computed with *nondiscounted* dollars at the beginning of this chapter. As the years go by, the difference becomes greater and greater, because the inflation rate compounds itself.

Thus, for both investors represented in Figure 4-1a and b, the rates of return actually start to decrease after year 4—in discounted values. Disregarding year 5, in which heavy amortization payments create a temporary negative cash flow, their net spendable income increases, while their actual buying power goes down—even more for the 50-percent bracket taxpayer than for the one in the 60-percent bracket. Either investor in this example might be overjoyed with the prospect of having more and more dollars with each passing year. However, they would, in reality, be edging towards a negative flow in present value figures. They must therefore be prepared to increase rents to stay in step with the eroding effects of inflation.

This example points out the inescapable need to weigh the effects of inflation into any calculation for rates of return. Without such considerations, the results are meaningless on a practical basis.

Does it make sense to increase rents to match the inflation rate and then turn around to reduce them by the same rate? The exercise seems to cancel itself out, as shown in Figure 4-2: The investor reflected in this figure raises the net operating income by 8 percent each year, then discounts it by an 8-percent present value constant. Why not simply work in nondiscounted dollars and tack on 8 percent each year to the rents?

The answer is that inflation does not affect all elements in your analysis uniformly. Specifically, the initial investment outlay stays the same number of dollars throughout the holding period. Note in Figure 4-1a, for instance, that the present value versions of net spendable income still

	Year					
	1	2	3	4	5	6
Net operating income	75,000	81,000	87,480	94,478	102,037	110,200
Present value constant, 8% discount	.925926	.857339	.793833	.735030	.680584	.630170
Present value	69,444	69,444	69,445	69,444	69,445	69,445

(a)

Present value of net spendable income, 50% bracket	18,062	18,411	18,818	19,265	Second Loan Payoff	23,058
Percentage increase over previous year	–	1.9%	2.2%	2.4%	–	19.7%[1]

(b)

[1]Over fourth year.

Figure 4-2.

increase every year (again with the exception of year 5). In Figure 4-2b, you see that this increase over the constant $92,000 outlay provides a steady increase in net operating income from one year to the next. In this way, inflation can actually benefit the real estate investor.

The Mathematics

What are the effects, specifically, of inflation on rental income from property? First, inflation obliges you to raise rents to obtain the number of dollars necessary to give you the equivalent value of the original, first-year rent. For example, after 1 year of 8-percent inflation, you need $108,000 in income to have the equivalent of $100,000 in income during the first year. Second, inflation diminishes the true value of the original $100,000. For instance, the worth of $100,000 after 1 year is only, roughly, $92,000.

The Future Value Constant. To keep pace with inflation, you must raise rents; that is, you must require tenants to pay more dollars to make up for the loss of value in each dollar. The future value constant tells you how much the rent has to be in any given year of the holding period, assuming an average rate of inflation. After the first year in which the inflation rate has effect (usually the second year of the holding period, since leases are typically negotiated annually), the $100,000 must be raised to $108,000. In the next (third) year, that rent has to be raised again by 8 percent of the $108,000—not of the original $100,000, because inflation has a compounding effect. For the amounts of subsequent years, see the third row of Figure 4-3a.

To calculate the constant, simply take the following year's "future value" and divide it by the original (present) value, which in this case is $100,000. For example, in Figure 4-3a, the constant for year 4 is 1.3605. This figure is the result of dividing years 5's future value ($136,049) by the present value:

$$\text{Future value constant} = \frac{\text{Future value of following year}}{\text{Present value}}$$

The Present Value Constant. Inflation also erodes the present value (let's say the "first-year" amount). As the years go by, the original $100,000 is worth less and less. To determine what it is worth in any given year, you need a present value constant for the year in question. That constant is calculated by dividing the present value by the following year's future value. That is

$$\text{Present value constant} = \frac{\text{Present value}}{\text{Future value of following year}}$$

—the opposite of the future value constant formula!

	Year					
	1	2	3	4	5	6
Future value	100,000	108,000	116,640	125,971	136,049	146,933
x Interest/ appreciation rate	.08	.08	.08	.08	.08	.08
= Amount of increase	8,000	8,640	9,331	10,078	10,884	11,755
+ Future value	100,000	108,000	116,640	125,971	136,049	146,933
= Following year's future value	108,000	116,640	125,971	136,049	146,933	158,688
÷ Present value	100,000	100,000	100,000	100,000	100,000	100,000
= Future value constant	1.08	1.1664	1.2597	1.3605	1.4693	1.5869

(a)

Present value	100,000	100,000	100,000	100,000	100,000	100,000
÷ Following year's future value	108,000	116,640	125,971	136,049	146,933	158,688
= Present value constant	.925926	.857339	.793833	.735030	.680584	.630170

(b)

Figure 4-3. (a) Future value constant. (b) Present value constant.

As an illustration, the present value constant for year 4 would be 0.735030, calculated by dividing year 5's future value ($136,049) by the present value ($100,000).

As a practical matter, you needn't do all this figuring. The effects of inflation on future income and present value are quickly determined from precomputed tables, which present such computations for a wide range of rates and years. Increasingly, this sort of work is done either on inexpensive calculators and microcomputers, or it is accessed from computers through telephone terminals. You must still, however, grasp the dynamics of future and present values to understand the rate of return and—the next step—the internal rate of return.

THE REQUIRED RATE OF RETURN UPON DISPOSITION

Often an investor begins the evaluation of prospective investments by establishing a required annual rate of return not only on income during the holding period, but also on sale proceeds upon disposition. This overall return is a much more meaningful measure of performance than the capitalization rate, which reflects only the ratio between net operating income and market value. In fact, if the market value were to increase at a greater rate than NOI, the "cap" rate would actually *decrease*—no matter how high either factor goes!

Let's say the investor is looking for the same 10-percent overall rate of return from income and disposition proceeds, as might be expected in the cap rate. If an 8-percent inflation rate also prevails, it reduces the present value of future cash returns by that rate. In Figure 4-4 (a, b, and c), the required 10-percent rate of return and 8-percent inflation rate are combined into a discount factor, which is then used to determine the point in the holding period of our hypothetical investment at which the required after-tax rate of return would be achieved through sale of the property. That point is passed when the "adjusted present value" (the present value of all future cash flows discounted at 18 percent, minus the present value of the investment outlay) becomes a positive number—in this case, sometime during the second year.

In other words, the rate of return is somewhat less than 18 percent at the end of the first year and somewhat more than that at the end of the second, because the respective APVs are −$25,679 (indicating a negative rate of return) and $10,347. But at which point in the holding period would the rate of return (with sale in the given year) be *exactly* 18 percent? Answer: When the adjusted present value is equal to *zero*. Turning the question

	Year				
	1	2	3	4	5
Present value of net spendable income	16,531	15,423	14,428	13,519	−16,444
Net present value	16,531	31,954	46,382	59,901	43,457
+ Present value of net sale proceed	49,790	70,393	86,404	98,456	136,274
= Total discounted cash flow	66,321	102,347	132,786	158,357	179,731
− Investment outlay	92,000	92,000	92,000	92,000	92,000
= Adjusted present value	−25,679	10,347	40,786	66,357	87,731

(a)

Net spendable income	19,507	21,475	23,705	26,210	−37,619
Present value constant, 18% discount	.847458	.718185	.608632	.515790	.437111
Present value of net spendable income	16,531	15,423	14,428	13,519	−16,444

(b)

Net sale proceed	58,752	98,015	141,964	190,883	311,761
Present value constant, 18% discount	.847458	.718185	.608632	.515790	.437111
Present value of net sale proceed	49,790	70,393	86,404	98,456	136,274

(c)

Figure 4-4. (a) Present value of net spendable income. (b) Net spendable income. (c) Net sale proceed.

around, we might ask, "Given net spendable income of $21,475 and a net sale proceed of $98,015 in the second year, what would the rate of return be?" Answer: Whatever discount rate makes the adjusted present value equal to zero; that rate is called the *internal rate of return.*

INTERNAL RATE OF RETURN

"Zero" is the key number in computing IRR, because this method:

1. "brings back" (or discounts) all cash flows generated by the investment—including the net or gross sale proceed;
2. weighs each cash flow according to when it is received; and
3. presents the result as an annual rate for each year through the year in which the property is sold (the year of "zero balance").

Many of us might find it simpler just to understand what the IRR method does and how to make use of it, than to wrestle with the procedure for computing it. For now, let's forget the calculations, and see if a few examples clarify how the method works. Figure 4-5 shows how the IRR works in various cases. In keeping with the zero balance called for by the IRR computation, try to view each of these tables as a see-saw or a scale, bearing on its opposite ends two bags of gold pieces worth $100,000 each. One bag (on the left) represents the initial investment outlay; the other the sale proceed.

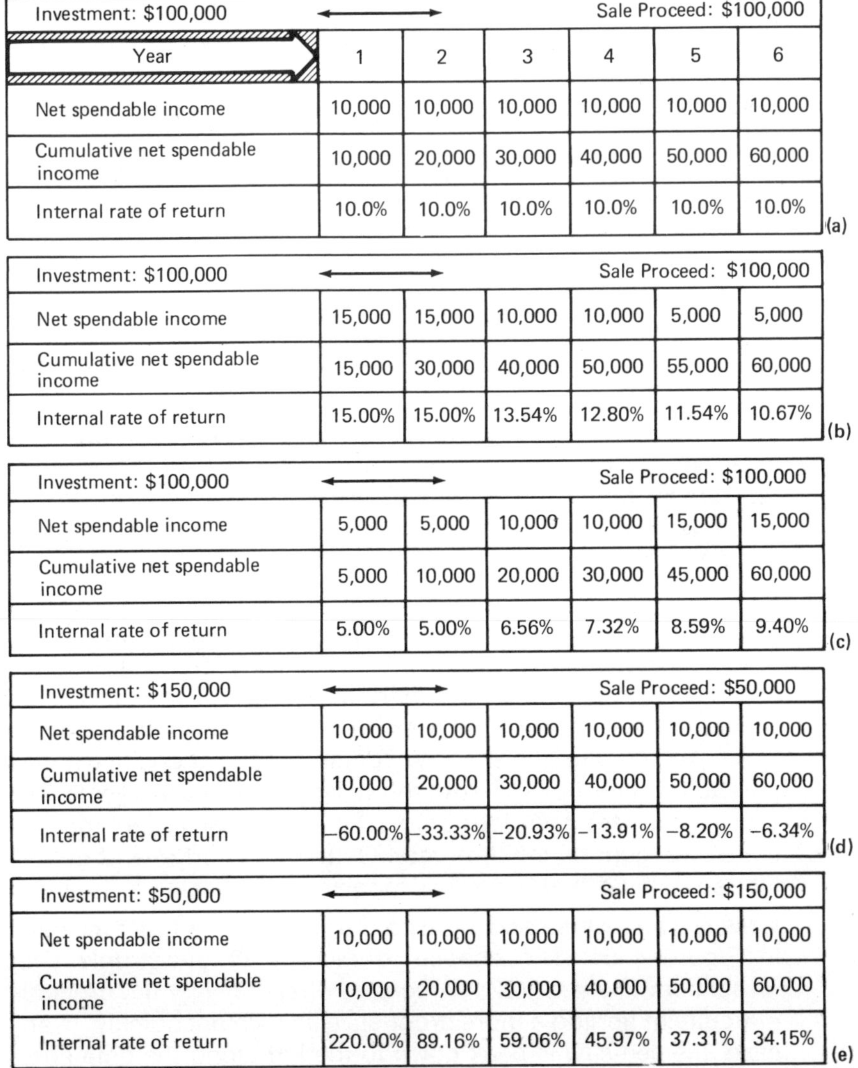

(a)

Investment: $100,000	⟷			Sale Proceed: $100,000		
Year	1	2	3	4	5	6
Net spendable income	10,000	10,000	10,000	10,000	10,000	10,000
Cumulative net spendable income	10,000	20,000	30,000	40,000	50,000	60,000
Internal rate of return	10.0%	10.0%	10.0%	10.0%	10.0%	10.0%

(b)

Investment: $100,000	⟷			Sale Proceed: $100,000		
Net spendable income	15,000	15,000	10,000	10,000	5,000	5,000
Cumulative net spendable income	15,000	30,000	40,000	50,000	55,000	60,000
Internal rate of return	15.00%	15.00%	13.54%	12.80%	11.54%	10.67%

(c)

Investment: $100,000	⟷			Sale Proceed: $100,000		
Net spendable income	5,000	5,000	10,000	10,000	15,000	15,000
Cumulative net spendable income	5,000	10,000	20,000	30,000	45,000	60,000
Internal rate of return	5.00%	5.00%	6.56%	7.32%	8.59%	9.40%

(d)

Investment: $150,000	⟷			Sale Proceed: $50,000		
Net spendable income	10,000	10,000	10,000	10,000	10,000	10,000
Cumulative net spendable income	10,000	20,000	30,000	40,000	50,000	60,000
Internal rate of return	-60.00%	-33.33%	-20.93%	-13.91%	-8.20%	-6.34%

(e)

Investment: $50,000	⟷			Sale Proceed: $150,000		
Net spendable income	10,000	10,000	10,000	10,000	10,000	10,000
Cumulative net spendable income	10,000	20,000	30,000	40,000	50,000	60,000
Internal rate of return	220.00%	89.16%	59.06%	45.97%	37.31%	34.15%

Figure 4-5.

Case 1. Figure 4–5a shows equilibrium: $100,000 is invested, thereby becoming a negative downward balancing force. But that negative force generates countervailing positive forces in the form of income: The investor derives a regular $10,000 (or 10.0 percent) per year until sale, at which time he or she *removes* the $100,000 outlay from the balance, thereby reducing everything to zero. The see-saw swings back to a horizontal position.

Case 2. In Figure 4–5b, the same $100,000 is invested, and the total income again comes to $60,000 over the 6-year holding period. When the $100,000 is removed from the balance at the end of 6 years, the scale returns to "zero balance." In this case, however, 40 percent of that $60,000 income is realized during the first half (3 years) of the period. In either of the first 2 years, the IRR is 15 percent per year, upon sale. From then on, the annual return, spread out over the holding period, becomes progressively lower for each additional year the investment is held. Because the left side of the see-saw leans down, the early disposition of this investment might be (or might have been) the most profitable alternative.

Case 3. Figure 4–5c suggests just the opposite. As is often the case in real estate investments, the cash flows from income weigh more heavily in the later years of the holding, so the trend of the IRRs nudges the see-saw down on the right. Judged ("internally") in terms of its own performance, this investment might be read to indicate an increasingly profitable holding. Indirectly, the figures also raise the question of whether some other investment might not be more so. In either event, the investor has some valuable guideposts in considering the matter.

Case 4. In Figure 4–d, the IRR is put to the unpleasant task of assisting in the judgment of when to get out (or to have gotten out) of an investment, given that the sale in *any* given year is going to mean a substantial loss over the initial investment outlay. In this case, the rate of loss merely diminishes in intensity with the passage of time, but a positive return is not realized in 6 years. The fifth year comes and goes before the rate of loss even approximates the general inflation rate. Getting out early—and getting into something that loses less money—would seem to be best.

Case 5. The reverse and more comfortable dilemma is presented in Figure 4–5e. The chance to more than quardruple your investment in a year (220 percent) is offset only by the probable difficulty in finding a more productive investment quickly. In any case, the see-saw is back down to the left along the time line.

In practical terms, the IRR is an investment analysis approach that accounts for *all* the factors in deriving the rates of return shown in Figure 4-1. As you saw in these cases, this method takes the year-to-year income flow, adds it to the anticipated sale proceeds, and distributes the sum over the years of the holding period. The resultant annual figures then represent discounted, and generally after-tax returns on investment for *each* year of the investment (see Figure 4–5). In this respect, the IRR method differs from a "straight" average annual rate of return, which does not consider the time value of money. The farther away from the beginning time it is that you receive the same amount of money, the less value it has, because of the time it was not earning returns for you.

In general, the preferred approach to real estate investment analysis is on an after-tax basis. Figure 4–6, however, shows the IRR computed on a before-tax basis for two reasons: First, the before-tax rate is put to practical use in comparing investment opportunities on a "tax-neutral" basis. (Some investors' investment income is tax-free due to various sheltering programs or other reasons, such as employment by certain international organizations.) Secondly, the before-tax figures can be contrasted with the after-tax returns to help measure the importance of tax factors in a given investment. Contrary to a notion that has far too wide currency, an investment made essentially for the tax benefits should be viewed with skepticism.

Let's delve into this method a little more deeply, using our hypothetical income property investment. Figure 4–6 shows how the values used directly in arriving at an IRR for this investment are derived from the key 15 analysis factors. The values needed for direct use in the computations are:

1. capital outlay,
2. periodic cash flows, and
3. withdrawal or disposition proceed.

Capital Outlay

The capital outlay takes the form of an initial investment consisting simply of a down payment and closing costs. Its combined present value is unaffected by time because it is entered into the equation at point zero, as in this example. Other capital outlays (such as replacing, as distinct from repairing, floors, roofs, furnaces, and the like) are entered in the year in which they are made. Capital outlays are negative values in the IRR computation.

Investment outlay: $92,000	Year					
	1	2	3	4	5	6
Gross spendable income	8,556	14,556	21,036	28,034	−31,040	52,036
Cumulative gross spendable income	—	23,112	44,148	72,182	41,142	93,178
Gross sale proceed	60,599	118,685	181,518	249,494	389,714	468,629
Before-tax IRR	−24.83%	25.08%	37.41%	40.61%	41.12%	39.96%

(a)

Purchase price	$690,000					
Other investment costs	23,000					
Annual depreciation 125%, declining balance	33,925	32,229	30,617	29,086	27,632	26,251
− Cumulative depreciation	33,925	66,154	96,771	125,857	153,489	179,740
= Adjusted basis (at time of sale)	679,075	646,846	616,229	587,143	559,511	553,260

(b)

Cumulative depreciation 125%, declining balance	33,925	66,154	96,771	125,857	153,489	179,740
Annual depreciation, straight-line method	27,140	27,140	27,140	27,140	27,140	27,140
− Cumulative depreciation, straight-line method.	27,140	54,280	81,420	108,560	135,700	162,840
= Recaptured depreciation	6,785	11,874	15,351	17,297	17,789	16,900
x Tax bracket	50%	50%	50%	50%	50%	50%
= Tax on recaptured depreciation	3,393	5,937	7,676	8,649	8,805	8,450

(c)

	Year					
	1	2	3	4	5	6
Sale price	745,200	804,816	869,201	938,737	1,013,836	1,094,943
− Sales commission	52,164	56,337	60,844	65,712	70,969	76,646
− Other sales costs	14,904	16,096	17,384	18,775	20,277	21,899
= Amount realized	678,132	732,383	790,973	854,250	922,590	996,398
− Adjusted basis	679,075	646,846	616,229	587,143	559,511	533,260
= Total gain	−943	85,537	174,744	267,107	363,079	463,138
− Recaptured depreciation	6,785	11,874	15,351	17,297	17,789	16,900
= Capital gain	−7,728	73,663	159,393	249,810	345,290	446,238
x Capital gain tax rate (40% x tax bracket)[1]	0.20	0.20	0.20	0.20	0.20	0.20
= Capital gain tax	−1,546	14,733	31,879	49,962	69,058	89,248

(d)

[1] 0.40 x 0.50 = 0.20

Figure 4-6.

Investment Outlay: $92,000	Year					
	1	2	3	4	5	6
Sale price	745,200	804,816	869,201	938,737	1,013,836	1,094,943
– Balance, first loan	548,897	545,469	541,683	537,498	532,876	527,769
– Balance, second loan	68,636	68,229	67,772	67,258	0	0
= Equity	127,667	191,118	259,746	333,981	480,960	567,174
– Sales commission	52,164	56,337	60,844	65,712	70,969	76,646
– Other sales costs	14,904	16,096	17,384	18,775	20,277	21,899
= Gross sale proceed	60,599	118,685	181,518	249,494	389,714	468,629
– Tax on recaptured depreciation	3,393	5,937	7,676	8,649	8,895	8,450
– Capital gain tax	–1,546	14,733	31,879	49,962	69,058	89,248
= Net sale proceed	58,752	98,015	141,963	190,883	311,761	370,931
Net spendable income, 50% bracket	19,507	21,475	23,705	26,210	–37,619	36,590
After-tax IRR,. 50% income tax bracket	–14.94%	25.06%	35.89%	39.06%	39.73%	38.39%

(e)

Gross sale proceed	60,599	118,685	181,518	249,494	389,714	468,629
Tax on recaptured depreciation[1]	4,071	7,124	9,211	10,378	10,673	10,140
Capital gain tax[1]	–1,855	17,679	38,254	59,954	82,870	107,097
Net sale proceed	58,383	93,882	134,053	179,162	296,171	351,392
Net spendable income, 60% bracket	21,697	22,859	24,239	25,846	–38,935	33,501
After-tax IRR 60% income tax bracket	–12.96%	25.05%	35.55%	38.70%	39.39%	38.01%

(f)

[1] Computed here for 60% tax bracket by same methods as in Figures 4–6c and 4–6d for 50% tax bracket.

Figure 4-6 (Continued).

Periodic Cash Flows

As usual in real estate investment analysis, the IRR is worked out on an annual basis, but it can be on a monthly or any other time increment basis. The cash flows can be positive, negative, or mixed. The periodic cash flows used in this example are gross and net spendable income, with a negative cash flow in the fifth year caused by the payoff of a second loan.

Withdrawal or Disposition Proceed

To find a rate that, by definition, equates the present values of cash flows into and out of an account, the account must be brought into balance. The "gross" disposition proceeds are those before taxes; the "net" proceeds represent the amount left after federal taxes on recaptured depreciation and capital gain.

Keep in mind that computing an IRR involves a cycle of cash flowing out as capital outlay, producing income over a period of time, and flowing back in in the form of withdrawal or disposition proceeds. If, in mathematical effect, that cycle occurs twice, there will be two IRRs—a potential limitation on the usefulness of the rate.

Computing the IRR

How do you compute the internal rate of return? Even a professional mathematician can compute the internal rate of return only by trial and error. The procedure is called an "iterative" process; that is, a trial rate is first selected by approximation. This "guesstimation" is then tested for accuracy, using present or future value factors. It may or may not "compute"—that is, it may or may not equate the present value of future cash flows (net spendable income and net sale proceed) to the present value of the initial investment outlay (down payment and closing and other investment costs). If it does not, then another rate is selected and tested. The process continues, literally, to *zero in* on the correct rate until it is selected and verified. The most efficient way to do the actual computation—or to check its accuracy—is to use a calculator or computer having the appropriate program. But in a pinch (or for instructional purposes), you can also use graphs and various interpolative and extrapolative processes.

Figure 4-8 (a, b, and c) presents a simplified demonstration of the iterative process. In this figure, our hypothetical investment is sold in the fourth year by an investor in the 50-percent tax bracket. Future value constants are used to test rates roughly estimated on each side of the correct after-tax IRR.

How do you make these estimates? One way is to get your first estimate by calculating the "average annual rate of profit (AARP)." As shown in Figure 4-7, the "AARP" is a ratio between the average yearly profit to the initial investment outlay. The AARP is an earlier alternative to the IRR—until computers and calculators made computation of the IRR inexpensive. Nowadays, because this rate does not account for the time

	Year			
	1	2	3	4
Net spendable income	19,507	21,475	23,705	26,210
Cumulative net spendable income	19,507	40,982	64,687	90,897
+ Net sale proceed	58,752	98,015	141,963	190,883
= Total receipts	78,259	138,997	206,650	281,780
−Investment outlay	92,000	92,000	92,000	92,000
= Total profit (cumulative cash flow)	−13,741	46,997	114,650	189,780
÷ Number of years held	1	2	3	4
= Average annual profit	−13,741	23,498	38,217	47,445
÷ Investment outlay	92,000	92,000	92,000	92,000
= Average annual rate of profit (after tax)	−14.94%	25.54%	41.54%	51.57%

Figure 4-7.

	Investment Outlay	Net Spendable Income			Net Spendable Income + Net Sale Proceed
Year	0	1	2	3	4
Cash flow	−92,000	19,507	21,475	23,705	217,043[1]
÷ Future value constant for 42% trial rate	1.0	1.42	2.0164	2.8633	4.0659
= Present value	−92,000	13,737	10,650	8,279	53,381
Net present value (cumulative sum)	−92,000	-78,263	-67,613	-59,334	-5,952

(a)

[1] 26,210 (net spendable income) + 190,833 (net sale proceed) = 217,043.

Cash flow	−92,000	19,507	21,475	23,705	217,043
÷ Future value constant for 38% trial rate	1.0	1.38	1.9044	2.6281	3.6267
= Present value	−92,000	14,136	11,277	9,020	59,846
Net present value	−92,000	-77,864	-66,587	-57,567	2,279

(b)

Cash flow	−92,000	19,507	21,475	23,705	217,043
÷ Future value constant for 39.06% rate	1.0	1.3906	1.9338	2.6891	3.7395
= Present value	−92,000	14,028	11,105	8,815	58,041
Net present value	−92,000	-77,972	-66,867	-51,043	2

(c)

Figure 4-8.

frame within which income is received, many investment analysts consider it useful only for "eyeballing" the IRR.

Let's go through a simplified iterative process just to demonstrate how it works. We assume that the holding will be sold in the fourth year. We also know that our analysis to this point has been based on an 8-percent inflation rate, and that the AARP method does not consider the time value of money. We therefore can surmise that the fourth-year rate derived by the AARP method would be higher than a rate derived by a method that does make such a consideration. So we begin our search for the IRR by knocking, say, 10 percent off the AARP of 51.5 percent and rounding it to 42 percent. Since this "classroom" computation rounds off a great deal, its results are less precise than if the calculations were left to a powerful computer.

Figure 4-8a shows the first computation to zero in on the IRR, using 42 percent as a trial rate. (The future value constants for all the trial rates in Figure 4-8 are computed by the method shown in Figure 4-3a.) Figure 4-8a shows that 42 percent is too high to be the IRR we seek because the net present value in the fourth year is a negative amount (-$5,952). So we drop the trial rate to 38 percent and repeat the procedure.

In Figure 4-8b, the net present value goes from -$5,952 to $2,279—a positive value. So the IRR is somewhere between 38 percent and 42 percent. Whether by graph, linear interpolation, and/or a hand calculator programmed for such a routine, the rate 39.06 percent should eventually be reached. That is the IRR in this example.

Figure 4-8c shows the computation down to "zero" ($2) net present value. If everything else is held constant, the 39.06-percent IRR holds through a net sale proceed of $217,043 to $217,099.[1]

IRR, INVESTMENT VALUE, AND NEGOTIATIONS

Price is the focal point in most negotiations involving the sale of almost anything. So keep in mind at least four important prices when participating in a real estate transaction:

[1]Those fascinated by mathematical fine points may note that a net sale proceed of $217,042 produces an IRR of 39.05-percent, while one of $218,000 produces a rate of 39.18 percent (on the hand calculator). For most practical purposes, the difference of 0.13 percent (or 0.01 percent), which would be made by a $1 change in net sale proceed, is much less important than many other factors in making an investment decision.

1. *The price above which the buying investor will not buy:* All other factors assumed to be optimal, the investor will not pay more either because the return on investment at that price is the lowest the investor is willing to accept, or because other, more favorable, investment opportunities become available at a higher price.
2. *The selling investor's offering price:* This price is likely to be close to the top price the buyer is willing to pay, since the seller (in the absence of misinformation, duress, or other extraneous factors) seeks the highest price the market will bear. But some sellers start high.
3. *The buyer's offering price:* This offer is likely to be on the low side of what the market will bear, since a low price favors maximum return, all other factors being optimal.
4. The final negotiated price.

In arriving at each of these prices, both the buyer and the seller should know the "investment value" of the property at each price. These values can in turn be used to find the IRR by a method slightly different from that reflected in Figures 4-6 and 4-7. All that information is important in the formulation of a sound negotiating posture on each side of the transaction. In the final analysis, *cash flows* are the objects being bought and sold.

Let's assume that the seller of our hypothetical investment places it on the market for $621,000, a price that would produce a sixth-year IRR of 38 percent if the available mortgages remain constant. Figure 4-9a shows how to derive a sale price from a given rate of return, in this case a 38-percent rate: The seller's offer is $702,948. The buyer, however, considers a 38-percent return to be minimal, and Figure 4-9b shows the same procedure for the 42-percent rate, upon which (we assume) the buyer bases an offer to purchase: The buyer's offer is $677,582. The method shown in either part of the figure holds the available mortgage loan amount, as well as closing and other investment costs, constant, while it discounts the after-tax cash flows from income and from the sale of the property. Thus it arrives at a *total* investment value. To that amount the available mortgage (minus investment costs other than the down payment) is added to arrive at a hypothetical sale price termed "total investment value." Let's assume that the buyer and seller negotiate a firm contract price of $690,000. A rate of return for that price can be calculated by the procedure in Figure 4-9c.

Though close to the 38.39-percent IRR shown at the end of the sixth year in Figure 4-5, the 40.04 percent in Figure 4-9c can be viewed as an IRR only with some qualification. For the most part, the procedure is sound. For instance, multiplying cash flows by present value constants, of course, is simply the reverse of dividing them by future value constants; only small discrepancies arise through rounding. Similarly, it is equally sound to add

Year	Net Spendable Income 50% Tax Bracket	Present Value Constant, 38% Rate	Present Value
1	19,507	.724638	14,136
2	21,475	.525100	11,277
3	23,705	.380507	9,020
4	26,210	.275727	7,227
5	−37,619	.199804	−7,516
6	385,209[1]	.144785	55,772
	Net present value or "investment value" of cumulative, after-tax, discounted cash flow.		104,948
	Available mortgage(s)		621,000
	Other investment costs		−23,000
	Total investment value		702,948

(a)

[1]36,590 (net spendable income) + 348,619 (net sale proceed) = 385,209.

1	19,507	.704225 [2]	13,737
2	21,475	.495933	10,650
3	23,705	.349250	8,279
4	26,210	.245950	6,446
5	−37,619	.173204	−6,516
6	385,209	.121975	46,986
	Net present value		79,582
	Available mortgage(s)		621,000
	Other investment costs		−23,000
	Total investment value		677,582

(b)

[2]Present value constants for 42% trial rate.

38%	=	702,900		
			12,900	
X%	=	690,000		
				25,300
42%	=	677,600		

(c)

38%	+	$(4\% \times \frac{12,900}{25,300})$	=	X%
38%	+	(4% x 0.50988)	=	X%
38%	+	2.04%	=	X%
40.04%			=	X%

(d)

Figure 4-9. (a) 38% IRR, the seller's offer. (b) 42% IRR, the buyer's offer. (c) the negotiated price.

a loan amount to cash flows and to subtract a down payment as part of an investment outlay (as in Figure 4–9).

Holding the loan amount constant, however, distorts the input data for computing an IRR. In reality, a change in sale price, by the operation of loan-to-value ratios, means a change in loan amount, down payment, and closing costs. An IRR computed with erroneous investment outlays is bound to be off to some degree. Nevertheless, even with that caveat, the computation of investment values by way of rates of return—and vice versa—can be a useful tool not only in the analysis of investment alternatives, but also in negotiating specific transactions.

IRR PLUS REINVESTMENT

If an investment produces positive cash flows, it generates funds that may be reinvested, rather like the compounding of interest in a savings account. For that reason, some real estate investment analysts believe that the IRR should be either computed with an allowance for reinvestment or supplemented with a second rate reflecting additional return through reinvestment. Hence "IRR plus reinvestment."

Of the various approaches to this matter, each must make assumptions about the rate of return on gross and net spendable income and on net sale proceed. One approach is to assume that such income earns the same return as the investment producing it. This premise is dubious: Because three cash flows and time frames are involved, no real estate investment is likely to parallel another investment so closely, and other real estate investments would not ordinarily be made piecemeal. Another more realistic approach is to select a reinvestment rate independent of the investment being studied and present it separately as a rate that can be useful in an investor's overall planning.

SENSITIVITY ANALYSIS

The question in sensitivity analysis is, "If I change a given element in an investment, how does that change affect all the other elements?" With the comprehensive investment analysis programs available today through terminals in the real estate brokerage offices of most major housing markets in the U.S., anyone with basic analytical skills in the field can learn quickly to perform "sensitivity analysis" of an investment under consideration. The procedure is simply a matter of keying in the necessary basic inputs and assumptions for the analysis, letting the results print out, then going back for additional printouts based on changes in one or more variables while all the others are held constant. Among the key factors that can be manipulated to produce a half-dozen or more variations in a few minutes are:

- purchase price,
- gross income,
- vacancy rate,
- operating expenses,
- inflation and appreciation,
- down payment,
- other investment costs,
- financing terms,
- tax bracket,
- depreciation factors, and
- future disposition costs.

With such a tool available, the analyst can view the full range of any investment's "best case" and "worst case" situations. For example, what happens to the after-tax annual cash flow, if the price and the loan amount are increased (or decreased)? What happens to cash flows and final yield if the vacancy rate averages 5 percent during a 5-year period? What if 10 percent? What are the effects of a different financing method? As programs are refined and made more widely available for office and home computers, analysts' ability to secure accurate readings almost instantly is limited only by their capacity to ask meaningful questions about a prospective investment or set of investment alternatives.

5

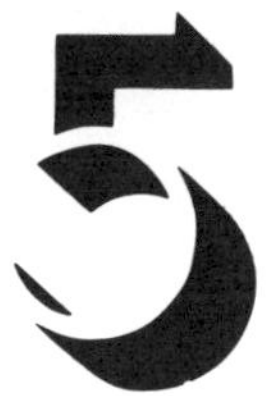

TOMORROW'S TECHNIQUES TODAY

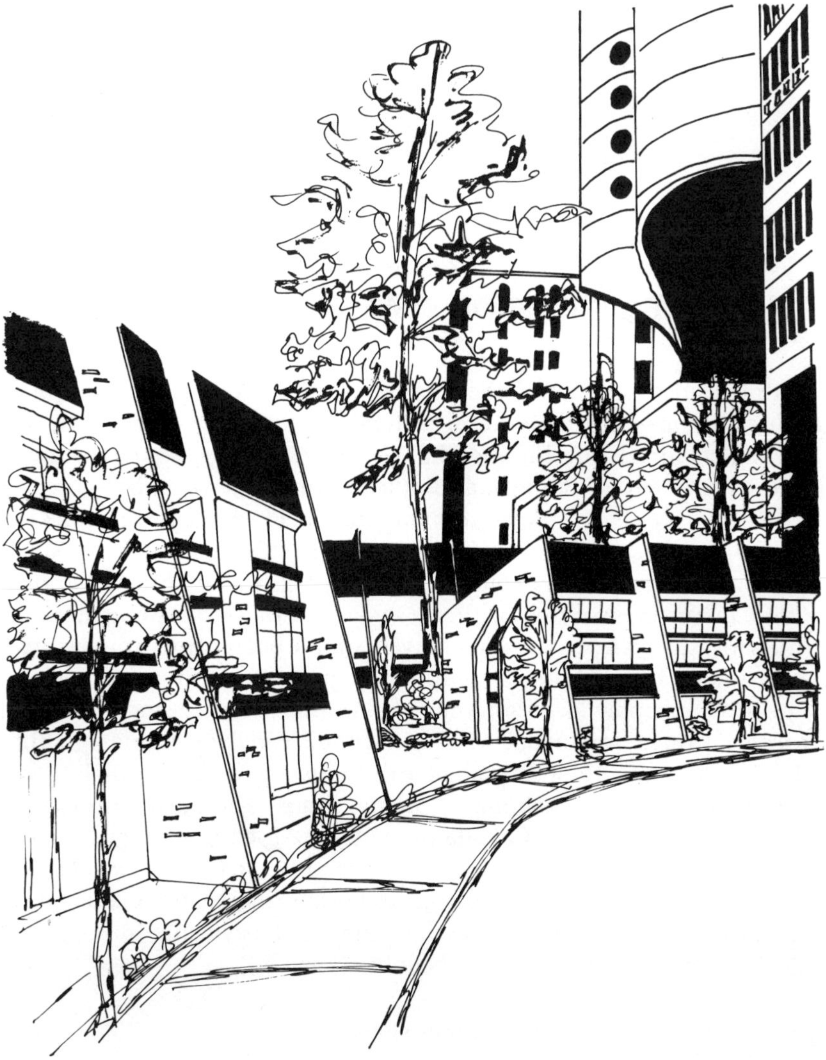

THE MONEY VALUE OF TIME

Let's consider something other than the time value of money: *the money value of time*—your time. Admittedly, the simpler functions of the basic investment anaylsis techniques that we have considered—such as figuring a down payment or adding and subtracting line items—can be figured and recorded with pencil, paper, and any handheld calculator as quickly as with the most sophisticated computer. In the case of such simple calculations, accessing a computer would just be wasteful. Yet in many other instances, working without some sort of electronic assistance is dramatically inefficient. Even relatively simple but repetitive procedures—such as loan amortization or compounding a sales price by an appreciation rate—can consume large amounts of time. Such procedures very quickly become wasteful for anyone who has to conduct analyses regularly without the assistance of a financial calculator. In just one complete analysis such computations are made many, many times. For such applications, calculators are a must. Calculators with the 5 basic financial keys are available at a purchase price lower than the cost of an hour or two of clerical time. Any clerk can learn to use one in far less time than it takes to do the computation by hand, such as figuring PITI payments[1] on a loan or working out an amortization schedule.

[1]Principal, interest, taxes, and insurance.

Calculators become even more essential for higher-salaried individuals. Anyone sophisticated enough in analysis to be weighing variations on the internal rate of return is likely to be earning enough in one hour to pay for a calculator that can present a string of results in a minute. If those results would take that person an hour or more to calculate by hand, the economies become self-evident. Even if the analyst is also working from a terminal linked into a more powerful computer's investment analysis program, the programmed financial calculator is cost-efficient for inputs and side computations too troublesome or trivial for the master program.

Programmability

Beyond piecemeal routines and built-in financial programs, calculators entering the market boast ever-increased "programmability." With this feature, you store sequences of keystrokes in the device and then call them out simply by entering one or more variables and running the program with one keystroke. You can not only display intermediate results with a pause or full stop, but you can also design the program to permit entry of new or changed data during the run cycle as well as at the beginning. Loan amortization and declining-balance depreciation schedules are typical of the many uses of calculator programmability, which both speeds up computations and minimizes the risks of error. Even if you have telephone terminal access to a powerful computer, such a calculator can be invaluable in covering routines not in the available programs or in replacing the computer when it is not available.

State of the Art

Today the firms of many real estate agents and investment specialists are wired into the national network of real estate computer services. These individuals have access to investment analysis programs that facilitate the complete financial planning of virtually any real estate investment, including new construction, within a few minutes. Such programs literally reduce the most sophisticated analytical techniques in current use around the nation to a streamlined set of keystrokes, making them intelligible to any subscriber who can master a few basic financial concepts. Accuracy and simplicity are the keys. The professional's time is spent applying meaningful principles rather than making elaborate or repetitive calculations.

Even as such programs come on line, competing real estate software firms continue to develop applications that:

1. expand the base of raw information about listings and real estate market factors;

2. make all analytical techniques with general validity available to subscribers;
3. cut user time and money costs through efficiencies made possible by technological advances;
4. open services to expanding user populations through cost efficiencies and simplified applications; and
5. increase sophistication and accuracy of new analytical techniques by lowering the cost of thoroughness.

ADVANCED ANALYSIS PROGRAMS

Because of the computer's speed in making detailed calculations, using such equipment routinely to replicate the full range of financial circumstances surrounding real-life investments has become practicable. The combination of increasing accuracy and simplicity with decreasing costs presents at least two options for any person who has been briefed on current techniques:

1. to use the *same amount of time* for multiplied and more accurate work product, and/or
2. to use *less time* for the same work product, with greater accuracy.

FINANCIAL MANAGEMENT ACCOUNT

A real estate investment inevitably has cash flows that are not accounted for in the traditional analytical methods. The net cash flow after expenses and debt service is likely to be either above or below zero in any given accounting period. If this cash flow is positive, the money is either withdrawn or reinvested. If the cash flow is negative, it must be covered in some way. The key element in an analysis that weighs the effects of irregular positive and negative cash flows is usually called the "financial management account." Whether handled as part of an overall computer investment analysis or otherwise, the "account" serves as an analytical tool in these three ways:

1. plans reserve account deposits and withdrawals for maximum interest earnings;

2. folds reserve account activity and earnings into all other cash flows generated by the investment; and
3. provides raw data for comprehensive rate of return measurement (the "financial management rate of return," FMRR).

The dynamics of this process are not difficult to understand, if broken down into specific steps, as follows:

Step 1. Establish a reserve account with two elements: (1) a "safe rate" balance and (2) a "reinvestment rate" balance. First, depending on applicable investor strategies, policies, or outside regulations, the safe rate (or rate X) balance may earn interest at the current passbook savings, money market fund, or other rate for funds sufficiently liquid to cover the projected negative cash flows. Second, the reinvestment rate (or rate Y) balance earns interest at the higher rate of a certificate of deposit, high-yield corporate or government bond, or some other investment that requires a minimum dollar input and that penalizes withdrawal prior to maturity. If all reserves are to remain in one balance, then no reinvestment rate or balance is established.

Step 2. Project the positive and/or negative cash flows for the maximum holding period, with the hypothetical disposition of property in any year during that time. Include income and outflow from rents, all expenses, debt service, capital additions (such as dollars invested in improvements or funded reserves), money brought in through new loans, interest earned on reserves, and tax payments or benefits.

Step 3. Fund the reserves. To arrive at a suitable amount for starting reserves determine the net present value of the negative net after-tax cash flows for the projected period of the analysis. The discount rate for the NPV determination is the FMRR safe rate.

Step 4. Set the criteria for the transfer of funds from the safe rate (X) account to the reinvestment rate (Y) account. The essential criterion is the minimum amount required for deposit or investment at the higher rate. The transfer takes place only if the principal and interest from the safe rate account are not needed to cover the projected negative cash flows from the property.

Step 5. Compute FMRR. The investment outlay consists of: (1) the net present value of the initial investment, (2) all annual after-tax negative cash flows, if any, and (3) the net sale proceed, if negative. The discount rate used to determine the NPV of those cash flows is usually the safe rate (X). The FMRR is computed simply by solving for the internal rate of return, using this investment outlay and all after-tax positive cash flows, including the net sale proceed if it is positive. The FMRR, in other words, is the interest (or discount) rate that makes the present value of the negative cash flows equal to the present value of the positive cash flows. (See the previous chapter, which explains IRR computations.)

INVESTMENT TAX CREDITS (ITC)

Under the tax law, at least from January 22, 1975 through 1980, an investment tax "credit" of one sort or another is available on the value of qualified personal property. The basic ITC is 10 percent. Eleven percent is permitted if the additional 1 percent is contributed by the taxpaying corporation to an employee stock ownership plan; 11.5 percent is allowed if the additional 0.5 percent is contributed by employees to such a plan. The credit may not exceed the taxpayer's tax liability in a given year, nor may it exceed $25,000 plus 50 percent of the tax liability in excess of that amount.

The taxpayer's reporting method affects the amount of ITC allowed. A husband and wife filing separately are limited, in their respective returns, to credits of $12,500 plus 50 percent of the excess over that amount, with this exception: If only one of them has no qualifying investment or unused credit, the other may use the entire $25,000 limitation plus 50 percent of his or her tax liability in excess of that amount. Special rules also apply to corporate groups, estates, and trusts.

For investors in residential income property, the investment tax credit has only limited applicability. Buildings and their components are not covered Section 38 Property. While elevators are among the types of tangible property included, property used to furnish lodging other than in a hotel or motel is specifically excluded. Yet coin-operated vending machines, washing machines, and dryers in lodging facilities do qualify.

For the periods subsequent to 1971, any part of the investment tax credit ITC not used in a given year because of the limitations outlined above is to be carried *back* 3 years and carried *over* 7 years. Under the tax code Sec. 46 (a) (1), ITCs are to be used up in the following order:

1. carryovers, from the earliest years first;
2. credits earned during the year; and
3. carrybacks, from the earliest years first.

Such Code provisions can be deciphered easily with a handful of mathematical signs as long as you have two extra fingers. (See Figures 8-8 and 8-11, lines 32 through 39 in each figure.) The detailed nature of the computation with all those variables, however, makes hand calculations impracticable in any situation requiring the rapid recomputation of all cash flows, as key factors are held constant while one or more of the others is changed. With a computer program handling all the repetitive calculations instantly, this sort of sensitivity analysis becomes almost routine.

LOAN INPUTS AND ANALYSIS

A good investment analysis program automatically computes the principal and interest payments for a first mortgage, amortizes the loan, and uses the results in calculating annual interest deductions and equity (market value minus loan balances). Secondary financing should also be covered.

In one of the most advanced programs widely available today, the analyst working at a terminal keyboard can enter any one or more of the following letters, each causing the computer to prompt for data entries related to the type of mortgage indicated:

C = Constant principal payment

B = Balloon

R = Refinanced at future date

F = Loan to start in other than first year

With such entry options available, the analyst can cover the five basic methods of loan amortization:

1. ***Fully amortized mortgage loan:*** In this method, constant periodic (usually monthly) payments of principal and interest (P&I) reduce the balance to zero at the end of the scheduled term.

2. ***Partially amortized mortgage loan:*** Periodic payments of P&I, usually based on a percentage of the principal amount, are insufficient to amortize the loan fully by the time of maturity. The remaining principal is then paid in a lump sum called a *balloon payment.* A fairly common practice is to schedule the payment of the balloon later than the time by which the buyer of the property believes it will have been sold at an appreciated price. Part of the proceeds can then be used to make the balloon payment. The effect of such an arrangement is to increase the investor's leverage by requiring a lower initial cash investment. Although such payments are sometimes associated with first trusts, they are far more typical of second mortgages.

*3. **Interest-only mortgage loan.*** In this "Interest-only" loan, periodic payments are set at the amount of interest due over the term, with the entire principal amount due at maturity. Today, again, such arrangements are most commonly associated with secondary financing.

*4. **Negatively amortized loan.*** P & I payment is too low to cover even interest due. Shortfall is *added* to principal balance at each payment period, and becomes part of balloon payment at end.

*5. **Straight loan.*** *No periodic payment* is made to either principal or interest during term. Entire amount is paid at end.

WRAP-AROUND MORTGAGE

A variation on secondary financing involves the creation of a *wrap-around* mortgage. Such an arrangement can work to the benefit of seller, buyer, or both. The possible loser is the holder of the existing first mortgage.

If the interest rate of the seller's existing mortgage is significantly lower than the rate that is available to the buyer for new financing, the buyer has a good reason to keep that mortgage in effect. If it is assumable without an escalation of the interest rate, the seller can offer the buyer a mortgage at a negotiated rate lower than that otherwise available, but higher than that of the existing loan. In the wrap-around setup the seller receives payments from the buyer at the "wrap" rate of interest, pays the holder of the existing mortgage at its rate, and pockets the difference. That difference in P&I payments between the existing and the wrap loans is referred to as *annuity income.*

In addition to an *annuity* (a series of cash flows consisting of the difference), the wrap holder receives a reversion if both loans are paid off earlier than maturity. The reversion comes from the *new money balance,* which is created because the amortization of the existing mortgage began earlier than that of the wrap and it is therefore being paid off faster than the wrap. The seller's yield from the wrap, computed from both the annuity and the reversion, varies from year to year, and upon payoff.

Figure 5-1 illustrates the workings of a wrap-around mortgage. In that example, the first mortgage is a fully amortized 30-year loan of $160,000 at 8.5 percent annual interest. In its third year, it is "wrapped" by a fully amortized 28-year loan at 11.5 percent annual interest, which is the rate that the wrap holder (seller) charges the borrower (buyer) on the wrap-around mortgage beginning at $224,474. The wrap holder's initial investment is $67,000, the amount of additional financing. The yield on that investment is computed as the internal rate of return on these cash flows:

1. the annual cash flows from annuity income,
2. a final cash flow consisting of the payoff year's annuity income, and
3. the ending new money balance, which includes the reversion.

The wrap may be structured in a number of ways, but the rate of return must involve the amortization of two loans, as well as the iterations

	Year					
	1	2	3	4	5	6
Wrap-around balance, beginning of year	0	0	224,474	223,323	222,032	220,585
− Payments to principal	0	0	1,151	1,291	1,447	1,623
= Balance, end of year	0	0	223,323	222,032	220,585	218,963
Interest payments	0	0	25,755	25,616	25,459	25,284
Existing loan balance, beginning of year	160,000	158,790	157,474	156,041	154,482	152,785
− Payments to principal	1,210	1,316	1,433	1,559	1,697	1,847
= Balance, end of year	158,790	157,474	156,041	154,482	152,785	150,937
Interest payments	13,554	13,447	13,330	13,204	13,066	12,916
Principal and interest payments, wrap-around mortgage	0	0	26,906	26,906	26,906	26,906
− Principal and interest payments, existing loan	14,764	14,764	14,764	14,764	14,764	14,764
= Annuity income	0	0	12,142	12,142	12,142	12,142
Wrap-around balance, end of year	0	0	223,323	222,032	220,585	218,963
− Existing loan balance, end of year	158,790	157,474	156,041	154,482	152,785	150,937
= New money balance	0	0	67,282	67,550	67,800	68,026
Rate of return	0	0	18.54%	18.50%	18.46%	18.41%

Figure 5-1.

of an IRR computation. The loans may be scheduled to mature at the same or different times. The payments on each may be constant or variable, as may the interest rates. One or more of the loans may involve a balloon payment. The only persistent requirement is that the arrangement meet the needs of the parties negotiating its terms. Such "tailoring" often requires several computations either of yield with new given money amounts or of terms needed to secure a given yield. For that reason, the best investment analysis programs have side routines specifically covering wrap-around mortgages.

Land Contract

If an existing loan is not assumable without interest rate escalation, you can work around the problem by combining a wrap-around mortgage with a "land contract." In this arrangement, most or all of the equitable interests in the property are transferred, including the rights to receive income, tax benefits, and future sale proceeds. But the legal title is held in escrow for transfer to the buyer at some future date.

Although this procedure is lawful, lending institutions often take the position that it violates mortgage provisions which prohibit the transfer of the property without prior lender approval and thereby empower them to "call the loan" or to escalate all payments due. In several states, that position has been upheld in court actions; in others the contrary position has prevailed. In most, at this writing, it has not been decided. Because of the legal intricacies of transactions involving land contracts, both the buyer and the seller must act under advice of an attorney. The land contract does not affect the dynamics of the wrap-around mortgage, although provisions may be made relating to the manner in which payments are to be handled.

Discounted Mortgage Yield

Although the seller usually holds a wrap-around mortgage to maturity, sometimes the seller needs cash. Very frequently the seller takes back a second mortgage from the buyer for a portion of the sale price, independently of other financing on the property. Such a mortgage may be held to maturity, sold immediately to a bank or to another third party to get the cash out, or sold later with or without partial amortization, depending on which kind of mortgage is involved. Various first mortgages are also actively traded.

As a general rule, the holder of a mortgage has to sell it for less than its remaining balance in order to secure the desired cash. Since those who buy such paper ordinarily require a higher yield than that of the note bought, it is often necessary to match the discounted purchase price to a required yield. Conversely, it often is necessary to determine the yield, given a specific price for the note.

> *Example:* A seller takes back a 5-year second loan for $10,000. He now wants to trade the note for cash. None of the payments, scheduled at $100 per month, has been made. The interest rate is 11 percent, and there is a balloon payment of $9,337 at the end of 5 years. The yield currently required by buyers of such notes is 18 percent. How much cash can the seller of the note expect to receive (or a buyer of it to pay)? The answer is $7,760, and it can be calculated fairly quickly on a financial calculator.
>
> So can the converse question: How much yield can the seller expect? In a given money market, the usual discount procedure is to reduce the remaining balance of a note by 5 percent for each year remaining to maturity. What is the effective yield of the note in this example, if bought at the indicated discount of 25 percent, that is, for $7,500? Again, the answer (18.97 percent) can be computed fairly quickly with a financial calculator. (See Chapter 9 for an overview on the use of financial keys. For the analyst working at a computer terminal, however, a programmed routine can be very convenient.)

VARIABLE PAYMENT LOANS

Graduated Payment Mortgages

Under FHA Section 245, mortgage loans are available in which the borrower has initial monthly payments that are lower than necessary to pay interest. Over periods of 5 or 10 years, depending on which of the 5 available schedules is used, the payments are increased by 2 percent, 2.5 percent, 3 percent, 5 percent, or 7.5 percent per year until they reach a level slightly higher than they would be with a regular FHA mortgage at current interest rates. Designed primarily for young owner-occupants who anticipate increased future income, graduated payment plans enable them to buy earlier than they would otherwise be able to do. Although such loans are not available directly to investors, they may be assumed without lender approval, like any FHA or VA loan. Because the entire amount of the initial payments go to pay interest, which can be deducted from taxable income, such loans can be desirable to investors if the timing is right.

Because such loans involve "negative amortization" (that is, the remaining balance actually increases slightly at some points initially) and

$100,000 Loan at 11% annual interest	Monthly Payments	
	First 5 Years	Last 20 Years
Straight 25-year amortization	$980.11	$980.11
Graduated amortization[1]	$936.96	$1,015.53

[1] First 5 years on 35-year schedule, remaining balance on 20-year schedule thereafter. The remaining balance to be amortized after five years is $98,386.29.

Figure 5-2.

other irregular patterns, you save a lot of time through computer programs that involve all the factors. Conventional graduated payment mortgages also have become available in recent years.

Graduated Amortization Loans

In another type of loan, sometimes used by investors, the initial payments are kept lower—for such reasons as minimizing start-up negative cash flows—by adjusting the amortization schedule. A 25-year loan, for example, may provide for payments scheduled during the first 5 years as though amortization were over a 35-year period. The remaining balance might then be fully amortized over the remaining 20 years. Figure 5-2 shows the effects of scheduling a $100,000 loan at 11-percent annual interest. The schedule can be whatever the parties negotiate. This type of loan can be accommodated easily by the loan inputs indicated in the table for a solid investment analysis program.

"FLIP" MORTGAGES

A final type of variable (graduated) payment loan is the Flexible Loan Insurance Plan (FLIP). In this type of loan, borrowers increase the loan amount for which they can qualify by, in effect, "insuring" a portion of the principal and interest payments in the early years. The "insurance" consists of the borrower's placing a substantial portion of the down payment in a special interest-bearing escrow account from which up to 25 percent of the initial monthly payments are made. As in the case of the FHA 245 loan, a higher anticipated future income covers the later increase of payments.

As this type of mortgage comes into greater use, computer programs are being designed to accommodate them. Like the financial management account, FLIP mortgages involve the automatic transfer of funds, interest earnings on variable balances, and other factors rendering hand computation impracticable where investment alternatives are being compared in detail.

VARIABLE RATE MORTGAGES

Because of uncertainties generated in today's inflationary economy, lenders have become reluctant to make long-term commitments of capital at interest rates that many people assume will just continue to increase. One consequence of this reluctance is that few conventional loans made in recent years are assumable without the escalation of interest to the current rate.

Another effect has been the emergence of variable *interest rates* in mortgage financing. The theory is that a variable rate enables mortgage lenders to loan money at current rates, rather than at rates set higher in anticipation of future market increases. In some such schemes, the monthly principal and interest payment remains constant. As the interest rate is increased or decreased, the amounts apportioned to principal and interest vary, thereby increasing the term of the loan if interest goes up and decreasing the term if interest goes down. The variations in interest rates may take several forms. They may be tied into a selected capital market rate, such as the prime rate charged by commercial banks to their preferred customers. Another method, called a "rollover mortgage," provides for the periodic renegotiation of the interest at 4, 5, or 6-year intervals.

Variable interest rate mortgages are accommodated by the best investment analysis programs. In fact, the analyst is able to enter loan date inputs year by year.

LEASE VERSUS PURCHASE

Sometimes an investor is presented with the alternative of either leasing or buying an investment property. At the simplest level, the choice is essentially whether (a) to free up capital for use elsewhere by taking a long-term lease on income property and deducting rent payments as expenses, or (b) to put money in, deduct depreciation and interest payments, and seek to realize a gain on future sale. On close examination, however, such a decision involves almost all of our so-called "key" factors. Advanced investment analysis programs, therefore, provide for the examination of cash flows and rates of return from leasing situations in such a way that they can be compared validly with the buying alternative.

TAX TABLES AND "BRACKETS"

Simplified investment analysis programs often prompt users to enter "tax bracket" as one of the variable inputs. This inclusion makes it easy for the program to compare the tax consequences of one investment alternative and set of circumstances with another.

While that approach is quite accurate if the tax bracket has been computed properly before its entry and if cash flows from the investment do not change the bracket, a more finely tuned program calls for the entry of "taxable income" rather than "bracket." As the federal income tax tables for the years from 1979 until amended (in Figure 5-3) show, several steps are involved in deriving someone's tax bracket. A single person with $50,000 in taxable income, for example, is in the 55-percent tax bracket. The ratios between taxable income and tax payable go up and down with the vagaries of government fiscal and social policies. An investment analysis program with "fine tuning" accepts that fact, carries the tax tables in memory, and automatically makes the kind of calculation reflected in Figure 5-4.

INCOME AVERAGING

Investors having substantial fluctuations in annual income may find it beneficial to "average" their income in peak years to avoid onerous tax payments. Under the tax law, as long as their income is more than $3,000, taxpayers may average—that is, spread—their income out over the previous 5 years' returns. Most types of income, including the ordinary income and capital gains associated with real estate investment, may be averaged. The following 10 steps are involved in income averaging:

Step 1. Average the taxable income of the previous 4 years.

Step 2. Establish a taxable income base (120% x 4-year average). The effect of this step is to project the 4-year average into the fifth (current) year, in order to treat it as the "norm."

Step 3. Determine your tax on the base; this tax is the "normal" tax.

For Use *Only* by Single Individuals for 1979 and following years

Taxable Income Over	Not Over	Pay	+	Tax Rate	On Excess Over
$	$ 2,300	$.....		....	$ .....
2,300	3,400	.....		14%	2,300
3,400	4,400	154		16%	3,400
4,400	6,500	314		18%	4,400
6,500	8,500	692		19%	6,500
8,500	10,800	1,072		21%	8,500
10,800	12,900	1,555		24%	10,800
12,900	15,000	2,059		26%	12,900
15,000	18,200	2,605		30%	15,000
18,200	23,500	3,565		34%	18,200
23,500	28,800	5,367		39%	23,500
28,800	34,100	7,434		44%	28,800
34,100	41,500	9,766		49%	34,100
41,500	55,300	13,392		55%	41,500
55,300	81,800	20,982		63%	55,300
81,800	108,300	37,677		68%	81,800
108,300	.....	55,697		70%	108,300

For Use *Only* by Married Individuals Filing Joint Returns and Certain Surviving Spouses for 1979 and following years

Taxable Income Over	Not Over	Pay	+	Tax Rate	On Excess Over
$	$ 3,400	$		.....	$ .....
3,400	5,500	.....		14%	3,400
5,500	7,600	294		16%	5,500
7,600	11,900	630		18%	7,600
11,900	16,000	1,404		21%	11,900
16,000	20,200	2,265		24%	16,000
20,200	24,600	3,273		28%	20,200
24,600	29,900	4,505		32%	24,600
29,900	35,200	6,201		37%	29,900
35,200	45,800	8,162		43%	35,200
45,800	60,000	12,720		49%	45,800
60,000	85,600	19,678		54%	60,000
85,600	109,400	33,502		59%	85,600
109,400	162,400	47,544		64%	109,400
162,400	215,400	81,464		68%	162,400
215,400	.....	117,504		70%	215,400

For Use *Only* by Married Individuals Filing Separate Returns for 1979 and following years

Taxable Income Over	Not Over	Pay	+	Tax Rate	On Excess Over
$	$ 1,700	$		.....	$ .....
1,700	2,750	.....		14%	1,700
2,750	3,800	147		16%	2,750
3,800	5,950	315		18%	3,800
5,950	8,000	702		21%	5,950
8,000	10,100	1,132.50		24%	8,000
10,100	12,300	1,636.50		28%	10,100
12,300	14,950	2,252.50		32%	12,300
14,950	17,600	3,100.50		37%	14,950
17,600	22,900	4,081		43%	17,600
22,900	30,000	6,360		49%	22,900
30,000	42,800	9,839		54%	30,000
42,800	54,700	16,751		59%	42,800
54,700	81,200	23,772		64%	54,700
81,200	107,700	40,732		68%	81,200
107,700	.....	58,752		70%	107,700

Figure 5-3. Income Tax Rates for Individuals, Estates, and Trusts (for 1979 and later years, these tax rates apply to individuals, estates, and trusts).

For Use *Only* by Head of a Household for 1979 and following years

Taxable Income Over	Not Over	Pay +	Tax Rate	On Excess Over
$	$ 2,300	$	....	$ .....
2,300	4,400	.....	14%	2,300
4,400	6,500	294	16%	4,400
6,500	8,700	630	18%	6,500
8,700	11,800	1,026	22%	8,700
11,800	15,000	1,708	24%	11,800
15,000	18,200	2,476	26%	15,000
18,200	23,500	3,308	31%	18,200
23,500	28,800	4,951	36%	23,500
28,800	34,100	6,859	42%	28,800
34,100	44,700	9,085	46%	34,100
44,700	60,600	13,961	54%	44,700
60,600	81,800	22,547	59%	60,600
81,800	108,300	35,055	63%	81,800
108,300	161,300	51,750	68%	108,300
161,300	.....	87,790	70%	161,300

For Use *Only* by Estates and Trusts for 1979 and following years

Taxable Income Over	Not Over	Pay +	Tax Rate	On Excess Over
$	$ 1,050	$	14%	$ .....
1,050	2,100	147	16%	1,050
2,100	4,250	315	18%	2,100
4,250	6,300	702	21%	4,250
6,300	8,400	1,132.50	24%	6,300
8,400	10,600	1,636.50	28%	8,400
10,600	13,250	2,252.50	32%	10,600
13,250	15,900	3,100.50	37%	13,250
15,900	21,200	4,081	43%	15,900
21,200	28,300	6,360	49%	21,200
28,300	41,100	9,839	54%	28,300
41,100	53,000	16,751	59%	41,100
53,000	79,500	23,772	64%	53,000
79,500	106,000	40,732	68%	79,500
106,000	.....	58,752	70%	106,000

Corporate Income Tax Rates. For tax years beginning after 1978, the old corporate system of normal tax, surtax, and surtax exemption is replaced by a graduated tax rate structure. The new rates are 17% on the first $25,000 of taxable income, 20% on the next $25,000, 30% on the next $25,000, 40% on the next $25,000, and 46% on taxable income above $100,000. These rate changes are to be treated as a change in tax for 1978-1979 fiscal-year corporations.

Figure 5-3 *(continued).*

Step 4. Determine one-fifth (1 year's worth) of the difference between the taxable income base (the "norm") and the current year's income (the "excess").

Step 5. Add the result of step 4 to the taxable income base, thus creating a new base that accounts for both "normal" and "excess" income.

Step 6. Determine your tax on the new base.

Step 7. Multiply that tax by 5, to establish the tax for the 5-year averaging period.

Before-tax cash flow from this investment	$9,000
+ Other taxable income (salary, etc.)	41,000
= Total taxable income[1]	50,000
– Base income[2]	41,500
= Excess over base	8,500
x "Marginal" or "ordinary" tax rate[2]	55%
= Tax on excess over base	4,675
+ Basic tax payment[2]	13,392
= Tax on taxable income	$18,067

[1] Positive or negative cash flows from investment under analysis may increase or decrease taxable income sufficiently to put taxable income in higher or lower bracket.
[2] From tax table.

Figure 5-4.

Step 8. Subtract the tax on old base (step 3) from the tax for the 5-year averaging period (step 7).

Step 9. Add the result in step 8 to the result in step 3. This is the tax liability for the year in which income averaging takes place.

Step 10. Subtract the tax with averaging from the computed tax without averaging, to determine whether and to what extent income averaging is beneficial.

Figure 5-5 illustrates the specific calculations involved with these steps. The percentage figures shown on lines 11,14, and 24 are derived by the method demonstrated in Figure 5-4. Programmable calculators can be programmed for such routines. But an advanced computer investment analysis program not only makes all the indicated tax and other calculations related to income averaging, but it also permits storage of all intermediate and final results for application at any useful point in the overall analysis.

RETURN ON INVESTMENT

There are numerous methods for measuring return on investment (ROI). Some, such as the capitalization rate, are meant to evaluate the income stream, with or without reference to financing. Some are concerned primarily with debt coverage and leverage. One method in particular, the average annual rate of profit, considers cash flows from both income and disposition, on a before- and/or after-tax basis, but it does not take the time

1	Average taxable income, past 4 years	$50,000
2	x Taxable income base factor	120%
3	= Taxable income base	60,000
4	Taxable income, current year	180,000
5	− Taxable income base	60,000
6	= Averagable income	120,000
7	x Averaging factor (1/5)	20%
8	= 1/5 (one year) of averagable income	24,000
9	+ Taxable income base	60,000
10	= Adjusted taxable income base	84,000
11	x Factor for base payment + payment on excess[1]	46.64%
12	= Tax on adjusted taxable income base	39,173
13	Taxable income base	60,000
14	x Factor for base payment + payment on excess[1]	39.91%
15	= Tax on taxable income base	23,943
16	Tax on adjusted taxable income base	39,173
17	− Tax on taxable income base	23,943
18	= Tax on 1/5 of averagable income	15,230
19	x Number of averaging years (five)	5
20	=Tax on averagable income	76,150
21	+ Tax on taxable income base	23,943
22	= Tentative tax, current year	$100,093
23	Taxable income, current year	$180,000
24	x Factor for base payment + payment on excess[1]	58.83%
25	= Tax without averaging	105,887
26	− Tax with averaging (from line 22)	100,093
27	= Amount saved with averaging	$5,794

[1] From tax table, single person.

Figure 5-5.

value of money into consideration. The internal rate of return (IRR) does so, but it requires modification to incorporate the effects of positive and negative cash flows. No known method accommodates all the factors "perfectly."

Although computers and calculators can speed up analyses and carry them out to many decimal places, they still depend on the logic of their programs—and hence on the logic of their programmers—for their reliability. Any computer program sophisticated enough to present the financial management rate of return (FMRR), for example, calls for data inputs from which any or all of the recognized rates of return can be computed. The difficulty for the program designer and the analyst is in deciding *which* measurements to present.

The problems in selecting valid measures are real (even though some methods of measuring return invite the deliberate distortion of data as a selling ploy). Like any business producing inventories, goods, or services, a real estate investment involves questions of finance and tax payments and benefits. Yet investors often enter into real estate investments with a much more passive involvement than they would have if they intended to operate a "regular" business. Further, individual investor needs and interests vary. A retired person, for example, might be interested mainly in receiving regular income, while an active professional person with expanding income might have a primary need for current tax deductions and deferred capital gains.

The following six measures of return on investment are, with the exception of the discounted annual rate of return (DARR), among the most common rates in use—and the most likely to be found in an advanced investment analysis program.

Capitalization Rate

As used most generally today, the "cap" rate—also called the "overall capitalization rate"—is simply net operating income (NOI) divided by market value. This calculation is a lot like figuring out a bond yield: you treat the hypothetical sale price of a property as the face value of a bond, and income as the annual dividend.

The simple cap rate can be useful if you keep its limitations in mind—that it:

1. cannot really compare a real estate investment with a bond, because the "face value" of the former is not fixed.
2. does not accurately reflect the value of the income from the investment over a period of time, because the cap rate actually goes *down* if income *increases* at a slower rate than the value of the property. Assuming that the value of an income stream decreases simply because the value of a property increases is simply not realistic.
3. does not consider the effect of financing.
4. does not consider the time value of money.

Cash-on-Cash

In the past, before computer/calculator technology made discounted cash flow computations a routine matter, analysts devised many manual shortcuts to add other factors into cap rates—beyond the relationship between a property's market value and NOI. One approach was to relate income after debt service (not NOI) to price. In this technique, analysts attempted to include the effects of financing by relating the equity investment amount (the down payment plus entry costs) to equity income (net annual cash flow—NOI minus P&I payments, but before tax payments and deductions). This technique is referred to as "cash-on-cash."

In this calculation, the net annual cash flow is divided by the equity investment, rather than by market value of the property. Since the initial investment is a constant, this method avoids the distortions suggested in the cap rate.

Cash-on-cash also adjusts for the effects of financing. If leverage is increased by securing a bigger loan, the down payment decreases but P&I payments go up, thereby decreasing net annual cash flow. Similarly, an increase or decrease in the interest rate changes debt service costs and net cash flow, and thereby the cash-on-cash rate.

The three main limitations in a cash-on-cash measurement are that it:

1. does not consider appreciation, depreciation, or future disposition returns.
2. does not ordinarily consider tax affects, although it can be computed on an after-tax basis.
3. does not consider the time value of money.

Discounted Annual Rate of Return

This method, a discounted cash-on-cash rate, is not currently in general use although computer/calculator technology renders it a relatively simple refinement of the cash-on-cash rate. Like cash-on-cash, the DARR is a rate of return based on the relationship between annual cash flow and investment outlay. Instead of dividing one by the other, however, the annual cash flow (preferably after tax) is discounted at the IRR (or preferably FMRR, if computed) for that year and then divided by the investment outlay. The reason for this is more simple than the words immediately suggest. As the IRR or FMRR becomes higher, it indicates that that property should be sold (and annual income thereby discontinued).

Discounting the annual income at the IRR or FMRR says that the incentive to keep annual income going decreases as the incentive to sell the property increases.

Figure 5-6a and b compares the cash-on-cash rate and DARR, given two variations on financing. Assume in the first figure that a $100,000 property is bought with an 80-percent loan at 12-percent annual interest, and in the second that a loan for 90 percent of the purchase price is assumed at an interest rate of 11 percent.

Pre-Tax IRR

This measure of return (discussed in detail in Chapter 4) treats all pre-tax cash flows—the initial investment (negative), income, and disposition—within the framework of the time value of money. The phrase "discounted cash flow" (DCF) is sometimes used in real estate investment analysis to mean the IRR.

Down payment: $20,000	Year					
+ Other investment costs: $2,000 = Equity investment: $22,000	1	2	3	4	5	6
Net operating income	10,000	12,000	13,000	14,000	15,000	16,000
− Payment and interest payments on 30-year loan of $80,000 at 12% interest	9,875	9,875	9,875	9,875	9,875	9,875
= Cash flow before tax	125	2,125	3,125	4,125	5,125	6,125
÷ Equity investment	22,000	22,000	22,000	22,000	22,000	22,000
= Cash-on-cash rate	0.57%	9.66%	14.21%	18.75%	23.30%	27.84%

Cash flow before tax	125	2,125	3,125	4,125	5,125	6,125
x IRR discount factor[1]	.909091	.756144	.578704	.409600	.401878	.432328
= Present value of CFBT	114	1,608	1,808	1,690	2,060	2,648
÷ Investment outlay	22,000	22,000	22,000	22,000	22,000	22,000
= DARR	0.52%	7.31%	8.22%	7.68%	9.36%	12.04%

Figure 5-6(a).

Down payment: $10,000	Year					
+ Other investment costs: $2,000 = Equity investment: $12,000	1	2	3	4	5	6
Net operating income	10,000	12,000	13,000	14,000	15,000	16,000
− Payment and interest payments on 30-year loan of $90,000 at 11% interest	10,285	10,285	10,285	10,285	10,285	10,285
= Net annual cash flow	−285	1,715	2,715	3,715	4,715	5,715
÷ Equity investment	12,000	12,000	12,000	12,000	12,000	12,000
= Cash-on-cash rate	−2.38%	14.29%	22.63%	30.96%	39.29%	47.63%

Cash flow before tax	−285	1,715	2,715	3,715	4,715	5,715
x IRR discount factor[1]	.909091	.756144	.578704	.409600	.401878	.432328
= Present value of CFBT	−259	1,297	1,571	1,522	1,895	2,471
÷ Investment outlay	12,000	12,000	12,000	12,000	12,000	12,000
= DARR	−2.16%	10.81%	13.09%	12.68%	15.79%	20.59%

[1] Assumed IRR	10.00%	15.00%	20.00%	25.00%	20.00%	15.00%

[1] See Figure 9–20 for calculator method to find discount factor.

Figure 5-6(b).

After-Tax IRR

The before- and after-tax IRRs (or DCFs) are computed from the initial investment outlay by the identical procedure (see Chapter 4). However, the pre-tax version relates that outlay to (before-tax) net annual cash flows and gross (before-tax) disposition proceeds. The post-tax approach relates it to after-tax annual cash flows and after-tax disposition proceeds. The before-tax measure is useful in comparing investments with each other, untailored to a particular investor's tax situation and related financial planning needs. The after-tax measure is a more accurate tailoring tool.

After-Tax FMRR

This measure does everything all the others do, but it also considers interest earnings on capital not invested in real estate and avoids mathematical problems sometimes associated with the IRR.

SAMPLE ANALYSIS, ADVANCED PROGRAM

Figure 5-7 (a, b, and c) presents a "blank" sample investment analysis form that is based on the most advanced and practical computer programs on line, or coming on line, in the early 1980s. Figure 5-8 (a–c) gives you a sample of this format. While the computerized version of this program does not in itself create new analytical techniques, it does facilitate developments on the existing ones and promote their wide application. It does not reduce the real estate professional or investor's need for substantive knowledge, but it does affect the manner, speed, and accuracy with which you can acquire the knowledge and put it to use.

In practice, you can alter the degree of detail in such a program as your needs dictate. The format shown in Figures 5-7 and 5-8 is more detailed than is necessary for many routine investment analyses. In actual usage, the lines of output would reflect the degree of detail that you choose through the inputs. Further, the better programs provide an optional summary format, as well as the option of selecting outputs by one or more headers—such as Annual Cash Flows, Reserve Account, Taxable Income, and the like. A summary format might present the following outputs on the same end-of-year basis (as shown in Figures 5-7 and 5-8):

- Loan Balances
- Pre-Tax Cash Flow
- Net After-Tax Cash Flow
- Pre-Tax Disposition Proceeds
- After-Tax Disposition Proceeds
- + Total Reserves
- = Net After-Tax Proceeds
- + Safe Rate Balance
- + Reinvestment Balance
- = Accumulated Wealth
- Net Difference in Accumulated Wealth[1]
- Capitalization Rate
- Pre-Tax IRR
- After-Tax FMRR

[1]Difference between "accumulated wealth" and after-tax balance if money invested had been in a safe rate account or investment.

(a)

Year						

Annual Cash Flows

1	Gross income					
2	– Vacancies					
3	– Credit losses					
4	–Operating expenses					
5	= Net operating income					
6	– Non-operating expenses					
7	– Reserve additions					
8	– Loan payments					
9	– Capital additions					
10	+ New loans					
11	+ Interest on reserves					
12	= Pre-tax cash flow					
13	– Income tax					
14	= After-tax cash flow					

Reserve Account

15	Starting reserves					
16	+ Interest on reserves					
17	+ Reserve additions					
18	= Subtotal					
19	– Offset of negative flow					
20	= Total reserves					

Taxable Income

21	Net operating income					
22	– Bonus depreciation					
23	– Depreciation: building or shell					
24	– Depreciation: components					
25	– Depreciation: new personal properties					
26	– Depreciation: used personal properties					
27	– Amortization					
28	– Non-operating expenses					
29	– Interest payments					
30	+ Interest on reserves					
31	= Taxable income					

Figure 5–7.

(b)

Year					

Investment Tax Credits (ITC)

32	ITC available					
33	+ Accrued ITC					
34	= Subtotal ITC					
35	− ITC used if held					
36	= Unused ITC if held					
37	− Additional ITC, if sold					
38	+ ITC recapture, if sold					
39	= Unused ITC, if sold					

Sale Proceed

40	Sale price					
41	− Loan balances					
42	= Equity					
43	− Transaction costs					
44	= Pre-tax proceed					
45	− Tax on recapitulation depreciation					
46	= Additional ITC available					
47	− Tax on capital gain					
48	+ Additional ITC available					
49	−ITC recapture					
50	= After-tax proceed					
51	+ Reserve balance					
52	= Net after-tax proceed					

Basis Adjustment

53	Original basis					
54	+ Depreciable capital additions					
55	+ Non-depreciable capital additions					
56	− Total depreciation taken					
57	− Amortization					
58	= Basis, if held					
59	+ Transaction costs					
60	+ Unamortized balance					
61	= Basis, if sold					

Figure 5-7 *(continued).*

(c)

Year					

Recaptured Depreciation

62	Total depreciation taken					
63	− Cumulative straight-line depreciation					
64	= Excess depreciation					

Capital Gain or Loss

65	Sale Price					
66	− Transaction costs					
67	= Amount realized					
68	− Adjusted basis					
69	= Total gain or loss					
70	− Recaptured depreciation					
71	= Capital gain or loss					

Financial Management Account

72	Reserve balance					
73	+ Interest income @ X%					
74	+ Interest income @ Y%					
75	+ After-tax cash flow					
76	= Financial management subtotal					

77	Safe rate balance					
78	+ Reinvestment balance					
79	+ After-tax sale proceed					
80	= Accumulated wealth					
81	− Future value of previous capital additions					
82	= Net accumulated wealth					

Returns on Investment

83	Capitalization rate					
84	Pre-tax cash-on-cash					
85	After-tax income IRR					
86	Pre-tax IRR					
87	After-tax IRR					
88	After-tax FMRR					

Figure 5-7 *(continued).*

	ANNUAL CASH FLOWS
1	Gross income: $ ____________ first year, ☐ Increase ☐ Decrease at ______% per year.[1]
2	Vacancy rate: ____________% of gross income per year.
3	Credit losses: ____________% of gross income per year.
4	Operating expenses: $________first year, ☐ Increase ☐ Decrease at ______% per year.[1]
5	Net operating income: (output)
6	Nonoperating expenses: $__________first year, ☐ Increase ☐ Decrease at ____%per year.[1]
7	Reserve additions to initial investment of $ ______________ computed automatically.
8	Loan payments (see Schedule A): includes principal, interest and mortgage insurance premium.
9	Capital additions, if any: input dollar amount by year.
10	New loans, if any: input dollar amount by year (see Schedule A for payments).
11	Interest on reserves: safe rate at __________%, and reinvestment rate at __________ %.
12	Pre-tax cash flow: (output)
13	Income tax: (output)
14	After-tax cash flow: (output)
	RESERVE ACCOUNT
15	Starting reserves: input first year. Subsequent years automatically computed.
16	Interest on reserves: see [11] above.
17	Reserve additions: automatically computed.
18	Subtotal (output).
19	Offset of negative flow: automatically computed.
20	Total reserves, E.O.Y. (output).
	TAXABLE INCOME
21	Net operating income (output): same as [5] above.
22	Bonus depreciation: 20% of basis (first year only) = $ ____________.
23	Depreciation: building or shell (see Schedule B).
24	Depreciation: components (see Schedule B).
25	Depreciation: new personal property (see Schedule B).
26	Depreciation: used personal property (see Schedule B).
27	Amortization, if any: input dollar amount by year.
28	Nonoperating expenses, if any: input dollar amount by year.
29	Interest payments: input via Schedule A.
30	Interest on reserves (output).
31	Taxable income (output).
	[1]ADDITIONAL NOTES, BY LINE
1, 4, 6	Variable inputs by years also possible.

(a)

Figure 5-8. *Courtesy of PRC Realty Systems, Inc.*

	INVESTMENT TAX CREDIT ACCOUNT
32	ITC available at beginning of year: dollar amount automatically computed.
33	Accrued ITC: input dollar amount by year.
34	Subtotal ITC: (output).
35	ITC used, if held: input dollar amount by year.
36	Unused ITC, if held: (output).
37	Additional ITC, if sold: automatically computed.
38	ITC recapture, if sold:
39	Unused ITC, if sold: (output).
	SALE PROCEEDS
40	Sale price: purchase price: $__________ appreciation rate __________%[2]
41	Loan balances: automatically computed.
42	Equity: automatically computed.
43	Transaction costs: input constant factor, or specific amount.
44	Pre-tax proceeds: (output).
45	Tax on recaptured depreciation: automatically computed.
46	Additional ITC available: (output).
47	Tax on capital gain: automatically computed.
48	Additional ITC available:
49	ITC recapture:
50	After-tax proceeds: (output).
51	Reserve balance: automatically computed.
52	Net after-tax proceeds (output).
	BASIS ADJUSTMENT
53	Original basis: input dollar amount.
54	Depreciable capital additions: input dollar amount, by year.
55	Nondepreciable capital additions: input dollar amount, by year.
56	Total depreciation taken: automatically computed (see Schedule B).
57	Amortization: amount amortized: $__________ Number of years __________.
58	Basis, if held: automatically computed.
59	Transaction costs: See [43] above.
60	Unamortized balance: automatically computed.
61	Basis, if sold (output).
	[2]ADDITIONAL NOTES, BY LINE
40	Variable inputs by dollar amount and year also possible.

Figure 5-8 *(continued).* (b)

	RECAPTURED DEPRECIATION
62	Total depreciation taken: automatically computed (see Schedule B).
63	Cumulative straight-line depreciation: automatically computed.
64	Excess depreciation: automatically computed.
	CAPITAL GAIN OR LOSS
65	Sale price: see [40] above, automatically computed.
66	Transaction costs: see [43] above, automatically computed.
67	Amount realized: automatically computed.
68	Adjusted basis: see [61] above, automatically computed.
69	Total gain or loss: automatically computed.
70	Recaptured depreciation: automatically computed (see Schedule B).
71	Capital gain or loss: (output)
	FINANCIAL MANAGEMENT ACCOUNT
72	Reserve balance at beginning of year: see [20] above.
73	Interest income @ X%: input "safe rate" interest: ______ %
74	Interest income @ Y%: input "reinvestment" rate: ______ %
75	After-tax cash flow: see [14] above, automatically computed.
76	Financial management subtotal: (output).
	(additional investment to extent [73] is negative, see also note below[3]).
77	Safe-rate balance: automatically computed.[3]
78	Reinvestment balance: automatically computed.
79	After-tax sale proceeds: see [50] above.
80	Accumulated wealth: (output).
81	Future value of previous capital additions.
82	Net accumulated wealth: (output).
	RETURNS ON INVESTMENT
83	Capitalization rate: automatically computed from inputs.
84	Pre-tax cash-on-cash: automatically computed from inputs.
85	After-tax income IRR, automatically computed from inputs.
86	Pre-tax IRR, automatically computed from inputs.
87	After-tax IRR, automatically computed from inputs.
88	After-tax FMRR, automatically computed from inputs.
	[3] ADDITIONAL NOTES, BY LINE
76 77	Transfer from safe-rate account to reinvestment account at specified level (input).

Figure 5-8 *(continued).* (c)

Finally, the best investment analysis programs include a "library" function by which an investment specialist can store not only the inputs for a particular investment, but also detailed data regarding the financial profile of a client-investor. Both kinds of data sometimes need to be recalled for the subsequent matching of financing, property, buyer, and seller. Because of the need for confidentiality, programs that store such data include protections against unauthorized access. Figure 5-9 is a flowchart showing the operation of a library function. Here are the inputs necessary for the sample analysis (see page 142 for list footnotes):

1. Taxpayer Reporting Method:[2]
2. Taxable Income:[2]
3. Market Value:[2]
4. Value Increase/Decrease Rate:
5. Down Payment:
6. Other Investment Costs:
7. Gross Income:[2]
8. Income Increase/Decrease Rate:
9. Vacancy Rate:[2]
10. Credit Loss Rate:[2]
11. Operating Expenses:[2]
12. Nonoperating Expenses:
13. Expense Increase Rate:
14. Starting Reserves:
15. Safe Rate:
16. Reinvestment Rate:
17. Minimum Reinvestment Amount:
18. Cash Portion of Reinvestment Yield:
19. Type of Loan (C, B, R, or F):[3]
20. Loan Amount:
21. Interest Rate:
22. Term:
23. Payments per Year:
24. P&I:
25. Balloon:
26. Basis, Building, or Shell (sch.#1):[4]
27. Useful Life (sch. #1):

28. Salvage Value (sch. #1):
29. Depreciation Method (sch.#1):
30. Basis, Components (sch. #2):
31. Useful Life (sch. #2):
32. Salvage Value (sch. #2):

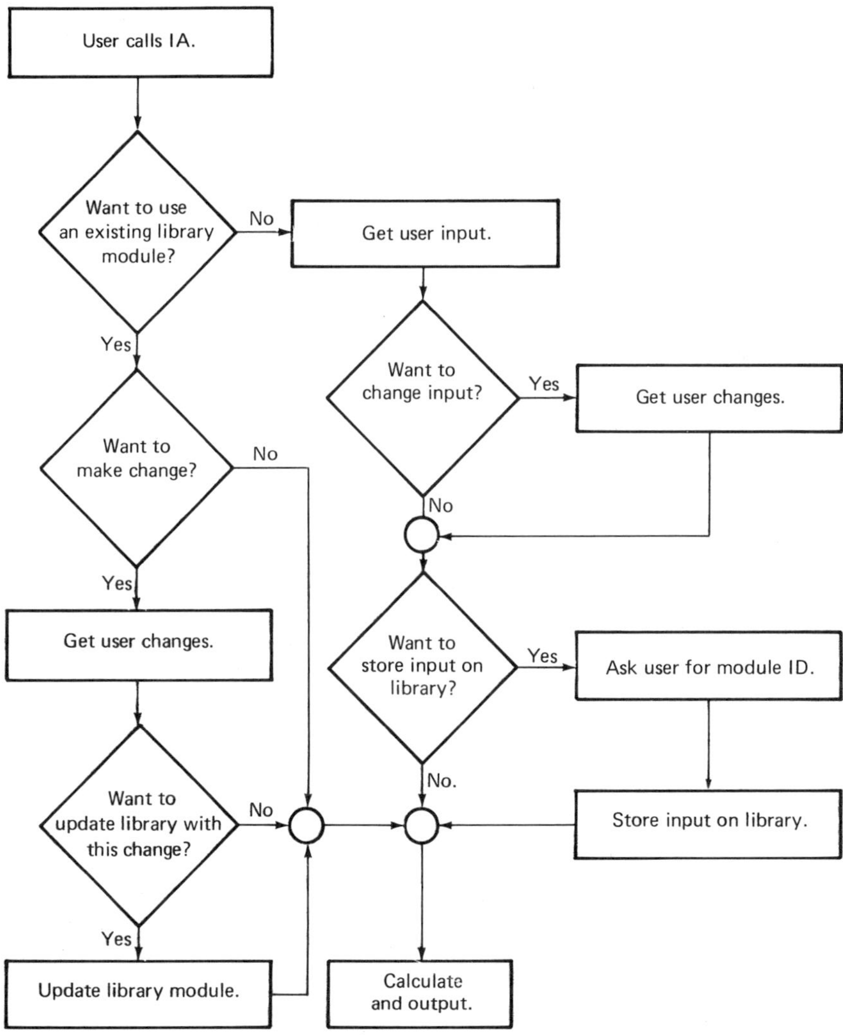

Figure 5-9. Library Module Initiation and Update. *Courtesy of PRC Realty Systems, Inc.*

33. Depreciation Method (sch. #2):
34. Basis, New Personal Property (sch. #3):
35. Useful Life (sch. #3):
36. Salvage Value (sch. #3):
37. Depreciation Method (sch. #3):
38. Basis, Used Personal Property (sch. #4):
39. Useful Life (sch. #4):
40. Salvage Value (sch. #4):
41. Depreciation Method (sch. #4):
42. Future Disposition Costs:
43. Further Considerations?[5]

Computerization of investment analysis not only has enabled investors and real estate professionals to apply complex established techniques simply and quickly, but it also has made practicable the development of more advanced and detailed analyses. As people with everyday general knowledge find such computer power in their hands, the need to be aware of current methods becomes a matter of significant advantage or disadvantage in investment negotiations and related decision making.

For a practical book of worksheets, reference tables, definitions, and line-by-line explanations relating current methods of analysis to current tax laws, see Paul Lyons, *Real Estate Investor's Tax & Profit Planner,* available through Reston Publishing Company, 11480 Sunset Hills Road, Reston, VA. 22090.

[2]These variable inputs can be changed as to the specific amounts or rates of increase/decrease in selected years or periods of years.

[3]The letters refer to the types of loan mentioned earlier. In practice, the computer prompts for additional loans after the entry of data related to each loan. Here just one is shown.

[4]As in the case of loan data entry, the computer prompts for additional depreciation schedules after the data for each is entered. If components (roof, plumbing, electrical and the like) are depreciated individually, many schedules may be involved. Amortization items are also covered in the depreciation input procedures.

[5]An affirmative response to "further considerations?" causes the computer to prompt for a series of more detailed or special inputs, such investment tax credit, installment sale, tax deferred exchange, and other data.

6

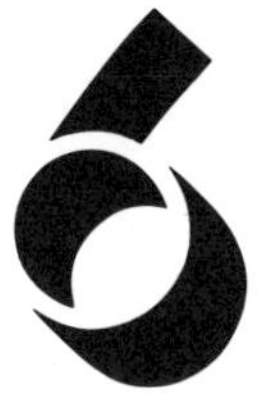

TAXES AND THE ACQUISITION PROCESS

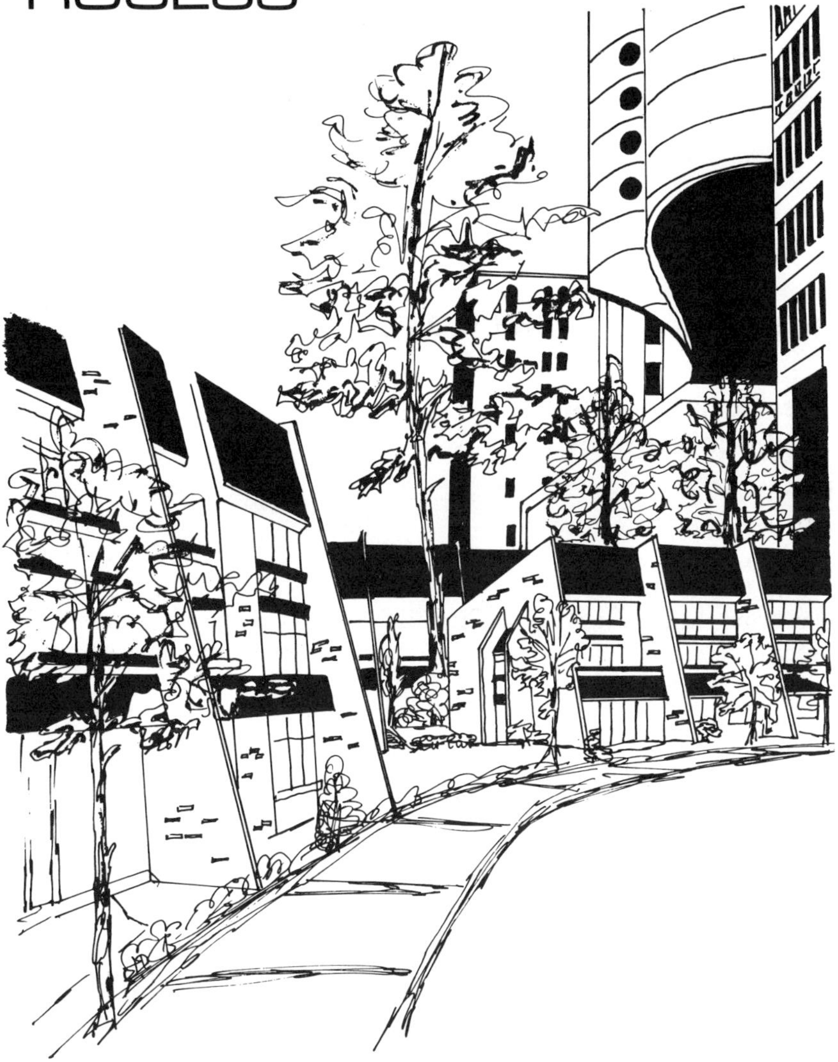

HOW TAX SHELTERS WORK

Real Estate Taxation and Public Policy

There is much controversy today over what some people see as inequitable tax advantages for those in the higher brackets. The many characterizations of the "tax shelter," however, sometimes make us lose sight of the basic tax laws and their underlying social policies, which make it possible to set up such shelters.The tax rules that make residential real estate attractive to investors flow from post-Depression era government policies that were originally designed to make adequate housing available to all—beginning with long-term FHA-backed amortized loans. Over the years, these government programs and policies have come to include interest deductions and accelerated depreciation deductions from taxable income during the holding period, favored tax treatment of capital gains as compared to ordinary income, rules enabling the investor to realize tax benefits on borrowed money, and other incentives to keep private capital invested in housing.

In some respects, the basic government policies concerning investment in real estate are the reverse of those covering investment in the securities market. In the stock market, the absence of rules discouraging marginal buying was viewed as a major cause of the 1929 crash. Subsequently, this market became one of the most highly regulated industries in the U.S. economy, with strict rules covering purchases on margin. In contrast, the policies that emerged regarding real estate, especially residential real estate, have encouraged precisely that kind of buying. This rather superficial parallel between buying stocks and improved real property with borrowed money gives rise to a question in some people's minds: Will the many years of buying real estate on margin eventually produce a "real estate crash"? Although such a thought might seem unthinkable to some, others are convinced that superficially similar patterns in history produce significantly similar repetitions of historical events. Some of the material covered in this chapter, as well as that covered throughout the book, might help readers to make their own judgments on this point.

ELEMENTS OF THE SHELTER

To understand the practical operation of a tax shelter, you have to compare the before-tax returns on an investment with those computed on an after-tax basis. [In this context, the measurement method most widely accepted among informed investors and investment counselors is the internal rate of return (IRR). (See Chapter 4.)] To the extent that tax considerations affect overall returns on a real estate investment, the basic elements in a program of tax "sheltering" are as follows:

1. leveraged tax benefits,
2. accelerated depreciation on deductions,
3. conversion of ordinary income into capital gain.

1. Leveraged Tax Benefits. Real estate investments are favored over others by rules that allow interest and depreciation to be deducted from gross income in amounts that are of larger proportions than the amount actually "at risk" would otherwise warrant. In other words, you can make a minimum down payment, add little or no closing and other investment costs, acquire a title to property valued many times higher than the initial outlay, use the property as security for a loan on the balance of the purchase price, and take annual interest and depreciation deductions based on that loan amount and purchase price.

2. Deferral of Tax Payments Through Accelerated Depreciation Deductions. As an incentive for investors to put risk capital into residential real estate, the tax laws allow a greater portion of the depreciation to be deducted in the early years of an investment than would be allowed by the straight-line method. Among others things, this "interest-free government loan" helps to offset the negative cash flows that tend to be greater in the early years of an investment (if they occur at all).

3. Conversion of Ordinary Income into Capital Gain. Earned income is taxable at a maximum rate of 50 percent, other "ordinary" income at 70 percent, capital gain at 28 percent (40% × 70%).[1] To the extent that the returns on a real estate investment come from appreciation rather than from current ordinary income, the investor can save up to $42 per $100 in income taxes due. Even for someone in the 30-percent tax bracket, the saving is $18. This is because such earnings are taxed at the capital gain rate, rather than the ordinary rate.

THE DEAL VERSUS THE SHELTER

Because the tax benefits attached to real estate investments can be substantial, some investors tend to think of real estate investments almost exclusively in terms of such benefits. In some cases real estate sales agents, investment advisors, syndicators, and others who stand to gain through these investments have encouraged such an inclination through their failure to conduct adequate investment analyses.

Acting on the all-too-common assumption that real estate investment *means* "tax shelter," some syndicators have even set up limited partnerships to take advantage of tax benefits from real estate investments that are of little attraction other than for those benefits. They have taken large management fees "up front," leaving the investors with optimistic projections and sometimes with lower returns than the use of their capital would justify—or than a more selective strategy would generate.

How do you avoid such "lopsided" investments? For starters, deal with advisors who you know are both trustworthy and knowledgeable. But perhaps the best way to avoid such oversights and abuses is to understand the dynamics of tax sheltering: Approach real estate investment as you would a business. Remember: Tax angles are an important part of running a business, but not the whole business. The shelter is part of the deal, not the reverse.

[1] Under the *Revenue Act of 1978,* the 28-percent maximum rate for capital gains results from the application of the maximum ordinary income tax rate to the taxable 40-percent (previously 50-percent) portion of the capital gain.

INDIVIDUAL AND GROUP INVESTMENT

The Acquiring Entity

You may invest in real estate as an individual or as part of a group. The various groupings of investors all have different legal status, tax obligations, and interrelationships. These legal entities (or "persons") can be classified in essentially the same manner as the basic types of business organization, as follows:

1. sole proprietorship,
2. general partnership,
3. limited partnership,
4. joint-stock company,
5. joint venture,
6. for-profit corporation,
7. subchapter S corporation,
8. nonprofit corporation,
9. government-related corporation, and
10. combination forms.

Sole Proprietorship

An individual investing alone in real estate operates as a *sole proprietorship*. All legal liabilities, as well as all returns associated with an investment, apply to the proprietor as an individual. So do income tax rules, both as to payments and benefits. This basic form of organization is popular among small investors because ownership is "personal"; the control of all investment decisions—when and how to buy, to finance, to rent, to fix, to sell, and so on—is completely in the hands of the investor. Sole proprietors have total personal control and flexibility in their investment strategy. These advantages, however, are offset somewhat by the limitation to one person's capital. Small investors might be excluded from opportunities that require more than their individual resources can cover at a given time or from those that entail a greater risk than they are prepared to take alone.

Partnerships

Partnerships, in their various forms, are not taxable entities as such. Generally, tax obligations and benefits are channeled through the partnership to the partners. In addition, the liabilities of individual partners are less limited than shareholders in a corporation—with some exceptions, as we shall see.

General Partnership

The simplest form of business organization for two or more individuals in a real estate investment is the *general partnership*. Although even a general partnership formed by oral agreement can hold title to real property, a written agreement is important because it defines the rights, duties, and liabilities of each partner. Such an agreement clarifies any misunderstandings—that may arise through a failure to reach an initial meeting of the minds—about such questions as capital contributions, division of profits and losses, methods for settling disputes, and provisions for termination of the partnership. Each general partner must also be concerned about the matter of personal liability: In the absence of specific written agreements to the contrary, each general partner is personally liable, along with all the others, for all the debts of the partnership—regardless of which partner or partners incur them.

As a rule, the income tax liabilities and benefits related to the real estate holdings of a general partnership may be shared by whatever arrangement the partners agree to, as long as it is consistent with the tax laws. Typically, tax gains and losses are passed through the partnership to each partner in proportion to his or her capital contribution. The partnership as such is not taxed. As a real estate investment produces positive or negative taxable income and/or capital gain, that income or gain is distributed among the partners. The portion attributable to each partner is then reported and taxed at that person's rate.

Because the partners may be in various tax brackets and because they have differing overall financial plans and positions outside the real estate investments of the partnership, they may not want to divide the tax benefits and liabilities in direct proportion to their capital contributions. One partner, for example, might find it beneficial to realize current tax losses, while another might benefit more by realizing current income, thus permitting others to take greater advantage of capital gain taxation at the time of disposition. Structuring the partnership in such a way that mutual needs can be accommodated is a relatively complicated matter that should be undertaken only with specialized legal and financial planning advice.

Limited Partnership. In a *limited partnership*, you can avoid the time and risk of active participation in the affairs of a general partnership, as well as personal liability for its debts. Many small investors are attracted by this business organization form, which permits the pass-through of the profits and tax benefits of a real estate investment without the disadvantages of a general partnership. The key characteristic of a limited partnership consists of limited partners, who offer only a passive form of investment and who enjoy only limited liability.

In addition to limited partners, a limited partnership must have at least one general partner with overall responsibility for the management of the partnership and with liability for its debts. Because the general partner is the active party and primary risk-taker in a limited partnership, he or she usually receives remuneration in the form of management fees, as well as a share in the profits that is greater than limited partners. The shares of the limited partners are determined essentially by what the entrepreneur-general partner finds must be offered to investors in order to attract their capital.

Because general partners have to solicit the capital of passive investors (whose liability is limited to the loss of their capital contributions, whether paid all at once or partly through subscription or assessment), the federal and many state governments regard the limited partnership in the same light as corporate securities, which are subject to regulations designed to protect investors against unscrupulous practices. Unlike a general partnership, which comes into existence through an oral or written agreement among two or more persons, a limited partnership is the creature of state law. Its enabling agreement *must* be in writing, and it must be recorded with the designated state government agency.

With regard to federal tax treatment, general and limited partnerships are treated in essentially the same manner. The limited partnership itself is not a taxable entity. Each year it files with the IRS an information return, Form 1065 (Schedule K), which shows the partnership's distributive income and loss items for the year. Each general and limited partner receives a copy of Schedule K (Schedule K–1), which in turn is attached to his or her own Form 1040, on which the partner's individual (or "distributive") shares of the partnership's tax benefits and liabilities must be separately reported.

Joint-Stock Company. Essentially a general partnership, the *joint-stock company* can be established in some states as a type of partnership. The partners have unlimited financial liability for the company's obligations, but they are passive in management, which is conducted by specified individuals. The joint-stock company is similar to a corporation in that respect, and insofar as it has continued existence separate from the partners.

As for tax consequences, it is normally treated as a partnership. Whether or not the joint-stock company is a recognized entity as such under state law, most of its characteristics can be approximated through the language of a partnership agreement, if that is desired.

Joint Venture. The final, and most amorphous, type of partnership is the *joint venture*. Basically a partnership rather than a corporation, its existence is by its legal nature of limited duration. Its business purposes are also limited, and usually very specific. The partners in the venture—individuals, other partnerships, corporations, hybrid entities—join capital and other resources for a particular project. Once that project is completed, the joint venture ceases to exist by previous agreement. It may buy land, develop and sell building lots, construct and sell the buildings, and do other specific things that do not entail liabilities for the co-venturers' financial obligations in any business activities beyond the single project. Whether the venture is treated as a partnership or corporation for tax purposes depends on the wording of its enabling documents and on the substance of its activities.

Corporations

For-Profit Corporation. The differences between the various forms of partnership and the various forms of corporation are significant both in overall legal effect and tax consequences. On a practical plane, the "For-Profit Corporation" is the "Standard" corporate form. The four basic legal characteristics of a corporation are as follows:

1. *Existence in perpetuity:* Unlike any kind of partnership, a corporation exists not only as a separate entity from its partners and as a creature of the state (either of which conditions may prevail to some extent in one form of partnership or another), but the corporation may also continue to exist even if all its current owners depart through death or otherwise. Partly to avoid the adverse consequences of being regarded by the IRS as a corporation, both general and limited partnership agreements usually contain clear provisions for the termination of the partnership at the end of a specified period of time.
2. *Management of the entity's affairs centrally and independently of the shareholders.* Limited partnerships also have this characteristic. General partnerships usually do not, except in the case of the joint stock company—which is one reason that such companies sometimes find themselves in court as "sue-able" entities separate from their owners.
3. *The limitation of shareholders' liability to the value of their share.* Limited partnerships usually also have this corporate characteristic to a point. Corporate stocks, however, are not ordinarily purchased by subscription, nor are the shares subject to subsequent capital assessments, as is fairly common with partnerships.
4. *Unconditional transferability of ownership interests.* Partnership agreements have provisions requiring the approval of any new

general partner by the others. General partners ordinarily also approve the entry of new limited partners, especially if limited partners are assessible for future capital contributions. Beyond the question of sound credit for assessments, the partnership agreement may require that new limited partners be approved by the other partners, a condition that helps to distinguish the partnership from a corporation for tax purposes.

As a general rule, the tax consequences of a for-profit corporation are negative. The corporation, unlike a partnership, is a separately taxable entity. Its income and capital gains are subject to corporate taxes, and any remaining profits, distributed to shareholders as ordinary dividends, are subject to tax as ordinary income received by the shareholder. (Only $100 is exempted for dividend income received from qualifying corporations.) *Beyond double taxation, corporation tax deductions do not pass through* to the owners, as in the case of partnerships. For those reasons, regular corporations have not been a popular vehicle among small investors in real estate.

Subchapter S Corporation. One way to sidestep the adverse tax consequences of a "standard" corporation, while retaining limited liability and freely transferable ownership interests, is the Subchapter S corporation. The Internal Revenue Code allows members of such a corporation to be taxed as individuals; the corporation itself is not a taxable entity. This business form, however, is practicable only for small corporations in businesses other than investment in real estate. No more than 15 shareholders are permitted, and no more than one class of stock. No more than 20 percent of corporate income can be passive, that is, derived from such sources as royalties, interest, dividends, and *rents.* Each stockholder must elect Subchapter S treatment, and the form must be approved by the IRS.

For any advantages the small investor in real estate might seek in a Subchapter S corporation, a limited partnership ordinarily serves just as well, without the concomitant disabilities. Liability is limited in both cases. Except for general partners, ownership interests are freely or easily transferable. The interests in either business form can be structured to be traded in organized securities markets, but in both cases this structure involves registration procedures beyond the normal scope of small investor activity. In both cases management is central.

Other Corporation Types. In addition to the regular for-profit corporation and Subchapter S corporation, many states provide for the establishment of *nonprofit corporations,* typically for charitable, educational, recreational, religious, and social purposes. Some jurisdictions permit several classes of nonprofit corporation, the common denominator being that they do not distribute profits as dividends to their members. Although they can own and operate real estate investments, they do not usually compare favorably with general or limited partnerships as a vehicle established primarily for that purpose.

Government and Quasi-Government Corporations. Such corporations as the U.S. Postal Service and Amtrak own and operate real estate. Established for various public purposes, generally on a very large scale, they are not available for creation as vehicles for small investor activity.

Combination Forms

Sole proprietorships and general/limited partnerships are by far the most popular business organization forms among small individual and group investors in real estate. For special purposes or transactions, however, the various forms can be combined in many ways. Individuals, general and limited partnerships, corporations, and joint ventures (consisting of two or more of those entities of the same or different kind) may all combine into various kinds of partnerships, "syndicates," corporations, or joint ventures. Their formations and activities are restrained only by federal and state securities regulations, as well as by the applicable tax consequences. What is to be promoted, how is it to be structured, how is it to be documented and marketed—these and other issues all enter into the decision as to which form best serves the purpose.

"DEALER" VERSUS "INVESTOR"

The form of business organization used by the acquiring entity in a real estate transaction is one question. Whether it acts as a *dealer or an investor* is quite another, with important tax consequences. If it acts as a dealer, gains from the sale of property are taxed as ordinary income, at rates from 14 to 70 percent. If it operates as an investor, gains are taxed as capital gains—that is, reduced by 60 percent before the application of ordinary income tax rates. The other side of that coin, however, is that dealers may claim tax *losses* at the higher ordinary income tax rates upon sale, while investors can only take capital losses at sale through additions to the adjusted basis. The effect of the capital loss approach is to reduce the dollar value of the tax *deduction* in question by 60 percent.

Which, then, is better: to be a dealer or an investor in acquiring, holding, and disposing of property in a given transaction or project? Ideally, of course, you would want to be a dealer in computing capital losses but an investor in computing capital gains. Since the tax laws do not permit such behavior, you must consider how the IRS is likely to view the question under a given set of circumstances. Those whose business is clearly that of buying and quickly reselling real estate through active sales efforts find themselves treated as dealers in transactions in which they carry on their regular business. A dealer, however, can set specified properties aside, hold them for income, and have them treated as investments for tax purposes. Acquiring entities that are ordinarily investors, on the other hand, may become involved in transactions or projects in which they are likely to be treated as dealers under current tax court and IRS rulings. The taxpayer should seek up-to-date readings of applicable law whenever the dealer/investor classification appears to be a potential issue of importance.

FORMS OF OWNERSHIP

The distinctions among the many forms of ownership of real property are often very important. They can be crucial in determining who has which rights and liabilities in the purchase, use, and disposition of particular property. We will concern ourselves, however, only with a summary of the tax consequences that the various forms of ownership may have on the interests of the small investor in residential real estate.

Legal Versus Equitable or Beneficial Ownership

It is possible to acquire, hold, and dispose of interests in real property in such a way that one person holds *legal title* to, and maintains formal control over, the property on behalf of one or more others who have rights to all ownerships *benefits* in the property, such as income, tax deductions, and capital gain. This arrangement can be done by agreement, by will, or by operation of specific state or federal statutes. The three main forms of such "trust" ownership are:

1. trust estates
2. real estate investment trusts (REITs), and
3. land trust act ownership.

1. Trust Estates. The trust estate is the mechanism commonly used to place assets "in trust." The trustee, who has essentially complete discretion in managing and disposing of the assets, has a strict legal obligation to act on behalf of the beneficiary or beneficiaries of the trust. Although the arrangement does not generally involve the double taxation that corporations undergo, either the trust as such or the beneficiary(ies) may be required to pay federal income tax, depending on whether and how the trust income is distributed or held in trust. If the beneficiaries exercise any control at all over trust assets, they risk assessment by the IRS of unanticipated tax liabilities.

Although trust estates may hold investment properties for beneficiaries without the adverse consequences of corporation taxation, their main purpose is to insulate certain individuals from the decision-making process regarding the management of assets from which they can gain financially. A typical reason is to protect a child from the effects of immature business judgment, or a political figure from appearing to have (despite the actuality) a conflict of interest.

2. Real Estate Investment Trusts (REITs). The creation of this type of trust is made possible by the *1960 Real Estate Investment Trust Act.* Like the more traditional trust estate, the REIT separates the owner of benefits (equitable interests) from the actual manager of properties. It is designed by public policy, however, more specifically for small investors than for children, political figures, and others in similar positions.

Shares in a REIT, usually established by one kind of chartered financial institution or another, are securities. Certificates of beneficial interest must be held by one hundred or more persons. Denominations are generally $100 per unit or less. Ninety percent of a REIT's income must be from real property, and 75 percent of its assets must be in real estate, cash, or government securities. It must pay dividends amounting to 90 percent of its income—leaving a margin of 10 percent for management-related fees or costs.

Beyond the low cost per ownership share, a key attraction to the REIT is that *the corporation itself is not taxed as a separate entity.* A glaring weakness in past performance has been an over-emphasis in mortgage money market investments at the expense of equity participation. Management costs also influence rates of return. For practical purposes, REITs compete more with money market instruments and publicly offered stocks and bonds than with direct real estate investments and partnership interests.

3. Land Trust Act Ownership. The land trust is a means by which the legal title to real estate can be separated from its control and the right to all its benefits. Under the procedure involved, the title is vested in a trustee whose only function is to hold and to relinquish title on behalf of those who own all the beneficiary rights to the property and who have all the concomitant liabilities. This arrangement includes the pass-through of all tax benefits and liabilities. The management and disposition of the property is by whoever would be designated for that purpose if the trust did not exist—such as a managing partner in a general partnership or a general partner in a limited partnership.

The main purpose of land trust ownership, which is provided for under the laws of five states at this writing, is to simplify real estate investment transactions where there are multiple owners, as in the case of partnerships. By allowing the beneficiary rights to be treated legally as personal property, the act makes it possible to avoid some of the cumbersome procedures involved in buying and selling real estate. Two such examples are seeking release of dower and curtesy rights from nonparticipants in the investment or arranging a transfer when one of the owners has died or become disabled. In addition, certain recording fees may sometimes be avoided. Although its use is not generally allowed to conceal conflicts of interest or to defraud others, it does result in privacy of ownership, in that only the name of the *legal* holder of title, the trustee, appears in public records.

ESTATES AND OTHER INTERESTS IN REAL PROPERTY

The law of real property abounds with classifications and subclassifications of ownership and other interests, each with potentially important legal implications (like determining whether a person owns a given property). The tax implications of the following broad forms of ownership are of interest to the small investor in residential real property:

1. freehold estates,
2. life estates,
3. leaseholds,
4. tenancies,
5. contract ownership, and
6. special types of interest.

Freehold Estates

The usual type of ownership associated with investment in residential real property is "fee simple absolute," through which the owner has all rights to possess, use, and dispose of the property in question, with no limitation as to time. Lesser types of freehold estate may be limited as to duration, transferability through inheritance or other disposition, or use.

As a general rule, the fee simple owner has all the income tax benefits and liabilities related to the property, including to some extent the right to transfer them to others.

Life Estates

Life estates carry almost all the rights associated with fee simple estates, except that life estates are by definition limited in duration to the lifetime of the grantee (owner) or some other person. The grantee has the right to income and other benefits of the property for the duration of the estate, but he/she cannot transfer a fee simple estate in it to anyone else. Life estates are typically set up to provide for someone's financial well-being during his or her life. They are sometimes established through the operation of law providing a spouse with protection through the operation of dower or curtesy. Most states also have homestead protective laws, which limit the action of creditors against a family's residence during the husband's and wife's lives.

Leaseholds

Leasehold estates consist of various rights to possess and use real property for given periods of time. For the investor in residential real estate, tenancies may be:

1. "for years" (leases with terms ending on specific dates),
2. "from period to period" (for a period of less than a year), and
3. "at will" (terminable by either landlord or tenant at any time, usually with prior notice).

Residential leaseholders do not have the basic rights and obligations to receive the income tax benefits and to pay the income taxes related to the real property. However, many contractual relationships can be established with that effect, such as when someone holding a long-term lease builds income-producing improvements on it and desires to take interest and depreciation deductions related to them.

Tenancies

In addition to types of leasehold estates, the term "tenancy" applies to the manner in which one or more persons may own specific real property separately or together. Here are the main classifications:

1. sole ownership,
2. tenants in common,
3. joint tenancy,
4. tenancy by the entirety, and
5. community property.

1. Sole Ownership. All rights acquired are owned by one person, subject to applicable state laws regarding dower, curtesy, and/or community propety if the person is married. Tax treatment may be individual or joint.

2. Tenants in Common. Two or more persons own *undivided* interests of *variable* proportions in *all* of a given property. Such interests or shares—as, for example, in the case of condominium apartment common areas—can be transferred separately from the interests of co-owners. Income tax benefits and liabilities may be apportioned or realized by an entity separate from the owners.

3. Joint Tenancy. Two or more persons own *undivided* but necessarily *equal* interests in *all* of the property (regardless of financial contribution), which must be acquired *simultaneously*. Both tenants are subject to the *right of survivorship;* that is, the death of a joint tenant causes his or her interests to pass automatically to the other joint tenants rather than into the decedent's estate. Tax treatment is essentially as in the tenancy in common.

4. Tenancy by the Entirety. In states where this form of tenancy is recognized, a husband and wife (and only a husband and wife) own undivided and equal interests in all of their property. Each has the right of survivorship, but neither may transfer any interest in the property without the consent of the other spouse. Tax treatment may be by individual or joint return.

5. Community Property. In states where this form of tenancy is recognized rather than tenancies by the entirety (and dower and curtesy rights), each spouse has a right to one-half of the interests in property acquired during the marriage (except through gift, devise, inheritance, or separately maintained funds). Either spouse may transfer his or her interests without the other spouse's consent. Although there are no rights of survivorship, the surviving spouse may have certain rights if the other dies intestate (without a will). Tax treatment is generally the same as for a tenancy by the entirety.

Contract Ownership

Valuable equitable interests in real property may be established in numerous contractual ways without passing any estate (or legal interest) to the purchaser. Typically, for example, a contract of sale is consummated on a property before the title is transferred at settlement. An option to buy a given property at a specified price within a definite period of time is also such an equitable interest in property.

Ordinarily, tax benefits and liabilities attach to the legal owner of real property, rather than to one with contract rights. An important exception —and one of interest to investors—is a sale by land contract. In residential real estate investment, this type of transaction occurs most commonly when a purchaser acquires the cash flows from income and tax benefits from a property having a mortgage loan that bears a low interest rate but that the lender will not permit a new owner to assume. In effect, the purchaser buys all the cash flows and the right to receive title in the future. In the meantime he/she makes the mortgage payments for the legal owner of title without actually "assuming" the loan. In some states, lending institutions have challenged this procedure, and the courts have upheld it. In others, the lenders have succeeded in calling loans when it has been done. IRS treatment is also not always certain in this controversial area. An investor should always seek specialized legal advice and up-to-date information before entering into such a transaction.

Special Types of Interest

Several types of interests fall short of estates. They are:

1. *restrictive covenants,* which limit the use and enhance the value of a property;
2. *profits,* which permit the removal of such things as crops, timber, and minerals; and
3. *easements,* which permit certain uses of real property.

The *historic easement* is a special type of property interest that can bring tax benefits of an unusual type to the investor in real estate, if the property has historic value of any kind. For example, the taxpayer might donate (by giving up) to the National Trust for Historic Preservation the right to destroy certain characteristics of a building (such as a unique facade) that are considered to be of historic value. The tax benefit is taken in the form of a charitable deduction; as an addition to the tax basis, it increases the annual depreciation deductions and reduces the capital gains tax, as well as the tax on recaptured depreciation upon disposition.

THE BASIS: KEY TO TAX BENEFITS

The real estate investor can receive *direct* financial returns from an investment in two ways:

1. *income* from rents and
2. *capital gain* from value increase and/or appreciation.

Conversely, the investor can receive *indirect* returns from an investment by taking federal income tax deductions in two general ways:

1. *Expense deductions,* which reduce annual taxable income. They can be broadly divided into: (a) operating expenses, (b) depreciation expense, and (c) interest expense.
2. *Capital gain reductions,* which occur through additions to the tax *basis* of the property value and result in a lower capital gain tax.

The dynamics of real estate investment taxation are essentially simple, since they all flow from these four factors: *returns* from (1) income and (2) capital gain, and *tax deductions* from (3) expenses and (4) reductions in the taxable capital gain.

Jargon associated with the "basis" can be confusing if the term is not broken down into its component parts and placed in context. The same word is often used to mean one of three different things:

1. The value for tax purposes (that is, for subsequent depreciation deductions and capital gain tax payments) at the *time of acquisition.*
2. The value that is reduced *annually* for the purpose of computing each subsequent year's depreciation deduction, if a declining balance method is used.
3. The value at time of disposition, after cumulative additions and reductions, that is subtracted from the amount realized (after sales commission, closing, and other sales costs) to determine the taxable depreciation recapture and capital gain.

As if to clarify the matter, the term "adjusted basis" is sometimes thrown in to describe the additions and reductions that affect it at acquisition, during the holding period, and upon disposition. In fact, the basis undergoes constant adjustment from the beginning of the investment cycle. Keep in mind (a) that *additions* to the basis are "good," because they increase depreciation deductions and reduce taxable gain and (b) that *reductions* are "bad," because they do the reverse.

To see how the basis operates in conjunction with the expense deduction procedures to produce tax gains and losses, let's trace its development through the three phases of the investment cycle.

Basis at Acquisition

Every time you spend money in connection with a real estate investment, you must account for the resulting cash flow in terms of either a capital expenditure or an expense. A capital expenditure is added to the basis and depreciated; an expense item is deducted from taxable income for the current year. A capital expense item reduces the future taxable gain by being added to the basis. In this case, the maximum future income tax saving for a person in the 70-percent bracket is 28 cents on every dollar by which the gain is reduced. An expense item reduces annual taxable income. In this case, the maximum tax saving is 70 cents on the dollar, taken annually. The comparative advantage in "expensing" an item rather than adding it to the basis holds for all tax brackets.

Acquisition by Purchase

Commonly, the property is acquired by purchasing it through a combination of cash and debt equal to the purchase price. That price, regardless of what portion is financed, is the first element in determining the initial basis.

How much of the property, however, is depreciable? Only improvements, not the land, are depreciable. Accordingly, the part of the acquisition cost that is attributable to land cannot be included in the basis for purposes of depreciation. In the case of new construction, the attributions are clear. With used properties, you must employ a reasonable measure of determination that is acceptable to IRS. The portion of value attributable to land varies with the type of building on it. Normally it is low for apartment buildings or condo apartment units, higher for townhouses, and higher still for detached houses.

Initial Additions to Basis

Next, other acquisition costs treated by the tax law as capital charges are added to the value of improvements. Ordinarily capital charges are items (other than prepaid interest) that are associated with the cost of acquisition and that by their nature are not likely to recur as annual operating costs. Lawyer's or other fees for clearing title, for preparing notes and mortgage instruments, and for closing are prime examples. Recording fees, notary fees, and fees paid for copies of needed public documents are also fairly clearly capital expenditures. The portion of a title insurance policy premium that the lender requires to protect itself is also a one-time expenditure necessary to close a transaction. A lender fee charged for the actual inspection of the property for loan approval would also be a capital expenditure rather than an expense item. The portion of the purchase price attributable to improvements, plus the foregoing charges, constitute the basis for depreciation. (A sample handheld calculator routine for this formulation is shown in Chapter 9.)

Expense Items at Closing

Not all items paid at settlement are capital expenditures. Items that are ordinarily prorated between the buyer and seller for periods of their respective ownership, as a general rule, are likely to be expense items. Property taxes, homeowner association dues, and hazard insurance premiums taken over by the purchaser are examples. Interest payments are also usually expense items, deductible annually from taxable income. Interest payments made on a new loan at the time of settlement for the remaining part of the month fall into that category. Prepaid interest, or "points," for a mortgage loan are given special treatment under the law.

Prepaid Interest

Under previous tax laws, investors could prepay as much as five years' interest in a given year and deduct the amount paid from that year's taxable income. Even prior to the *1976 Tax Reform Act,* the IRS restricted the practice on the grounds that it was a material distortion of income. Under current law, in the case of investment property, prepaid interest—typically in the form of loan points—must be "deducted ratably" or "amortized" over the term of the loan. In this context "amortized" means deducted in equal annual installments over the term of the loan on which the points are paid. It makes no difference that most mortgage loans are amortized through equal payments with declining proportions paid on interest.

Points paid on a home mortgage, if at the prevailing rate for the geographical area, are deductible currently. A penalty charge for prepayment of a mortgage, whether on a home or an investment, is also deductible as interest in the year paid.

Basis in Other Forms of Acquisition

For properties acquired by some means other than purchase with cash-plus-financing, the rules for determining the basis are pretty much the same. However, allowances are made for the whole or partial replacement of money in the transactions, and additions to the initial basis differ somewhat. These are the most common variations:

Purchase with Personal Property. The fair market value of such personal property as furniture, appliances, securities, collectibles, or other items can form part of the purchase price. If the total is less than the fair market value of the property purchased, the buyer is considered to have realized a gain, which must be reported to IRS.

Exchange with Other Realty. If properties of "like kind" are swapped (such as 12 condominium units held as an investment for two quadraplexes held as an investment), the effect may be simply a change of persons attached to the respective cash flows, with no different tax consequences to the properties themselves. (Tax-deferred exchanges are discussed later.)

Inheritance. In this case the equivalent of the purchase price is the fair market value at death. But if an estate value above $60,000 requires filing a federal estate tax return, the fair market value may be the value 6 months thereafter, at the taxpayer's option.

Gift. If the property is a gift, the amount of a gift tax, if paid, can be added to the adjusted basis. Otherwise, the donee takes over the donor's basis.

Exchange for Services Rendered. In this case the basis, to which additions are made, is the fair market value of the services rendered in return for the property given in compensation. The purchaser reports that compensation as ordinary income separately from the tax structure of the investment property itself.

Foreclosure. If the seller is a lender who has foreclosed on a loan and taken possession of the property in question, the new buyer's basis consists of:

1. the amount unpaid on the loan,
2. plus the seller's cost of having foreclosed,
3. plus any gain recognized for tax purposes.

Involuntary Conversion. Sometimes a real property investment is converted into cash or into something else through an action contrary to the investor's wishes—such as condemnation or a natural disaster. In these instances, the amount of the proceeds affects the basis of any replacement property. If that amount is greater than the fair market value of the property destroyed, a gain is realized, for which the investor can postpone tax liability until the end of the second year thereafter. If a replacement property is acquired prior to the second year, its basis is reduced by the amount of the untaxed gain. If the replacement property is acquired at a price or value of a lesser amount than proceeds from the conversion, the difference is taxed as a capital gain in the current year. For property held to produce income, or held otherwise as an investment, the replacement property need not be similar in use or in function to that destroyed.

PERSONAL RESIDENCE VERSUS INVESTMENT

If you plan to use a property as a primary residence prior to operating it as an income-producing investment, keep in mind several points when deciding what to claim as capital expenditures for addition to the basis. Interest payments and property taxes—not any other operating expenses or depreciation—are the only items currently deductible from the owner's taxable income in the case of a primary residence. For this reason, the owner of noninvestment residential property should try to include as many items as possible in additions to the basis, to reduce the *future* taxable capital gain. In other words, the "close" capital-expense questions should be resolved in favor of capitalizing; for example, claim a capital improvement rather than lose a tax gain from an item that might also be regarded as a repair. However, once you make such a decision, you cannot subsequently receive the more favorable treatment as currently deductible expenses.

7

HOLDING PERIOD EXPENDITURES AND DEDUCTIONS

Operating expenses, interest, depreciation—these are the three basic kinds of expense associated with an investment in income-producing real estate. The effects of each on the investment's cash flows before taxes are different from the others. The tax treatment and effects of each also differ. Let's review them briefly, to place the later detailed coverage in perspective:

Operating Expenses. These expenses are defined as all expenses, other than interest and depreciation expenses, that occur in connection with an income property, that do not add any improvement to the property with a useful life of more than one year, and that are not associated directly with the disposition of the property. Such expenses include property taxes, hazard and liability insurance, repair and maintenance costs, and other expenses likely to recur monthly, annually, or otherwise.

Operating expenses are deducted annually from taxable income. They are not normally subject to the long-term amortization procedures affecting interest payments. They do not produce the accelerated deductions, as does depreciation, without a current out-of-pocket expenditure. In an economy with an inflationary trend, operating expenses tend to increase over the holding period.

Interest Expense. Also generally deductible currently during the holding period, interest payments differ from operating expenses in that they are scheduled in advance over a long term. Also, they usually either decrease periodically over the holding period (as in the standard amortized first mortgage) or remain constant until payoff of principal (as in the interest-only second mortgage). The tax treatment of interest payments, which we will discuss, also differs from that of operating expenses.

Depreciation Expense. Depreciation expense is similar to operating and interest expenses in that they are taken in the form of annual reductions in taxable income. Like interest deductions, they are also scheduled in advance over a long term. Those reductions ordinarily either decrease annually during the property's useful life (as in the case of accelerated depreciation under a declining balance method), remain constant (straight line), or decrease, then become constant, with a crossover from declining balance to straight line.

Depreciation differs significantly from both operating and interest expenses in that it does not involve a current expenditure by the investor. Also unlike both of the others, depreciation deductions reduce the basis of the property, thereby increasing the future capital gain and the tax on it. That difference is significant. Another distinction: Operating and interest expenses, while they constitute deductions, exist apart from tax considerations; depreciation generates tax losses and valuable current deductions which, in the absence of the tax law, would be lower or nonexistent.

OPERATING EXPENSE VERSUS CAPITAL IMPROVEMENT

Should an expense be put into the books as an operating expense or as a capital improvement? Let's look at an example. An investor in the 50-percent tax bracket spends $1,000 to "repair" a roof of an income property. As an expense, that money is deductible from the investor's taxable income in the year spent; in other words, with $1,000 less to be taxed at 50 percent, the investor has $500 more in pocket after taxes than if the deduction had not been taken. If that same $1,000 were spent to "replace" the roof, the expenditure is for a capital improvement. Its value is then added to the basis, the effect of which is to reduce the investor's future taxable capital gain by $1,000. Only 40 percent of that gain ($400) is taxable at the investor's rate ($400 × 0.50 = $200). The tax saving is $300 (or 60 percent) less than if the work on the roof had been treated as a "repair" or "maintenance" rather than as a "capital improvement" or "replacement." Even if the replacement is depreciated over its useful life, the annual deductions are reduced in value because they are received over time rather than currently.

So which is it? The answer is not at all clear in every case, and much tax litigation centers on such distinctions. As a general rule of thumb, repair and maintenance are actions that keep the property in good condition or prevent its deterioration but that do not increase its useful life. A replacement or other capital improvement is either an addition with a useful life of more than one year or something that prolongs the useful life of the property.

INTEREST PAYMENTS: AMORTIZED OR DEDUCTED CURRENTLY

As mentioned already, prepaid interest must be amortized or "deducted ratably" over the term of the loan. This procedure is not the same as either a full deduction in the current year or depreciation, since depreciation involves reductions of the basis and tax savings only at the capital gains rate. Since amortized deductions are at the ordinary income rate, they are preferable to depreciation deductions. Although the general rule is that interest payments are a currently deductible expense, there are three notable exceptions other than the most common one related to prepaid interest:

1. *Unimproved and unproductive real property:* The taxpayer may *elect* to capitalize and amortize interest and finance charges.
2. *Construction period:* Interest and taxes payable during that period *must* be capitalized and amortized over ten years.
3. *Excess investment interest:* If an investment in a rental property is structured in such a way that income is in effect guaranteed, the property may lose the normal treatment as "trade or business" property and be treated as being "held for investment." The effect of this, most likely to occur in the case of a *net lease,* is that a *portion* of an individual taxpayer's deduction is disallowed for interest payments if they exceed the property's income. The basic limitation on interest deductions, not applicable to corporations, is $10,000 per year, plus the taxpayer's net investment income. Disallowed amounts are subject to carryover into future years. The detailed rules are complex and not widely applicable to small investors.

DEPRECIATION: FROM BASIS TO CAPITAL GAIN

The depreciation process is inextricably involved in each phase of an income property's investment cycle. At *acquisition* one or more tax bases must be established for subsequent depreciation deductions. During the *holding period* those deductions are taken annually at ordinary income rates, with each deduction reducing the basis for future capital gains computations. On disposition, the cumulative depreciation deductions that were taken during the holding period and that exceeded those allowable under the simple straight-line method are subject to tax at ordinary income tax rates. The cumulative depreciation deductions also affect the capital gains tax, as shown below.

Depreciation is not entirely a fabrication of statute designed to attract investors into residential real estate investments. Even without such devices as accelerated depreciation deductions, the economic value of a structure declines over time relative to similar structures built subsequently in the same market. If the difference is not reflected in sales price, it shows up in higher repair and maintenance costs for the older structure—assuming that well-informed investors have negotiated at arms' length. From another point of view, you're forced to say that owning and operating rental property is considered a *business.* As real and personal property used in connection with a business ages, its ability to produce net income declines relative to similar property which is new. This economic reality is sometimes recognized better by the tax laws than by the small investor. Nevertheless, the tax laws have taken depreciation beyond the realm of common-sense economics. Because of the intricate interrelationships with all the other aspects of a real estate investment, it may be helpful to review the ten basic steps involved in depreciation calculations before we examine those needing detailed treatment.

Step 1. Establish Initial Basis or Bases. The depreciation methods and time frames may vary according to whether the depreciable asset is personal property, commercial or residential real estate, the building shell or a component, new or used.

Step 2. Select Optimum Depreciation Method(s) for Annual Depreciation Deductions. This choice is a matter of financial planning. If your taxable income from sources other than the investment in question is expected to be constant, selecting methods that allow the greatest deductions in early years would normally be most advantageous. If you anticipate substantial increases in other taxable income needing shelter, the reverse strategy might be appropriate.

Step 3. Estimate Salvage Value. Salvage value is the projected future market value of a depreciated asset if it were torn down or sold for its component parts. If applicable for a given type of depreciation, salvage value is subtracted from the initial depreciation basis.

Step 4. Estimate Useful Life. For how many years will you be able to operate an asset for reasonable (as IRS might conceive the term) income and profit? The shorter the useful life, the greater the depreciation deductions.

Step 5. Establish Depreciation Schedule(s) for Annual Deductions. The rate for equal annual depreciation deductions under the straight-line method, if only one rate is used, is simply 100 percent (or 1.00) divided by the number of years of useful life (for example, $1.00 \div 25 = 0.04$). That rate is multiplied by the basis to determine the amount of the annual depreciation deduction (for example, $0.04 \times \$53{,}890 = \$2{,}156$).

For an accelerated depreciation rate, multiply that same rate by the percentage figure of your choice—125, 150, or 200 percent. For deductions under a declining balance method, for example, figure $0.04 \times 1.25 = 0.05$. The resulting rate, in turn, is multiplied by the basis to determine the amount of the first year's depreciation deduction under such a method: to illustrate, $0.05 \times \$53{,}890 = \$2{,}695$. It is also multiplied each year against the declining balance, which is the basis adjusted downward by each year's deduction. Hence the amount of each subsequent year's depreciation deduction is calculated as follows: $\$53{,}890 - \$2{,}695 = \$51{,}195 \times 0.05 = \$2{,}560$, the second year's depreciation amount. (Additional details on these and other depreciation methods and calculations follow.)

Step 6. Make Annual Depreciation Deductions. The deductions are taken on the schedule or schedules established as indicated in the previous steps. Each year, the basis is adjusted downward by the amount of applicable deduction.

Step 7. Crossover Depreciation Methods and Schedules. In an accelerated deduction method, a year will come in which the allowable amount of the annual deduction under that method is less (and will remain less in subsequent years) than would be allowable under the straight-line method. You may cross over to the straight-line or to a "lower" declining method without prior approval by the IRS. Any other crossover requires specific IRS approval.

Step 8. Compute Tax on Recaptured Depreciation at Time of Disposition. The cumulative amount of annual *accelerated* depreciation deductions, at the time of sale, in *excess* of the cumulative amount of depreciation deductions which would have resulted from the *straight-line* method is subject to taxation at ordinary income rates on the excess.

Step 9. Compute Adjusted Basis at Time of Dispostion. Adjusted basis is the initial basis, *plus* the cost of capital improvements, *minus* cumulative depreciation deductions, and *minus* such previously deducted items as uninsured casualty losses. Keep in mind that each *addition* to the basis *reduces* the taxable capital gain, while each *subtraction increases* it.

Step 10. Compute the Capital Gain Tax. The total taxable gain is the "amount realized" at sale (the sale price minus broker fees and other sales costs), minus the adjusted basis at time of disposition. The capital gain is total gain minus recaptured depreciation. Capital gain times the investor's capital gains tax rate (40% × ordinary rate) is the capital gain tax. Methods for the deferral of capital gains taxes through disposition other than by straight sale are discussed elsewhere.

DEPRECIATION METHODS AND CALCULATIONS

Figure 7-1 presents an overview of the depreciation methods specifically recognized by IRS and the types of property for which each can be used. Any depreciation method that makes sense in the context of your business and financial planning and that is consistent with sound accounting practices *may* be approved by the IRS. The maximum accelerations permitted in the recognized methods shown in Figure 7-1, however, make it clear that the direction of policy is to limit the extent to which a taxpayer may weight a depreciation schedule in favor of deductions in the earlier years of the holding period. Accelerated deductions are allowed to the highest degree with new residential income property and personal property used in business, to encourage capital investment in both. The need to provide such incentives for investment in used commercial real estate is not recognized in the tax policy at all. In any event, the total deductions during the first two-thirds of the useful life cannot be greater than the total allowable under the declining balance method.

Applications	METHOD						
	Straight-Line			Declining Balance			Sum of the Years Digits
	Short Formula	Standard Formula	Component Composite	125%	150%	200%	
Is salvage value deducted from basis?	No	Yes[1]	Yes[1]	No	No	No	Yes[1]
New commercial real property	Yes	Yes	Yes	Yes	Yes	No	No
Used commercial real property	Yes	Yes	Yes	No	No	No	No
New residential income property	Yes	Yes	Yes	Yes	Yes	Yes	Yes
Used residential income property	Yes	Yes	Yes	Yes	No	No	No
New personal property used in business	Yes[2]	Yes[3]	Yes	Yes	Yes	Yes	Yes
Used personal property used in business	Yes[2]	Yes[3]	Yes	Yes	Yes	No	No

[1]No salvage value need be deducted from the basis of personal property if the salvage value is estimated to be less than 10% of the original value *and* the useful life is estimated to be more than 3 years.

[2]Personal property, however, is not distinguished from real property in this approach.

[3]But personal property remains exempt from salvage subtraction from basis if salvage value is less than 10% and useful life more than 3 years.

Figure 7-1.

In calculating the annual depreciation deductions under the various methods, follow these steps:

Step 1. *Establish basis.*

Step 2. *Subtract salvage value* (in standard straight-line and sum-of-years-digits methods only) or use the basis to establish depreciable value.

Step 3. *Determine useful life.*

Step 4. *Determine the annual depreciation rate.*

Step 5. *Apply that rate annually according to the method used.*

For all methods, Step 1 is the same, but the basis has already been described.

If salvage value (Step 2) is applicable, a common rule of thumb is 10 percent of the original value of a building. In the case of personal property, the IRS rule is that salvage value need not be subtracted to establish depreciable value if:

1. salvage value is estimated at 10 percent or *less* of the original value, and
2. its useful life is estimated as *at least* 3 years.

Determining useful life (Step 3) is, like Step 1, common to all methods. IRS guidelines (Revenue Procedure 62-21) suggest useful lives of 40 years for such buildings as apartments and hotels, 45 years for dwellings, and 10 years for depreciable equipment used by such service businesses as hotels. The guidelines are not binding, but they reflect positions that the IRS might take. In estimating useful life, the investor may take into consideration normal wear and tear, economic changes in an industry, climate and other local factors, and the investor's own policies regarding maintenance and replacement. As a general rule, the investor finds the shortest useful life most beneficial.

The differences in the depreciation methods start to appear in Steps 4 and 5. Here is the way those rates are determined and applied under the various methods:

Straight-Line

Short Formula. This is the simplest method. The cost of the building is 100 percent of the amount to be depreciated. Divide 100 percent by the number of years of useful life (such as 100% ÷ 25 years = 4% per year, or an annual rate of 0.04). To apply the rate annually simply multiply the rate by the basis (0.04 × $53,890 = $2,156). No distinction is made among the building shell, other components, and personal property. No salvage value is subtracted from the basis. There is one depreciation schedule, and all deductions under it are the same for each year of its duration.

Standard Formula. In the straight-line "standard" formula, the building and all its real property components are depreciated on one schedule, while the personal property acquired with it (such as refrigerators, window treatments, window units as distinct from central air conditioning, and the like) is depreciated on a separate schedule. Since personal property ordinarily has a shorter useful life than real property, this method increases current depreciation deductions. They are reduced somewhat, however, by the fact that IRS requires that salvage value be considered in this formula. To illustrate, assume you have purchased with real property $5,000 in personal property, with 7 years' useful life and a salvage value of less than $500 (10 percent). Application of the standard formula would result in your deduction is shown in Figure 7-2.

Component/Composite. There are two approaches to component depreciation under the straight-line method. In both, the real property components of the property (shell, roof, plumbing, and so on) are broken down for separate treatment for depreciation purposes. In one approach, a separate depreciation schedule with a different annual depreciation rate is

	Total	Building	Personal Property
Basis	53,890	48,890	5,000
– Salvage value (at 10%)	4,889	4,889	NA[1]
= Depreciable value (rounded)	49,000	44,000	5,000
x Annual depreciation rate	(two rates)	0.04	0.14[2]
= Annual depreciation deduction	2,460	1,760	700
– Short formula straight-line deduction	2,156	—	—
= Increase, with standard formula	304	—	—

[1]No salvage value deducted with value under 10% and life over 3 years.

[2]1.00 ÷ 7 = 0.14, rounded.

Figure 7-2.

Component	Percentage of Building	Depreciable Value (After Salvage)	Useful Life in Years	Annual Depreciation Rate	Annual Depreciation Deduction
Shell	40.0	17,600	25	0.040	704
Roof	8.0	3,520	12	0.083	292
Floor	8.0	3,520	12	0.083	292
Plumbing	11.0	4,840	12	0.083	402
Electrical	17.0	7,480	10	0.10	748
Central Heat–A/C	13.0	5,720	10	0.10	572
Parking Area Pavement	3.0	1,320	8	0.125	165
Total	100.0	44,000	—	—	3,175
Average	—	6,286	15	0.088	454

Figure 7-3.

established for each component. In the other approach, the disparate annual rates are averaged to create one rate and one schedule. Personal property, as in the standard formula, is depreciated separately. In both approaches the salvage value must be considered.

Component and composite depreciation is most frequently used with new buildings, for which the respective costs of components is easier to determine. However, it can also be applied to used buildings. If you apply this method to used property without a prior IRS review, keep records (ideally with an independent appraiser's report) to support the valuations of components. Component/composite depreciation may also be used with the accelerated depreciation methods, subject to the recapture rules (which

	Total	Building	Personal Property
Depreciable value	49,000	44,000	5,000
Annual depreciation rate	(various rates)	(various rates)	0.14
Annual depreciation deduction	3,875	3,175	700
Short formula deduction	2,156	0	0
Increase with component/composite	1,719	0	0

Figure 7-4. Approach 1.

	Total	Building	Personal Property
Depreciable value	49,000	44,000	5,000
Annual depreciation rate	(two rates)	0.088[1]	0.14
Annual depreciation deduction	4,572	3,872	700
Short formula deduction	2,156	0	0
Increase, with component/composite	2,416	0	0

[1] Average of annual depreciation rates.

Figure 7-5. Approach 2 (Composite Rate).

will be discussed), but prior IRS approval is required to cross over to component/composite depreciation from another method.

Given the additional information on the components that is shown in Figure 7-3, look at the overall effects of component/composite depreciation, as demonstrated in Figures 7-4 and 7-5. Note the dramatic increases for annual depreciation deductions by both component depreciation approaches. An important reason for this increase is that we are employing them on a used building, whose shell (the major component) is assumed to have 25 years' remaining useful life, rather than the more common 40-45 years for a new dwelling. In tax parlance, this is an "aggressive" approach toward the IRS, and it would be more so if an accelerated depreciation method were used.

Declining Balance

For each of the three declining balance methods, the annual depreciation rate is determined and applied annually in the same manner. The annual depreciation rate is a constant 125, 150, or 200 percent of the straight-line rate. (See Figure 7-6.) Once the annual rate is determined, it is simply applied each year to a basis that has been adjusted downward by the amount of the depreciation deduction taken for the previous year. In other

	Declining Balance Factor		
	125%	150%	200%[1]
Straight-line percentage of basis	100%	100%	100%
÷ Useful life, in years	25	25	25
= Straight-line depreciation rate (annual)	0.04	0.04	0.04
x Declining balance factor	1.25	1.50	2.00
= Declining method rate	0.05	0.06	0.08

(a)

Declining balance factor	1.25	1.50	2.00
÷ Useful life, in years	25	25	25
= Declining method rate	0.05	0.06	0.08

(b)

[1] Commonly referred to as "double declining balance," an effect of which is to double the first year's depreciation deduction, over the straight-line deduction.

Figure 7-6. (a) Declining Balance Method. (b) More Direct Method.

words, *the rate is applied to an annually declining balance.* No salvage value is subtracted from the basis to determine the depreciable amount for either real or personal property.

> *Example: The investment in the preceding example is a 25-year-old income-producing townhouse that is depreciated at the maximum accelerated rate of 125 percent on the declining balance. The used personal property purchased with it is depreciated at the maximum rate of 150 percent on the declining balance for the seven years of its useful life. Figure 7–7 shows how the depreciation schedule works out over the 7-year period.*

Sum-of-the-Years-Digits (SOYD)

Like the double-declining balance method, the SOYD method may be applied to depreciation of new residential income property and to new personal property for use in business. Although this method also produces initial payments higher than straight-line depreciation would and although, like all methods, it produces a declining balance, it is not a "declining balance" method because the annual depreciation deductions are (ordinarily) computed independently of the annually adjusted basis. Instead, they are computed by a formula derived from the number of years of useful life—specifically, from the sum of all the digits in that number. In

	Total	Building Depreciated at 125% on Declining Balance for 25 Years	Personal Property Depreciated at 125% on Declining Balance for 25 Years	Personal Property Depreciation Schedules Without Crossover to Straight-line[1]: 150%	Personal Property Depreciation Schedules Without Crossover to Straight-line[1]: Straight-line
Basis	53,890	48,890	5,000	5,000	5,000
First-year deduction	3,516	2,445	1,071	1,071	714
Remaining balance	50,376	46,446	3,929	3,929	4,286
Second-year deduction	3,163	2,322	821	841	714
Cumulative deductions	6,679	4,767	1,912	1,912	1,428
Remaining balance	47,209	44,123	3,086	3,086	3,572
Third-year deduction	2,867	2,206	661	661	714
Cumulative deductions	9,546	6,973	2,573	2,573	2,142
Remaining balance	44,342	41,917	2,425	2,425	2,858
Fourth-year deduction	2,702	2,096	606[2]	520	714
Cumulative deductions	12,248	9,069	3,179	3,093	2,856
Remaining balance	41,640	39,821	1,819	1,906	2,144
Fifth-year deduction	2,597	1,991	606	408	714
Cumulative deductions	14,845	11,060	3,785	3,501	3,570
Remaining balance	39,043	37,830	1,213	1,497	1,430
Sixth-year deduction	2,498	1,892	606	321	714
Cumulative deductions	17,343	12,952	4,391	3,822	4,284
Remaining balance	36,546	35,939	607	1,176	716
Seventh-year deduction	2,499	1,892[3]	607	252	716
Cumulative deductions	19,844	14,844	5,000	4,074	5,000
Remaining balance	34,047	34,047	0	924[4]	0

[1] See discussion below under "crossover to straight-line."
[2] First year of crossover to straight-line method, for personal property.
[3] First year of crossover to straight-line method, for building.
[4] This would be amount of lost depreciation deductions on the depreciation schedule for personal property at 150% declining balance, if crossover to straight-line were not made.

Figure 7-7.

the case of a seven-year depreciation schedule, for example, the sum of the years is:

$$7 + 6 + 5 + 4 + 3 + 2 + 1 = 28$$

An easier formula is:

$$\frac{(n \text{ Years} \times n \text{ Years}) + n \text{ Years}}{2} = \text{SOYD}$$

or:

$$\frac{(7 \times 7) + 7}{2} = 28$$

Or by calculator:

(Algebraic logic): 7[×]7[=]49[+]7[=]56[÷]2[=]28

(RPN logic): 7[ENTER]7[×]49, 7[+]56, 2[÷]28

The sum-of-the-years-digits (in this case, 28) becomes constant for the depreciation schedule. It serves as a denominator in a fraction in which the numerator is the number of years of remaining useful life. This fraction changes for each year in which the depreciation deduction is computed. For example, in the first year of a 7-year schedule, you have 7 years of useful life remaining. The fraction then becomes 7/28 for the first year (see Figure 7-8). That fraction is then multiplied by the basis *after salvage value has been considered,* to determine the deduction for the year, as in Figure 7-8, which assumes that the personal property in the previous example is new rather than used.

Additional First-Year Depreciation

For Personal Property. Under the *1978 Revenue Act,* depreciable personal property that costs up to $10,000 ($20,000 on a joint return), that is used in a business or for the production of income, and that has a useful life of at least 6 years, is eligible for a first-year "bonus" depreciation deduction of 20 percent of the cost (after considering salvage value). The bonus is first taken on the basis. Then the remaining balance is used to establish a

Years Remaining	Sum of Years Digits Fraction	Fraction Converted to Decimal		Basis (Salvage Considered)[1]		Depreciation Deduction for Year
7	7/28	0.2500	x	5,000	=	$1,250
6	6/28	0.2143	x	5,000	=	1,072
5	5/28	0.1786	x	5,000	=	893
4	4/28	0.1429	x	5,000	=	715
3	3/28	0.1071	x	5,000	=	536
2	2/28	0.0714	x	5,000	=	357
1	1/28	0.0357	x	5,000	=	177[2]
				Total	=	$5,000

[1] Salvage value not subtracted because it is less than 10%, and useful life is more than 3 years.

[2] Because of the cumulative effects of earlier rounding, application of the last sum of years digits fraction would result in a deduction of $178.50, which is reduced by $1.50 on the principle that an asset cannot be reduced below a value of zero.

Figure 7-8.

depreciation schedule in accordance with whichever method you select. Assuming that the personal property in the preceding examples is new furniture, appointments, and appliances, Figure 7-9 shows how it would be depreciated with the bonus deduction under the various methods.

Crossover to Straight-Line

No examination of the common depreciation methods is complete without a discussion of crossover from a *declining balance method* to straight-line depreciation. You may change from SOYD to straight-line,

	Straight-Line	Declining Balance			Sum of Years Digits
		125%	150%	200%	
Basis	5,000	5,000	5,000	5,000	5,000
x First year bonus rate	0.25	0.25	0.25	0.25	0.25
= Bonus deduction	1,250	1,250	1,250	1,250	1,250
Adjusted basis	3,750	3,750	3,750	3,750	3,750
Regular first-year deduction	536	670	804	1,071	938
Total first-year deduction	1,786	1,920	2,054	2,321	2,188
Remaining balance	3,214	3,080	2,946	2,679	2,813
Second-year deduction	536	550	631	765	804
Cumulative deductions	2,322	2,470	2,685	3,086	2,992
Remaining balance	2,678	2,530	2,315	1,913	2,009
Third-year deduction	536	452	496	547	670
Cumulative deductions	2,858	2,922	3,181	3,633	3,662
Remaining balance	2,142	2,078	1,819	1,367	1,339
Fourth-year deductions	536	371	390	390	536
Cumulative deductions	3,394	3,293	3,571	4,023	4,198
Remaining balance	1,606	1,707	1,429	976	804
Fifth-year deduction	536	305	306	279	402
Cumulative deductions	3,930	3,598	3,877	4,302	4,600
Remaining balance	1,070	1,402	1,123	697	402
Sixth-year deduction	536	250	240	199	268
Cumulative deductions	4,466	3,848	4,117	4,501	4,868
Remaining balance	534	1,152	883	499	132
Seventh-year deduction	534	206	189	143	132
Cumulative deductions	5,000	4,054	4,306	4,644	5,000
Lost deductions	0	946	694	356	0

Figure 7-9.

but doing so is not likely to make good business or investment sense. Crossing over to straight-line, on the other hand, is an extension of the declining balance methods—flowing from the mathematical eccentricities built into them.

Figure 7-7 presents a typical problem. After large initial deductions, the declining balance method produces a schedule with lower current deductions than straight-line, which thereafter make the whole declining balance schedule less favorable than straight-line. Figure 7-9 illustrates the problem in greater detail and suggests a cause (and effect) of it: At the projected end of a declining balance depreciation schedule, the method does not produce a zero balance, like both straight-line and SOYD. With schedules of relatively short duration (such as 7 years), the lost depreciation can be greater than the first deduction on a declining balance schedule.

Figure 7-10 translates the numbers in Figure 7-9 into graph form. Whereas straight-line and SOYD methods have definite points on the graph where they begin and end, the declining balance methods never quite seem to touch the horizontal axis. To use an example not shown in the figures, a $5,000 asset is depreciated at 125 percent on a declining balance for 7 years, at which time the adjusted basis (or remaining balance) is $1,262, and the scheduled depreciation deduction is $274. After 50 years, there is still a balance of $405, with a scheduled deduction of $20. After crawling down to a balance of $31 at 100 years with a deduction of $1.56, the truly persistent investor could look forward to a balance that has declined to $0.18 at 200 years, with the prospect of a deduction rounded up to one cent. (The curious reader may note the affinity of such a schedule to a Zen Koan: "How close can you get to something without actually touching it?" One of the answers is that you can always divide the remaining distance and thus never touch.

As Figures 7-9 and 7-10 show, the declining balance methods generate larger than straight-line deductions in the initial years, but only at the cost of lost deductions if you remain on the same schedule. Under IRS rules, you may:

1. Change to *any* method of depreciation with prior IRS approval. (Such a change is regarded as a change in accounting method.)
2. Change from an accelerated method to straight-line, or to a "slower" accelerated rate, without prior IRS approval.
3. Change to a method of depreciating residential rental property (such as a property that was previously "commercial" in use) that is permitted or required for residential rental property, without prior IRS approval.

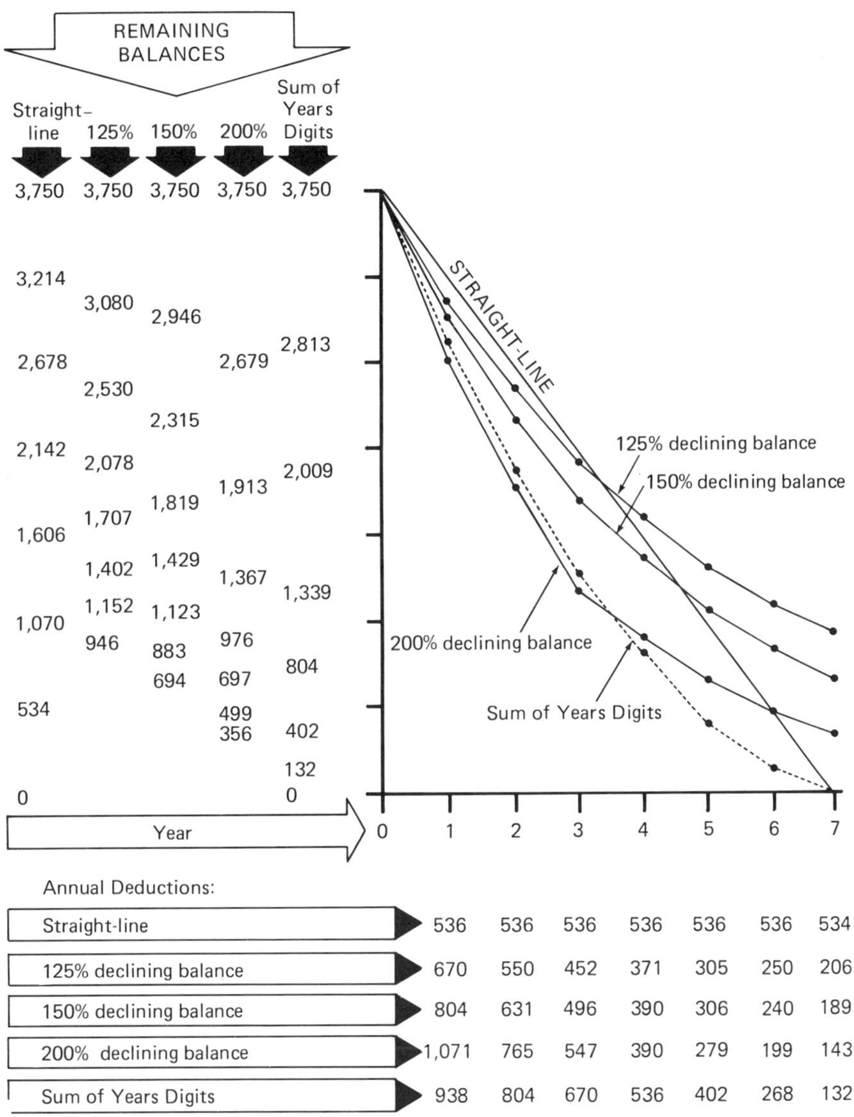

Annual Deductions:	1	2	3	4	5	6	7
Straight-line	536	536	536	536	536	536	534
125% declining balance	670	550	452	371	305	250	206
150% declining balance	804	631	496	390	306	240	189
200% declining balance	1,071	765	547	390	279	199	143
Sum of Years Digits	938	804	670	536	402	268	132

Figure 7-10.

Timing the Crossover. What's the best time to make the crossover? Let's seek out some answers through examples.

Example 1: In Figure 7-7, the investor should change from 150 percent to straight-line after the third deduction of $661 has been taken and before the fourth deduction of $520 is taken, if the investor wants maximum early deductions. In crossing over, a new annual depreciation rate is derived from the remaining years on the depreciation schedule (0.20 for 5 years or 0.25 for 4 years) and applied to the balance remaining before the first deduction is taken under the crossover rate.

Example 2: The switch may also be made after the second-year's deduction of $841 to avoid falling below the $714 straight-line deduction in the third year (with its 125-percent deduction of $661). In this case, the new 5-year annual depreciation rate of 0.20 would be applied to a balance of $3,086 (0.20 × $3,086 = $614) to arrive at the new annual deduction—which turns out to be $47 *lower* than $661.

Example 3: If the switch is made the next year, the new 4-year annual rate of 0.25 is applied to a remaining balance of $2,425 (0.25 × $2,425 = $606)—which turns out $86 *higher* than the $520 deduction scheduled under the 125 percent method.

Example 4: By similar reasoning, you arrive at the seventh year as optimal for a crossover from 125 percent to straight-line for the 25-year depreciation schedule on the building.

These tables and charts help to make the procedure clear. As a practical matter, however, the determination of the crossover point can be accomplished quickly and accurately by the use of a relatively simple calculator routine or program.

8

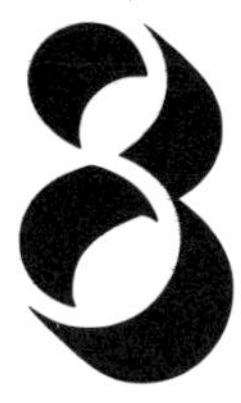

DISPOSITION TAXES AND TAX DEFERRAL

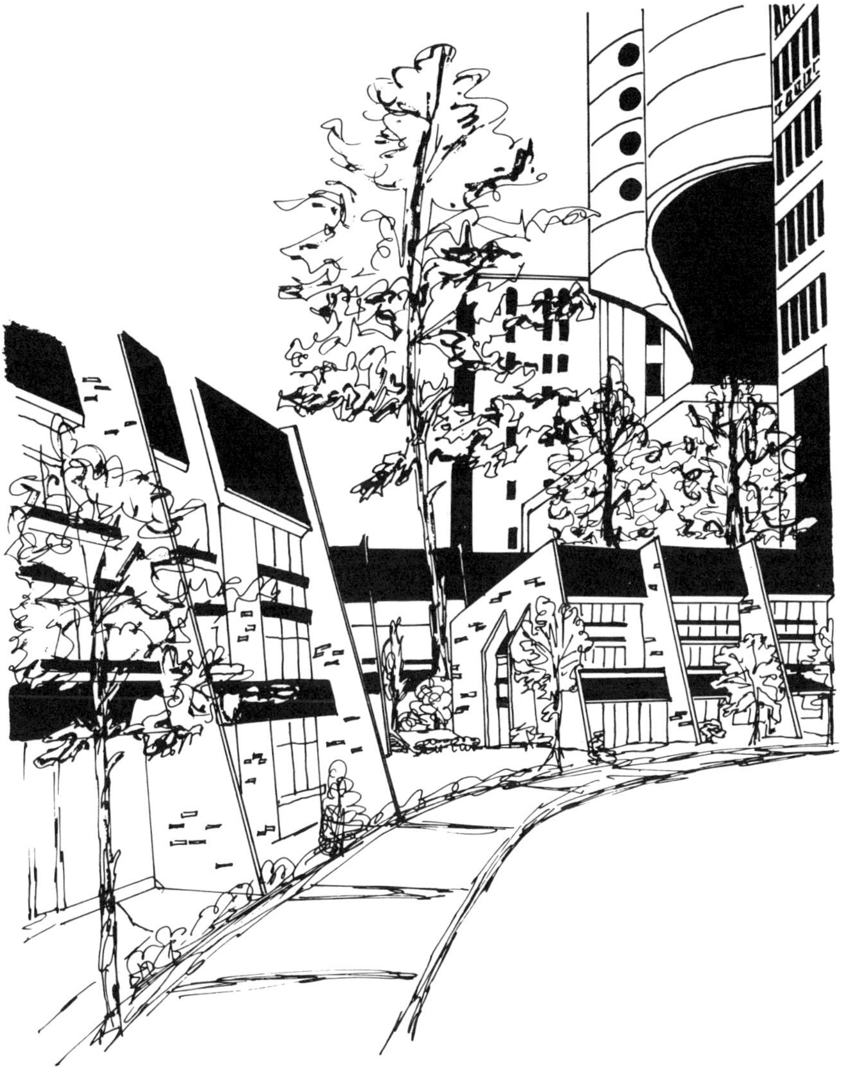

TAX ON DEPRECIATION GAINS

All depreciation deductions, unlike those for interest and operating expenses, produce current tax benefits without current cash outlays. Accelerated depreciation methods are designed to encourage capital investment even more than the ordinary straight-line method by increasing depreciation deductions in the early years of a holding. Those early deductions help to offset the start-up period negative cash flows, if any. Public policy justification for such tax incentives diminishes as the investment matures. Market economy theory, which usually forms the basis for debate about tax laws, encourages the belief that individuals should take their own economic risks.

But nothing is free. Deductions for depreciation aren't complete give-aways. If the risk-taker is successful in a real estate investment and realizes gain through appreciation at the time of disposition, current tax law treats the depreciation deductions as an interest-free loan from other taxpayers, or from "the government." Any gains subsidized by such a loan, the law says, must be shared with those lenders. The method of sharing is called *recapture.*

DEPRECIATION RECAPTURE FOR PERSONAL PROPERTY

Although the tax definition varies slightly from the legal definition, "personal property" generally means such items of interest to the residential real estate investor as furnishings, appointments, and appliances. For purposes of initial tax benefits, personal property is treated more favorably than real property through the first-year additional depreciation bonus. For purposes of recapture, it is treated less favorably.

The rule governing recapture for personal property is relatively simple. Regardless of the depreciation method employed during the holding period, that portion of any gain realized as a result of depreciation deductions is subject to tax as ordinary income (gain × tax bracket = tax), rather than the capital gain rate (40% of gain × tax bracket= tax).

CAPITAL GAIN AND THE ADJUSTED BASIS

The total gain on personal property is computed in the same way as the total gain on real property. It is the amount realized from disposition (after broker commissions and other disposition costs, if any) minus the "adjusted basis." For both types of property, *capital gain* is found by subtracting recaptured depreciation from *total gain*. The adjusted basis at the time of disposition is the original depreciable value minus any depreciation that has accumulated over the holding period and any other items that have reduced the basis in real estate investments. Recognized losses on involuntary conversions, as well as casualty losses not covered by insurance, would increase the basis. *Why* is capital gain computed this way? The answer can be presented in these eight steps:

1. The tax "basis" is the initial *cost* of the investment, including both the acquisition price and associated entry costs (legal and recording fees, and so on).
2. The difference between what you *pay* for an asset (the cost, or basis) and what you *receive* for it upon disposition is obviously a profit or gain if the cash return is greater than the outlay.

3. Anything that makes the capital *outlay* greater (in relation to the cash return) *reduces gain* or profit.
4. Anything that makes the capital *outlay lower* relative to the cash return *increases gain* or profit.
5. Depreciation deductions *lower the outlay,* or make the "adjusted basis" lower, because they are *returns of capital invested,* paid back annually to the investor at ordinary income tax rates (depreciation deduction × tax bracket = cash benefit or return).
6. Depreciation deductions thereby *increase gain* by reducing the adjusted basis.
7. Having been received by the investor at the ordinary income rates, which are favorable for deductions, depreciation deductions subject to recapture are taxed at those same rates when disposition produces a gain.
8. If disposition produces no gain (that is, no cash return above the adjusted basis), there is no taxable gain.

DEPRECIATION RECAPTURE FOR REAL PROPERTY

The rules for tax on recaptured depreciation of real property tightened up progressively during the decade of tax reform culminating in the *Revenue Act of 1978.* Thereafter, the general rule is that 100 percent of the capital gain resulting from the *accelerated portion* of the cumulative depreciation deductions[1] is subject to taxation at ordinary income rates. The only exception that remained intact was certain low-cost housing. For eligible properties of this sort, the accelerated portion subject to tax on recapture is 100 percent *minus* 1 percent for each full month the property is held in excess of 100 months (8⅓ years). So if the investor holds eligible property for 15 years (180 months), only 20 percent of the accelerated portion of the cumulative depreciation deductions is subject to tax on recapture. Hence the main application is to new subsidized housing with long depreciation schedules.

[1]That is, the portion in excess of what would have resulted from a straight-line depreciation schedule.

COMPUTING DISPOSITION TAXES

Upon disposition of an income-producing investment property—at the time that capital gain is realized—four types of income taxes must be accounted for, taxed, or deferred:

1. *Depreciation recapture tax on real property: The full amount of the accelerated portion* (except for low-cost housing) of cumulative depreciation deductions is taxed at the taxpayer's ordinary income rate.
2. *Depreciation recapture tax on personal property:* The full amount of *both straight-line and accelerated cumulative depreciation* deductions is taxed at the taxpayer's ordinary income rate.
3. *Capital gains tax on real property:* Forty percent of any gain over the amount on which depreciation recapture tax is payable is taxed at the taxpayer's ordinary income rate.
4. *Capital gains tax on personal property.* Same as for real property.

Figures 8-1 and 8-2 use basic numbers from previous examples to show the computation of the four types of tax upon fifth-year disposition. Figure 8-1 assumes that the real property portion has appreciated to a market value of $81,000 and that the personal property has declined in value to $2,000. The interrelationships among the applicable rules can be put into perspective by considering what each "table" shows in this figure:

Table A—Calculating Excess Depreciation. Personal property, depreciated over 5 years at either 125-percent or 150-percent declining balance, shows cumulative depreciation deductions in excess of what they would be on a straight-line method basis from the beginning. In the case of the real property, that "excess" depreciation is used for computing the tax on recaptured capital gain in Table E.

Table B—Calculating the Amount Realized. Disposition costs include such items as brokerage, legal, recording fees, and other direct costs of disposition.

Table C—Arriving at the Adjusted Basis. Keep two points in mind when considering the adjusted basis at the time of disposition:

Line	Computation	Total	Real Property	Personal Property
	Table A			
1	Cumulative depreciation deductions (actual)	14,845	11,060	3,785
2	– Depreciation deductions (straight-line method)	13,348	9,778	3,570
3	= "Excess" depreciation	1,497	1,282	215
	Table B			
4	Disposition price	83,000	81,000	2,000
5	– Disposition costs	5,900	5,800	100
6	= Amount realized	77,100	75,200	1,900
	Table C			
7	Purchase price plus investment costs	53,890	48,890	5,000
8	– Cumulative depreciation deductions	14,845	11,060	3,785
9	= Adjusted basis	39,045	37,830	1,215
	Table D			
10	Amount realized	77,100	75,200	1,900
11	– Adjusted basis	39,045	37,830	1,215
12	= Total gain (or loss)	38,255	37,370	685
	Table E			
13	Depreciation recapture	1,967	1,282	685
14	x Ordinary income tax rate[1]	0.40	0.40	0.40
15	= Tax on recaptured depreciation	787	513	274
	Table F			
16	Portion of gain taxable at capital gains rate	36,088	36,088	0
17	x Ordinary income tax rate x 40%	0.16	0.16	–
18	= Capital gains tax	5,774	5,774	–
	Table G			
19	Tax on recaptured depreciation	787	513	274
20	+ Capital gains tax	5,774	5,774	–
21	= Total income tax on disposition	6,561	6,287	274

[1] It is assumed here that the investor is in the 40% tax bracket.

Figure 8-1.

1. It remains the same regardless of the sale or other disposition price; and
2. It is by definition the amount by which depreciation deductions have reduced the original depreciable value.

Table D—Computing Capital Gain or Loss. The personal property has produced a capital gain in spite of the fact that the amount realized on disposition ($1,900) is $3,100 *less* than the original cost basis ($5,000). All the gain comes from depreciation deductions.

Table E—Computing Tax on Recaptured Depreciation. Only the accelerated portion, or "excess," of depreciation (from Table A) is taxable at the taxpayer's ordinary rate. The full amount of the excess depreciation shown for the real property is taxable at that rate.

Table F—Figuring Capital Gains Tax. The same amount (capital gain) is not taxed twice. Thus the portion of the gain that is already taxed as

Disposition price, personal property	500	10,000
– Disposition costs	50	1,000
= Amount realized	450	9,000
– Adjusted basis	1,215	1,215
= Total gain (or loss)	–765[1]	7,785

Depreciation recapture	0	3,785[2]
x Ordinary income tax rate	—	0.40
= Tax on recaptured depreciation	—	1,514

Portion of gain taxable at capital gains rate	0	4,000
x Ordinary income tax rate x 40%	—	0.16
= Capital gains tax	—	640

Tax on recaptured depreciation	—	1,514
+ Capital gains tax	—	640
= Total income tax on disposition	—	2,154

[1]Under tax rules effective beginning with the 1978 tax year 50% of net long-term capital losses may be deducted from ordinary income, up to a maximum of $3,000 in a year, if the taxpayer's capital losses exceed capital gains. Allowable deductions above that annual maximum may be carried over into subsequent years. The same rules apply to short-term capital losses, except that the full loss is deductible.

[2]No more than the full amount of depreciation deductions is subject to depreciation recapture tax.

Figure 8-2.

recaptured depreciation (in Table E) is subtracted from the total gain to determine which portion is to be taxed at the capital gains rate: for the real property, \$37,370 − \$1,282 = \$36,088; for the personal property, \$685 − \$685 = 0. In the latter case, the full amount of the gain has come from depreciation and is already taxed as recaptured depreciation in Table E. Note that the capital gains tax can be computed in two ways:

1. First multiply the gain by 0.40, and then multiply the result by the taxpayer's ordinary rate: for example, \$36,088 × 0.40 = \$14,435 × 0.40 = \$5,774.
2. Multiply the ordinary rate by 0.40, as in Table F: for example, 0.40 × 0.40 = 0.16.

Table G—Total Tax This table simply totals the taxes involved in this case.

Figure 8-2 shows the effects of changing the disposition price of the personal property portion of the transaction first to \$500 and then to \$10,000. In the first case, no tax is payable because there is no capital gain. In the latter, the portion of the gain beyond the amount on which depreciation recapture is payable is shown to be taxable at the capital gains rate.

DISPOSITION TAX DEFERRAL

In some financial planning situations, it makes sense for the investor to dispose of a property so that the payment of disposition taxes is deferred until a later time. However, since both the individual's needs and the potential "side effects" are so variable, you can't make a general statement of this sort "stick" in every case. For those who feel that tax deferral is desirable, there are three common methods:

1. a *tax-deferred exchange,* by which like property and other goods or services are exchanged *in lieu* of cash, for all or part of the disposition price;
2. *sale-and-leaseback,* a form of tax deferral exchange by which the seller immediately enters into a lease of 30 years or more with the new owner; or
3. *installment sale,* by which a portion of the sale price is received directly by the seller from the buyer in no fewer than 2 tax years.

Tax-Deferred Exchange

As a starting point, let's imagine that two properties are identical in age, investment use, cash flow position, tax structure, and market value. These two properties get together to trade their respective owners and adjusted bases. In such a hypothetical situation, nothing with immediate tax consequences has occurred. Each property continues its business activities, producing its same patterns of income, expenses, and deductions. But it does so for a new owner, and it carries along a new adjusted basis toward some eventual transfer involving the payment of taxes.

In real life, of course, an exchange does not occur in quite that manner. Instead, *people* get together and negotiate exchanges involving the transfer of properties that are similar but not identical. Entering into negotiations are such considerations as cash, dissimilar property, debt relief, and tax benefits. Eventually the two owners arrive at what they consider to be a mutually advantageous trade. Ordinarily part of the transaction is tax-free and part not. Here are the basic rules applicable to such trades:

1. Although more than two parties may be involved in an exchange transaction, the protection of tax-deferred status requires that the specific exchanges occur directly between principals.
2. No taxes are paid at the time of transfer on that portion of the transaction that involves the exchange of "like property," regardless of the difference in its respective market value.
3. On the portion of the transaction that involves the payment of *cash,* if any, the party receiving it realizes a taxable capital gain in that amount. Since unlike property is called "boot," cash is sometimes also referred to as boot.
4. On the portion of the transaction that involves the exchange of *unlike property* (boot), its *fair market value* is translated into monetary terms and treated like cash as a taxable capital gain by the party receiving it.
5. On the portion of the transaction that involves *cash payments for unlike property,* the tax treatment is as for a separate transaction: Taxable capital gains and losses, if any, for the respective parties are computed on the differences between the adjusted bases and the fair market values of the property in question.
6. On the portion of the transaction that involves an exchange of *mortgage debt obligations,* only the *difference between the respective mortgage amounts* is treated as taxable gain to the party favored by the difference.

7. Like disposition by sale, all direct transaction costs (such as brokerage, legal, recording and other fees and expenses) reduce net transaction proceeds and thereby the taxable gain.
8. The parties retain the adjusted bases and remaining depreciation deductions on the property they give away, subject to the effects of boot in the transaction. The procedure is called "substituted basis."

Like Property. What constitutes "like" property? The like properties traded and received in tax-deferred exchanges must both be held either for business or trade or as investments. Stock in trade and property held in inventory for resale, however, do not qualify. In the case of personal property, "likeness" is sometimes rather narrowly defined. For example, a truck may be traded for a machine used in business. So can stocks in the same corporation be exchanged for each other or, in the case of reorganizations, for those of another corporation—or even for U.S. bonds, insurance policies, or other types of securities. But livestock of different sexes, for example, are not considered to be of "like kind."

In contrast, almost any kind of real property held for business or investment can be traded tax-free for any other real property so held—but no personal property. For instance, an apartment may be swapped for an office building or for a tract of unimproved land. A leasehold of 30 years or more for business or investment is also treated by the IRS as "like kind" to other real estate.

Effects of an Exchange on Basis. In an exchange of only like property, each party retains the basis of the property being given up, adding on (as with a sale) disposition costs. If one of the parties receives boot in the form of cash as part of the consideration for the property given up, that payment constitutes a capital gain. It is "recognized" (that is, taxable) as such and must be reported. It is then *added to the basis of the new property* so that it is not taxed again as a capital gain when the property is eventually sold. In the case of boot in the form of *unlike property,* its fair market value applies.

At this point, you must distinguish between gains or losses that are *indicated* or *realized* and those that are *recognized* or *taxable. Indicated* gains or losses are not paid or deducted currently. Such a gain or loss is simply the difference between the market value and the adjusted basis, with transaction costs also deducted. The whole point of the tax-free portion of a property exchange is that neither party's indicated gain is paid at the time of the exchange and that neither party's indicated *loss,* if any, can be deducted. Both indicated gains and indicated losses are, in effect, carried over to each party's new property, which assumes the adjusted basis of the old property. *Recognized* gains and losses are payable or deductible currently. Gains that come about from cash or boot in an otherwise tax-free property exchange fall into that category.

Once the tax-free exchange is completed, each party's cash flows, as affected by the tax consequences of the exchange, become the other's. The present and projected future values of those cash flows are then studied separately from the immediate effects of the exchange.

Key Tax-Deferred Exchange Computations. Figure 8-3 presents a basic analysis of a hypothetical property exchange that is partly tax-free, except that cash is paid by investor A to investor B. Property 1 is based on the figures from previous examples with some additional assumptions, as indicated. (You need not, however, refer to earlier figures for the computations in Figure 8-3.) Whereas property 1 is assumed to be a furnished rental townhouse, property 2 is a furnished rental condominium unit. The unlike property consists of the furnishings and appointments.

When you look over Figure 8-3, don't despair if the dynamics seem a challenge to understand. After all, the tax consequences of four distinct transactions are involved: Each investor acquires more than one kind of property with more than one kind of tax treatment, and each disposes of a similar package. Each item that is a plus to one party shows up in some way as a minus to the other. The mathematics of all these transactions is sometimes elusively simple. As Figure 8-3 shows, the whole process is no more than a matter of adding and subtracting values to and from each other. In fact, such additions and subtractions define most terms: For example, "equity" is only the market value minus loan balance; "indicated capital gain" is the market value minus adjusted basis, minus transaction costs; and so on.

All these effects are summarized by a review of the four "tables" in Figure 8-3:

Table A shows the standard computation for equity. The difference (in this case, $8,000) determines what payments in cash, boot, or net mortgage relief must be made to equalize the equities.

Table B applies directly only to the properties traded off. The adjusted bases and transaction costs, however, are added together and carried forth as the adjusted bases for the respective parties' *acquired* properties.

Table C shows two key factors:

1. adjustments needed to equalize the equities, and
2. the taxable capital gains resulting from that for each party.

Investor A *receives* net mortgage relief of $18,000 (the difference between mortgage balances in Table A) and $1,200 in boot for a total value

	Investor A		Investor B	
	Property 1 Traded Off	Property 2 Acquired	Property 1 Acquired	Property 2 Traded Off
Table A				
Market value	81,000	55,000	81,000	55,000
– Mortgage balance	50,000	32,000	50,000	32,000
= Equity	31,000	23,000	31,000	23,000
Table B				
Market value	81,000	—	—	55,000
– Adjusted basis	37,830	—	—	30,000
– Transaction costs[1]	4,500	—	—	3,100
= Indicated capital gain[2]	38,670	—	—	21,900
Table C				
Cash received	0	—	—	11,200
– Cash paid	11,200	—	—	0
+ Mortgage relief	18,000	—	—	0
– Mortgage liability	0	—	—	18,000
+ Other boot received	1,200	—	—	2,000
– Other boot paid	2,000	—	—	1,200
– Transaction costs	4,500	—	—	3,100
= Recognized capital gain[3]	1,500	—	—	9,100
Table D				
Adjusted basis carried over	—	42,330	33,100	—
+ Recognized gain[4]	—	1,500	0	—
– Recognized loss[5]	—	0	0	—
= Adjusted basis after exchange	—	43,830	33,100	—

[1]Added to adjusted basis carried over, thereby reducing future capital gain.
[2]This is gain on which party trading off avoids current capital gains tax. No loss can be recognized in this part of the transaction.
[3]Currently payable capital gains tax. "Negative gain" does not create deductible loss.
[4,5]Added to or subtracted from basis to avoid double taxation or deduction.

Figure 8-3.

of $19,200. That relief is offset by the $8,000 difference in equity (Table A), leaving a balance of $11,200 in investor A's favor.

Investor B starts with $18,000 *transferred* as net mortgage relief to A, plus $1,200 *in favor of A*. That transfer is offset by $2,000 in boot, plus $8,000 in equity, leaving investor B to equalize the equities. The rest of the table reflects the capital gains tax consequences: little for A ($1,500 × 0.16 = $240) assuming the 40-percent tax bracket, and none for B.

Table D adds up the pluses and minuses to arrive at the adjusted basis that each investor has with the new property. Each starts with the adjusted basis of the respective old property, plus his or her own transaction costs for the exchange. Any capital gain recognized (taxed) is added to that amount. Recognized uninsured casualty and other losses (which would be deducted) are subtracted. The new adjusted bases are the values for future depreciation deductions and capital gains and losses on the property acquired.

Sale-and-Leaseback

In a sale-and-leaseback arrangement, the owner sells property and immediately leases it back from the new owner. The seller–lessee is often a corporation that needs the cash or that can do better with the sales proceeds than it can do with the property itself. If the lease is for 30 years or more, the IRS treats the leasehold equivalent to ownership of the property itself. Hence the whole transaction would be considered a sale. The following table summarizes what the parties receive:

Seller–Lessee	***Buyer–Lessor***
Cash	Property ownership
Relief of mortgage debt	Long-term lease
Continued long-term use of property	Interest and depreciation deductions
Deductions of rent expenses at ordinary income rate	Appreciation and residual interests at end of term

From the standpoint of the seller, the blessings of the sale-and-leaseback are mixed. If a capital gain is recognized through the receipt of cash, it is taxable. If a loss is sustained on the sale (that is, if the amount realized is less than adjusted basis), it is not deductible, due to its tax deferred status. The main advantage is usually the cash. But the seller should weigh:

1. the trade-off between, on one hand, the existing interest and depreciation deductions plus future disposition returns and, on the other hand, the rental expense deductions without residual rights;
2. additional tax considerations concerning options to renew the lease or to repurchase the property; and

3. to the extent that sale-and-leaseback is a method of raising capital, current loan-to-value ratios, interest rates, and other money market conditions. Is there a better way?

Installment Sales

The installment sale is a more common method for the small investor to defer payment of capital gains taxes. In an installment sale, the seller enters into an agreement *directly with the buyer* to receive *no more than 30 percent of the sale price in the first year,* with *payments of principal made in at least two tax years.* If a sale is consummated under such terms, the seller can defer payment of capital gains taxes over the years during which the installment payments are scheduled.

To secure such tax-deferred treatment, you have to follow the rules carefully, of which the "30-percent rule" is the most troublesome. In fact, the 30-percent rule is so central to installment sales, that the main question is whether the sale can be kept within the 30-percent rule. Any of the following items can be added to amounts received to increase the total beyond 30 percent:

- *Payments other than by cash:* As in the case of boot in a tax-free exchange, such payments are credited at their fair market value.
- *Principal paid off on existing loan.*
- *Any prepayments of principal due in the future,* on a loan taken back by seller.
- *The assumption of payments to third parties,* such as liens, taxes, and expenses related to the property, if called for in the sales contract.
- *A mortgage assumption in excess of the seller's adjusted basis:* The amount by which an assumed mortgage exceeds the adjusted basis (including disposition costs) is treated as a first-year payment.
- *Assumption of mortgage with third party,* if placed on property in year of sale to avoid 30-percent rule.
- *Cancellation of existing debt* owed to buyer by seller, if in contract terms.

Interest payments under an installment sale are *not* considered to be payments under the 30-percent rule, since they are normally treated as income. However, if the installment sale is financed with a loan by the seller to the buyer, it may have the effect of bringing payments above 30 percent if the contract or note call for no interest or for interest at a rate lower than 6-percent simple interest.

In such a case, IRS imputes a rate of 7 percent. In effect, the IRS *reduces the sale price* by the total amount of the interest payments due under the loan on a 7-percent amortization schedule.

> *Example:* The seller grants the buyer an interest-free, 3-year installment loan of $56,700 (70 percent of $81,000) with monthly payments plus a first-year payment of $24,300. (There is no existing mortgage.) This loan seems to fall within the 30-percent rule. If, however, the IRS imputes 7-percent interest, the resultant $6,326 in interest charges over the period would reduce the sale price to $74,674. The first-year payment of $24,300 would then be 32.5 percent of that amount, which knocks it out of coverage by the 30-percent rule. So the seller must either charge interest of at least 6 percent, *or* increase the loan amount to compensate for IRS-imputed interest of 7 percent per year, *or* take less cash.

Higher loan balances, relative to the market values, obviously make it more difficult for the sale to qualify. In the case of property 1 in Figure 8-3, for example, the buyer's paying off of the loan balance of $50,000 would disqualify the transaction, because that amount is 61.7 percent (well over 30 percent) of $81,000. If the same loan were *assumed* by the buyer, the difference between the loan amount and the adjusted basis ($50,000 − 37,370 = $12,630, using the basis from Figure 8-4) must be added to the first year's payment *and* added to the contract price for the purpose of computing the deferred capital gains tax, as we will explain. The effects of the assumption, therefore, would be to reduce the cash that the buyer could receive in the first year from $24,300 (30 percent of $81,000) by $12,630 to $11,670, along with the amounts subject to capital gains tax.

	Property 1	Property 2
Sale price	81,000	55,000
Existing loan balance	50,000	32,000
Equity	31,000	23,000
Excess of assumed mortgage over adjusted basis[1]	12,630	0
Contract price	43,630	23,000
Capital gain[2]	37,370	21,900
÷ Contract price	43,630	23,000
= Gain-to-equity ratio	0.8565	0.9522

[1,2] Separately computed for purposes of this example.

Figure 8-4.

Second Mortgage: $19,330 36 Months @ 10% Interest per Annum	First Year	Second Year	Third Year	Fourth Year
Payments received	11,670	7,704	7,705	7,704
Payments to principal	11,670	5,691	6,413	7,226
x Gain-to-equity ratio	0.8565	0.8565	0.8565	0.8565
= Amount subject to capital gains tax	9,995	4,874	5,493	6,189
x Capital gains tax rate x 0.40	0.16	0.16	0.16	0.16
= Capital gains tax	1,599	780	878	990
Payments to interest	0	2,013	1,292	478
x Investor's ordinary income tax rate	0.40	0.40	0.40	0.40
= Ordinary income tax	0	805	517	191
Cumulative capital gains tax	1,599	2,379	3,257	4,247
+ Cumulative ordinary income tax	0	805	1,322	1,513
= Cumulative total income tax	1,599	3,184	4,579	5,760
Cumulative after-tax cash return from regular sale[1]	18,913	18,913	18,913	18,913
Cumulative after-tax cash return from installment sale[2]	4,271	10,390	16,700	23,223

[1]Equity interest – Disposition costs – Total tax on disposition ($31,000 – $5,800 – $6,287 = $18,913).

[2]First year: Payments received – Disposition costs – Capital gains tax ($11,670 – $5,800 – $1,599 = $4,271); subsequent years: Annual payments – Capital gains – Ordinary taxes paid.

Figure 8-5.

Installment Payments of Gains Tax

The gain-to-equity ratio determines the principal portion of each installment payment—that is, the portion subject to the capital gains tax. This ratio is derived by dividing the seller's capital gain by the contract price. Except in the case where the remaining balance of an assumed loan is higher than the seller's adjusted basis, the "contract price" is simply the equity interest—sales price minus the existing loan balance.

Figure 8-4 shows the gain-to-equity ratios for the two properties in question. (The gains from either or both of the properties in this figure could be given installment sale treatment since tax-free exchange proceeds are also eligible.) To continue with Property 1, however, the next step after determining how much cash can be received in the first year ($11,670) and the gain-to-equity ratio (0.8565) is to apply the ratio to the *principal* portion of installment payments—to determine the annual amount subject to the capital gains tax. The entire *interest* portion is subject to tax at the ordinary income rate.

In this case, the amount that the seller receives in payments to principal after the first year is $19,330 (equity of $31,000 − first-year payment of $11,670). For this example we assume that the seller is in the 40-percent income tax bracket, and that a 3-year second mortgage has been negotiated at 12-percent interest per annum, to be paid in 36 equal payments of $642 each. (Computations of the amortization schedule are not shown here.) Figure 8–5 shows the allocations to principal, interest, and income taxes annually and cumulatively.

TWENTY INVESTOR SHORTCUTS ON A HANDHELD CALCULATOR

THE LOW COST OF "AUTOMATION"

Today handheld calculators that cost about the same as a stop at the gasoline pump boast the ability to:

1. add;
2. subtract;
3. multiply;
4. divide;
5. use these four basic functions in built-in computer-style programs for numerous algebraic and trigonometric functions;
6. employ those functions, in turn, in specialized programs for such fields as statistics, science, engineering, and finance for which the particular calculator is designed; and
7. store and recall intermediate results for use from one computation to another.

For the approximate cost of a family shopping visit to the supermarket, you can purchase a calculator–computer that can be programmed for elaborate, multi-step computations in a wide range of practical applications. These applications include iterative procedures such as finding the internal rate of return by selecting, through trial and error, an interest rate that equates numerous and variable cash flows over a sometimes lengthy period of time to an investment outlay.

Inexpensive electronic hardware with such capabilities has come about much more rapidly than the concomitant "software" *programs,* which you need to use them most effectively. Yet these programs, in turn, have been developed much more rapidly than potential users have come to understand the tools at their disposal and learned to put them to practical use.

For the small investor, for the realtor, and for other real estate professionals, the implications of all these developments are far-reaching. Printed tables, which saved so much time when pencil and paper calculations were the alternative, are now just cumbersome time-killers if you are figuring PITI, balloon payments, remaining balances, present and future values, and other real estate numbers. Nowadays you can learn sophisticated analytical procedures and quickly apply them to subject investment properties with far greater accuracy and in less time than you could with the "shortcuts" of the past. Programs that, in recent years, were accessible only through computer terminals employed by specialists in commercial real estate investment analysis can now be carried around in the hip pocket of anyone who can afford to gas up a car and go shopping at the supermarket.

This chapter deals with the calculators that now have—or that soon will have—the capability to run such programs. No particular brand or make of calculator is recommended. Even if such recommendations were appropriate for a book of this nature, the variety of products and rate of technological advancement in the field would require another book to make the recommendations intelligible. Our limited purpose is to suggest some practical applications of this growing technology to problems of interest to the small investor.

TWO KINDS OF LOGIC

A handheld calculator can offer one or the other of two basic systems of logic, by which problems are keystroked or "punched." The more common one is the *algebraic method.* In this method of entry, problems are solved through the traditional sequences of numbers and functions that most of us learned in school: for example, 2[+]2[=]**4**; 0.02[×]200[=]**4**; 4[÷]0.02[=]**200**;

etc. (For purposes of notation, let's say that a number in roman type (such as 2) has to be entered, while a boldface number (such as **4**) indicates a result.) The main advantage in this method of entry is its familiarity. Problems are entered pretty much as most people would work them out on paper.

Less common, but easy to learn and considerably more efficient to use, is the so-called *RPN method* of entry. Based on a system of mathematical notation devised by a Pole in the early 1950s, RPN logic is sometimes referred to as "reverse Polish notation." This method is characterized primarily by the presence of an [ENTER] key and the absence of an [=] key. The first number in a two-number or chain calculation is simply punched in, then separated from subsequent numbers by hitting the [ENTER] key. The desired function key [+, −, ×, ÷], instead of [=], is hit after each subsequent number to arrive at a result: for example, 2[ENTER] 2[+]**4**; 0.02[ENTER]200[×]**4** 4[ENTER]0.02[−]**200**; and so on. The main advantage in this method of entry is that it eliminates the need for many extra steps in more elaborate calculations, thereby speeding up the process and reducing the risk of error. Some of the routines presented in this chapter may illustrate this point.

Beyond differences in the basic method of entry, most makes and models bear many similarities to one another in their key sysmbols and sequences. Each manufacturer also tends to maintain still greater consistency from one model of its own to the next. Accommodating the habits and expectations of users sometimes makes more sense than making minor "objective" improvements piecemeal with each new product.

The shortcuts and basic investment analysis routines in this chapter are presented generally in the order in which they occur when you examine investment property alternatives. The sequence progresses from down payment at acquisition to IRR and FMRR upon sale or other disposition. By and large, the computations move from the simple to the more complicated. The simplest can be worked out on any four-function (add, subtract, multiply, divide) calculator. As the routines become more advanced, the efficiencies of using calculators with financial programs and programmability become increasingly significant . . . and increasingly apparent.

Details in routine vary so much from one make and model to the next, that treating each variation separately is just not practicable. The most basic and common approaches have been selected for both the algebraic and RPN methods. In many cases the routines are "ready" enough to apply directly to a problem. In some cases you might have to adjust for the operating characteristics of a particular calculator. If you are already accustomed to the unit in question, you can often do so without even referring to an owner's manual. Otherwise, using the manual, you should be able to match your equipment easily to any problem within its range of operations.

Here are the twenty "shortcuts":

1. DOWN PAYMENT

VA Loans. The most simple to compute of the three basic types of down payment is for a VA loan. It is either zero or another difference between the sales price and the maximum VA loan allowed on the property by a lender. (See Figure 9-1.)

Conventional Loan. Calculating a down payment for a conventional loan is just as easy. The percentage of the down payment is dictated by the lender. Simply multiply it against the sale price. After the down payment is subtracted from the sale price, the balance is the loan amount. (See Figure 9-2.)

FHA Loans. FHA down payments, with the settlement fold-in feature, are a little more involved. First, determine a "total acquisition

Term	Algebraic		RPN	
	Key	Example	Key	Example
Sale price		105,000		105,000
Maximum loan[1]	[−]	100,000	[ENTER]	100,000
Down payment	[=]	5,000*[2]	[−]	5,000*

[1]With $25,000 VA loan eligibility and 75% loan-to-value ratio.

[2]Note: Asterisk * indicates a result. Numbers without asterisks are to be punched in.

Figure 9-1. Minimum VA Down Payment.

Term	Algebraic		RPN	
	Key	Example	Key	Example
Sale price		58,000		58,000
Percentage down	[−]	20	[ENTER]	20
Down payment	[%]	11,600*	[%]	11,600*
Loan amount	[=]	46,400*	[−]	46,400*

Figure 9-2. Conventional Down Payment.

cost" by adding the closing costs that are allowable for the purposes of the formula, which are taken from a table published by FHA for the particular area. Next, establish the maximum FHA loan by subtracting from the total acquisition cost the "normal" FHA down payment based on this formula: 3 percent on the first $25,000 of sale price, 5 percent on the amount above $25,000 to the maximum loan amount. Finally, subtract that loan amount from the sales price to determine the required down payment. The overall effect of this formula is to permit the buyer to finance some or all of the buyer's closing costs. Since figures in the formula are revised periodically, check the details before using these routines directly. (See Figure 9-3.)

Term	Algebraic		RPN	
	Key	Example	Key	Example
Sale Price		58,000		58,000
First $25,000	[−]	25,000	[ENTER]	25,000
Amount on which 5% down is paid	[=]	33,000*	[−]	33,000*
Five percent	[x]	0.05		5
5% down portion	[=]	1,650*	[%]	1,650*
	[STO] [1]		[STO] [1]	
First $25,000		25,000		25,000
Three percent	[x]	0.03	[ENTER]	3
3% down portion	[=]	750*	[%]	750*
5% down portion	[+] [RCL] [1]	1,650*	[RCL] [1]	1,650*
Down payment	[=]	2,400*	[+]	2,400*

(a)

Term	Algebraic		RPN	
	Key	Example	Key	Example
Sale price		58,000		58,000
Closing cost allowance	[+]	1,350	[ENTER]	1,350
Total acquisition cost	[=]	59,350*	[+]	59,350*
FHA-formula down payment[1]	[−]	2,500		2,500
Maximum FHA loan	[=]	56,850*	[−]	56,850*
Sale price	[−]	58,000		58,000
	[X⇌Y]	56,850*	[X⇌Y]	56,850*
Down payment	[=]	1,150*	[−]	1,150*

(b)

[1] Same routine as in Figure 9-3(a), applied to total acquisition cost of 59,350. Resulting down payment is rounded up to the nearest $50.

Figure 9-3. (a) FHA Down Payment, No Fold-In. (b) FHA Down Payment, with Fold-In.

2. BUYER'S SETTLEMENT COSTS

Besides the necessary down payment, settlement costs are the next concern in the initial capital investment. When running quick but accurate analyses of numerous investment property alternatives, you have to make reasonably close estimates of those costs. But even if you are working with a computer terminal or a calculator, the time it takes to use the itemized settlement cost sheets found in every real estate office renders the procedure impracticable. Therefore, once you understand the specific items that constitute settlement costs, itemizing them for each analysis is wastefully redundant. Using constants or multipliers makes much more sense. Properly derived, they are every bit as accurate as the itemized estimates, but they work in a fraction of the time.

Despite many variations in fees, taxes, and other settlement charges from one jurisdiction to another, the basic cost structure remains essentially the same. There are three kinds of costs:

1. those based on a percentage of the sales price—deed recordation, fire insurance and property tax escrows, and so on;
2. those based on a percentage of the loan amount—title insurance, loan placement fees, prepaid private mortgage insurance, recordation of trust of mortgage documents, initial loan interest payments, and the like;
3. flat rate items—fixed or estimated fees for survey, money market placement charges, FHA/VA assumption fee, recordation taxes, legal fees, and so on.

These three groups of costs can be pieced together easily into three constants, which can then be applied to figures from each transaction to estimate the buyer's settlement costs quickly. At least six sets of constants should be on hand:

- three for conventional loans at 5, 10, and 20 percent down,
- one each for FHA and VA loans with the minimum down payment, and
- one for assumptions.

Figure 9-4 is an example of a form used in one area for estimating purchaser settlement costs. Let's apply a hypothetical tax rate of $1.54 per $100 of assessed value, where the assessed value is 100 percent of market value. Divide the decimal figure of 0.0154 (annual rate) by 6 (0.0154 ÷ 6 = 0.0026). The result (0.0026) is a constant that is applicable to the sale price

Address: ______________________________

____

Sales Price: ______________________

		Type of Loan					
		Conventional			FHA (Minimum Down)	VA (Minimum Down)	Assumption ☐ Conventional ☐ FHA/VA
		5% Down	10% Down	20% Down			
Percentage of sales price:[1] Sales price x 0.0045 →							
% of Loan[2]	5% Down: Loan x 0.03 →		—	—	—	—	—
	10% Down: Loan x 0.025 →	—		—	—	—	—
	20% Down: Loan x 0.020 →	—	—		—	—	—
	FHA/VA: Loan x 0.020 →	—	—	—			—
Conventional Assumption: Add 1% of loan amount or actual fee, if known →		—	—	—	—	—	
Two-month tax escrow: annual tax amount ÷ 6 →							
Flat rate items[3] →		$350	$350	$350	$275	$275	$250
Subtotal							
Deductions							
Total							

[1] Includes deed recordation, one year's fire insurance, and two-month fire escrow.

[2] Loan costs: title insurance, placement fee prepaid PMI, trust recordation, and first (partial) interest payment.

[3] Includes fixed or estimated fees for survey, money market placement, FHA/VA assumption, recording, tax, and legal.

Figure 9-4. Purchaser's Settlement Cost Estimates.

Term	Algebraic		RPN	
	Key	Example	Key	Example
Sale price		58,000		58,000
Sale price constant	[x]	0.0071	[ENTER]	0.0071
Settlement costs based on sale price	[=]	412*	[x]	412*
	[STO] [1]		[STO] [1]	
Loan amount (20% down payment)		46,400		46,400
Loan amount constant	[x]	0.02	[ENTER]	0.02
Settlement costs based on loan amount	[=]	928*	[x]	928*
	[+][RCL][1]	412*	[RCL] [1]	412*
Settlement costs based on sale price and loan amount	[=]	1,340*	[+]	1,340*
Flat rate items	[+]	350		350
Total settlement costs	[=]	1,690*	[+]	1,690*

Figure 9-5. Buyer's Settlement Costs.

and that determines the 2-month tax escrow required at settlement. That constant, in turn, can be added to the sum of other constants applicable to the sale price (0.0026 + 0.0045 = 0.0071) to arrive at one overall applicable constant. Go through this same process—of deriving individual constants and adding them up—to develop an overall constant applicable to the loan amount. (See Figure 9-5.)

3. PRINCIPAL AND INTEREST (P&I) PAYMENTS

You can compute principal and interest payments on an amortized loan on any calculator with the five basic financial keys, which are now found on a wide selection of inexpensive models. (See Figure 9-6.) Here are the keys:

- [*n*] *The number of periods.* For example, if monthly payments are to be made on a 30-year loan, multiply the number of years by 12 (30 × 12 = 360) to arrive at the number of payments. That number is entered.
- [*i*] *Interest rate per period.* If the interest rate is annual (say 11 percent) and the payments are monthly, the annual rate must be divided by 12 (11 ÷ 12 = 0.9167) to arrive at the monthly rate. The rate entered via the [*i*] key must be *per the number of periods* entered via the [*n*] key.

- [PV] *Present value.* In computing periodic loan payments, enter the loan amount with this key.
- [PMT] *Payment.* With the appropriate entries made via the other keys, punching this one solves for the periodic payment.
- [FV] *Future value.* This last of the 5 basic financial keys is not needed in computing payments on an amortized loan. Like the other keys, it can be used either for an entry or, after appropriate entries via the other keys, for a solution. It shows up in routines later in this chapter.

4. PITI

"T&I" is the other portion of the "PITI" payments. Principal, interest, taxes, and insurance are all commonly treated as one monthly obligation to the lender in real estate transactions. The borrower's monthly payments include enough of a T&I amount to fund an escrow account. The lender uses this account, in way of self-protection, to pay annual property taxes and hazard insurance premiums on behalf of the property owner.

Programmable financial calculators can be set up to run the whole PITI computation with a minimum number of keystrokes. With the less elaborate models, you can arrive at PITI by:

1. computing P&I,
2. adding the product of the sale price times the T&I constant.

Example: The monthly P&I payment is $441.88 (Figure 9–6), the tax rate is 0.0154, and the annual hazard insurance premium is $3 per $1,000 of market value (making an insurance constant equal to 0.003). Adding the two constants (0.0154 + 0.003 = 0.0184) results in an annual T&I constant for the jurisdiction in question. That constant divided by 12 (0.0184 ÷ 12 × 0.001533) is the monthly T&I constant. P&I is then added to T&I—obviously—to arrive at PITI. (See Figure 9–7.)

5. BALLOON PAYMENTS

A balloon payment is the disproportionately large payment due at the end of a loan's term when the previous payments are not large enough to reduce the balance to zero at the end of that term. A common example is the interest-only second mortgage, on which the borrower makes only interest

Term	Algebraic		RPN	
	Key	Example	Key	Example
Loan years		30		30
Payments per year	[x]	12	[g] [12x][1]	
Number of periodic payments entered	[=] [n]	360*		360*
Annual interest rate		11		11
Payments per year	[÷]	12	[g] [12÷][2]	
Periodic (monthly) interest rate entered	[=] [i]	0.9167*		0.9167*
Loan amount		46,400		
Monthly principal and interest payment	[PV] [PMT]	441.88*	[PV] [PMT]	−441.88*[3]

[1] The [12x] entry is part of the [n] key and automatically enters the [12x] result in the [n] program memory.
[2] The [12÷] entry is part of the [i] key and automatically enters the [12÷] result in the [i] program memory.
[3] RPN logic employs the "cash flow sign convention," by which all income is presented and entered as positive numbers, and all outflow (e.g., capital outlay, loan payments) as negative numbers.

Figure 9-6. Principal and Interest Payments.

Term	Algebraic		RPN	
	Key	Example	Key	Example
Sale price		58,000		58,000
T&I constant	[x]	0.001533	[ENTER]	−0.001533
T&I	[=]	88.93	[x]	−88.93
P&I (from figure 9−1)	[+]	441.88		−441.88
PITI payments	[=]	530.81	[+]	−530.81

Figure 9-7. PITI Payments.

payments during the life of the loan and then pays the entire principal at the end of the term agreed to in the covering note.

> Example: Half of the $11,600 down payment ($5,800) in the previous routines were to be borrowed in the form of a second mortgage at 12-percent annual interest (that is, 1 percent per month). In this case, the balance would be $5,800 at the end of the 5-year term (or any other term), because only interest payments have been made.

What would the balance be at the end of 5 years if the loan amount and interest rate remained the same, but if the monthly payment were increased

Term	Algebraic		RPN	
	Key	Example	Key	Example
Loan years		5		5
Payments per year	[x]	12	[g] [12x]	
Number of periodic payments entered	[=] [n]	60*		60*
Annual interest rate		12		12
Payments per year	[÷]	12	[g] [12÷]	
Periodic (monthly) interest rate entered	[=] [i]	1.0*		1.0*
Loan amount		5,800		5,800
Monthly P&I payment	[PV]	75	[PV]	−75
Balloon payment at end of five years	[PMT] [FV]	4,411.62*	[PMT] [FV]	−4,411.62

Figure 9-8. Balloon Payments.

to $75 per month in order to reduce the principal by some amount? In the past, that amount might have been found most efficiently by looking up a constant in a table, and then multiplying the loan amount by that constant. Now the following routines are faster and less susceptible to error. (See Figure 9-8.)

6. DEPRECIATION BASIS

The amount to be depreciated in a real estate investment consists of the value of the improvements (the physical realty other than land) and such other investment expenses as settlement costs. Although the market value of land can decrease, it is not depreciable for tax purposes. As a general rule, 80 percent of the value of a detached house may be attributed to

Term	Algebraic		RPN	
	Key	Example	Key	Example
Sale price		58,000		58,000
Percentage of value which is improvements	[x]	0.90	[ENTER]	0.90
Amount of value which is improvements	[=]	52,200*	[%]	52,200*
Other investment costs	[+]	1,690		1,690
Depreciation basis	[=]	53,890*	[+]	53,890*

Figure 9-9. Depreciation Basis.

improvements, 90 percent of the value of a townhouse, and 95 percent of the value of a condominium unit or apartment building. (See Figure 9–9. For a detailed discussion of tax considerations, see Chapters 6 and 8.)

For the purposes of the routines in Figure 9–9, let's assume that we seek to establish the depreciation basis for a $58,000 townhouse and that other investment costs consist of settlement costs of $1,690.

7. DEPRECIATION DEDUCTIONS

Variables in depreciation schedule computations include the depreciation basis, the period of depreciation in years, and the method (straight-line, 125, 150, or 200 percent on a declining balance, or sum-of-the-years-digits). Programmable calculators provide the most efficient means for working out depreciation schedules over a period of years. The following routines illustrate the basic calculations involved. Assume that the $58,000 townhouse in the previous example, with its basis of $53,890, is to be depreciated over a 25-year period at 125 percent on a declining balance. Two years' depreciation are presented in order to show you operation of the declining balance method. (See Figure 9–10.)

8. APPRECIATION

As a rate affecting the value of an economic good, including real property, appreciation works like compound interest. Given a constant appreciation rate over a period of time, the base amount is increased by that rate. Then the amount to which the base is increased is again increased by the same rate—and on the process goes for as many periods as are affected. For example, if $100 appreciates by 10 percent for three years, the figures work out this way:

100 [×]0.10[=]**10**[+]100[=]**110**[×]0.10[=]**11**[+]110[=]**12**[×]0.10[=]**12.1**[+]121[=]**133.1**.

Even such a relatively simple chain calculation is time-consuming and, with each keystroke, increasingly subject to error. In the past, again, tables with constants provided the best alternative. Now the solution to such problems is computed almost instantly with a few keystrokes on the simplest financial calculator. For the following routines, assume that the investor wants to know what the value of the $58,000 townhouse will be at the end of 6 years if it appreciates at 15 percent per year. (See Figure 9–11.)

Term	Algebraic		RPN	
	Key	Example	Key	Example
Basis		53,890		53,890
Depreciation years	[STO] [1] [÷]	25	[STO] [1] [ENTER]	25
Annual depreciation straight-line method	[=]	2,156*	[÷]	2,156*
Basis	[÷][RCL][1]	53,890*	[RCL] [1]	53,890*
Annual straight-line depreciation rate	[=]	0.04*	[÷]	0.04*
Percentage, accelerated method		125		125
Annual accelerated rate, declining balance method	[%]	0.05*[1]	[%]	0.05*[1]
Basis	[x][RCL][1]	53,890	[RCL] [1]	53,890
First-year depreciation deduction	[−]	2,695*	[x]	2,695*
Basis	[RCL] [1]	53,890*	[RCL] [1]	53,890*
First-year depreciation deduction	[−]	2,695	[ENTER]	2,695
First-year adjusted basis	[=]	51,195*	[−]	51,195*
Accelerated rate	[x]	0.05[1]		0.05[1]
Second-year depreciation deduction	[=]	2,560*	[x]	2,560*

[1]In calculators with more than one memory available to the user, this rate can also be stored for recall in each year's depreciation computation. Otherwise, it can be stored at the point of the first-year's computation. Financial keys can also be used for finding the adjusted basis.

Figure 9-10. Depreciation, Declining Balance Method.

Term	Algebraic		RPN	
	Key	Example	Key	Example
Purchase price		58,000		−58,000
Number of compounding periods	[PV]	6	[PV]	6
Interest (appreciation) rate	[n]	15	[n]	15
Appreciated value	[i] [FV]	134,158*	[i] [FV]	134,158*

Note: The sequence of [PV], [n], and [i] entries does not affect the result.

Figure 9-11. Appreciation.

9. INFLATION

Inflation affects value in the same way as appreciation—but in the opposite direction. To take again the example of $100, we can *reduce* it by 10 percent a year for 3 years with a chain calculation: 100[×]0.10[=]**10**[−]100 [$x = y$][=]**90**[×]0.10[=]**9**[−]90[$x = y$][=]**81**[×]0.10[=]**8.1**[−]81[$x = y$][=] 72.9. The financial calculator routine is simply a matter of entering the interest (inflation) rate as a negative factor. (See Figure 9-12.)

Term	Algebraic		RPN	
	Key	Example	Key	Example
Purchase price		58,000		−58,000
Number of compounding periods	[PV]	6	[PV]	6
Interest (inflation) rate	[n]	−15	[n]	−15
Value after effects of inflation	[i] [FV]	21,875*	[i] [FV]	21,875*

Figure 9-12. Inflation.

10. CASH FLOWS FROM INCOME

Five key cash flows from income are ordinarily analyzed for various purposes:

1. Gross income (maximum possible rent): Simply the basic annual rent before any deductions are made for vacancies, operating expenses, debt service, or income taxes.
2. Effective gross income: Annual gross income reduced by an allowance for vacancies.
3. Net operating income (NOI): Effective gross income (if separately computed) reduced by operating expenses, *or* gross income reduced by vacancies and operating expenses.
4. Gross spendable income (net annual cash flow): NOI reduced by loan payments. Dividing by 12, gives you the monthly positive or negative cash flow.
5. Net spendable income (annual after-tax cash flow): Gross spendable income reduced or increased by income tax payments or benefits.

The following routines use inputs from the previous examples for the $58,000 townhouse shown, with the additional assumptions as indicated. (See Figure 9–13.)

11. GROSS INCOME MULTIPLIER

Gross income multipliers are useful on a limited basis. For one thing, you can compare investment property alternatives in terms of their relative potential to produce income on a before-costs basis. Or you can determine

Term	Algebraic		RPN	
	Key	Example	Key	Example
Gross income		4,200		4,200
Vacancy rate (1 month)	[–]	8.33	[ENTER]	8.33
Vacancy cost	[%]	350*	[%]	350*
Effective gross income	[=]	3,850*	[–]	3,850*
Operating expenses	[–]	1,200		1,200
Net operating income	[=]	2,650*	[–]	2,650*
Loan payments (monthly P&I x 12)[1]	[–]	6,203		6,203
Net annual cash flow	[=]	–3,553*	[–]	–3,553*
Income taxes (investor in 40% bracket)	[–]	–3,430[2]		–3,430[2]
Annual after-tax cash flow	[=]	–123*	[–]	–123*

[1] Includes first and second mortgage payments.
[2] The negative figures here indicate *tax benefits* to, rather than tax payments by, the investor.

Figure 9-13. Cash Flows from Income (End of First Year).

whether the price of a given property is "in the ballpark," by checking it with such a multiplier. If an investor is using, say, 13 to multiply against gross income and thereby to estimate the price of a rental townhouse in a particular market, the "negotiating" price is shown in Figure 9-14a. Figure 9-14b shows the actual multiplier for the townhouse in the previous examples, at the $58,000 price. The lower the multiplier the better.

Term	Algebraic		RPN	
	Key	Example	Key	Example
Gross income		4,200		4,200
Gross rent multiplier	[x]	13	[ENTER]	13
Indicated price	[=]	54,600*	[x]	54,600*

(a)

Term	Algebraic		RPN	
	Key	Example	Key	Example
Offering price		58,000		58,000
Gross income	[÷]	4,200	[ENTER]	4,200
Gross rent multiplier	[=]	13.8*	[÷]	13.8*

(b)

Figure 9-14. (a) Income and Gross Rent Multiplier for Price. (b) Price and Income for Gross Rent Multiplier.

Term	Algebraic		RPN	
	Key	Example	Key	Example
Net operating income		2,650		2,650
Market value, end of first year[1]	[÷]	66,700	[ENTER]	66,700
Capitalization rate	[=]	3.97*	[÷]	3.97*

[1]Often computed from beginning of year value.

Figure 9-15. Capitalization Rate.

12. CAPITALIZATION RATE

The capitalization rate—NOI divided by the market value—is a more meaningful tool of analysis than gross income multipliers because it takes into consideration the differences in vacancy rates and operating expenses from one property to the next. Yet the calculator routines are as simple as for the GIM. The roles of division and multiplication are reversed in the two calculations: When initially comparing income properties with each other, keep in mind that the higher the cap rate the better. (See Figure 9-15.)

13. GROSS SALE PROCEED

At the time of sale, the amount remaining to the seller after paying off loans is the "equity reversion." The further deduction of the sales commission and other sales costs from equity results in the before-tax or "gross" sale proceed—the amount with which the seller walks away from the settlement table, so to speak.

On a "Seller's Net Sheet" (Figure 9-16) you add up flat rate items and treat them separately from those that are based on a percentage of the sale price, of the new loan amounts, or of some other factor. Because charges and kinds of charges vary according to the lending institution, the jurisdiction, the money market, and the transaction, developing a set of blanket constants to estimate the settlement costs is far more difficult for the seller than for the buyer.

For the following routines, therefore, the broad assumption is that the sales commission is 6 percent and other costs 2 percent. When you are getting down to a final selection and an offer to buy or sell, you need more detailed estimates, of course. (See Figure 9-17.)

Address: ______________________________________ Sales Price: ______________

____

Other Terms: ______________________________________

	Conventional			FHA Minimum Down or $____	VA Minimum Down or $____	Assumption ☐ FHA/VA ☐ Conventional
	5%	10%	20%			
Legal fees	$100	$100	$100	$100	$100	$100
First trust release fee	50	50	50	50	50	50
Termite inspection	20	20	20	20	20	20
Lender inspection	75	75	75	75	75	—
Subtotal	240	240	240	240	240	165
Realtor fee						
Prepayment penalty				—	—	—
Loan placement points						—
Interest to date of first trust payoff						—
Estimated first trust payoff						—
Estimated second trust payoff						
Other lien payoffs						
Association dues						
Tax stamps: sales price x 0.001						—
Assumption tax stamps: amount over trust x 0.001	—	—	—	—	—	
Estimated total charges						
Sales price or (assumption) amount above trust	$	$	$	$	$	$
Estimated total charges	—	—	—	—	—	—
Seller's net	$	$	$	$	$	$

Figure 9-16. Seller's Net Sheet.

14. TAX AT SALE: DEPRECIATION RECAPTURE

At the end of the holding period, accelerated depreciation deductions taken during that period may be greater than the deductions that would have been taken with the straight-line method. If the accumulation for the accelerated method is greater, and if there is a gain upon disposition, the difference between the two cumulative figures is (subsequent to December 31, 1975) subject to tax as ordinary income as "recaptured depreciation." Computing tax on recaptured depreciation involves running two depreciation schedules and multiplying the results by the investor's tax rate.

In Figure 9-18, three years of depreciation (computed separately from these routines) are presented to show how recapture works, using figures from the previous examples. Because of the numerous keystrokes and the need to project figures over a period of years, programmable calculators are especially useful if taxes on recaptured depreciation are to be computed frequently.

15. TAX AT SALE: CAPITAL GAIN TAX

Total gain is the difference between amount realized and the adjusted basis. The amount realized is the price at sale *minus* the sales commission and other sales costs. The *adjusted basis* is the original purchase price

Term	Algebraic		RPN	
	Key	Example	Key	Example
Sale price		88,200		88,200
Balance, first loan [1]	[STO][1][−]	45,698	[STO] [1] [ENTER]	45,698
	[=]	42,502*	[−]	42,502*
Balance, second loan [1]	[−]	5,068		5,068
Equity reversion [2]	[=][STO][2]	37,434*	[−][STO][2]	37,434*
Sale price	[RCL] [1]	88,200*	[RCL] [1]	88,200*
Constant for disposition costs	[x]	0.08		0.08
Disposition costs [3]	[=]	7,056*	[%]	7,056*
Equity reversion	[RCL][2][−]	37,434*	[RCL] [2]	37,434*
Disposition costs	[X⇌Y]	7,056*	[X⇌Y]	7,056*
Before-tax (gross) sale proceed [4]	[=]	30,378*	[−]	30,378*

[1] Financial calculators have variety of routines for amortizing loans.
[2] No number is placed after the [STO] or [RCL] keys with calculators having only one memory available at a time. In using such a calculator a subsequent number wanted for later recall would have to be punched in at the time it is needed, if the single memory is already in use.
[3] Includes sales commission, legal, recording, and loan-related fees, and other closing costs.
[4] For purposes of settlement, this "gross" (before-tax) figure is often referred to as the "seller's net."

Figure 9-17. Gross Sale Proceed.

Term	Algebraic		RPN	
	Key	Example	Key	Example
Cumulative depreciation 125% declining balance method		2,695		2,695
Cumulative depreciation straight-line method	[−]	2,156	[ENTER]	2,156
Recaptured depreciation (excess over SLM)	[=]	539*	[−]	539*
Tax rate	[x]	0.40		0.40
Tax on recaptured depreciation	[=]	216*	[x]	216*

(a)

Term	Algebraic		RPN	
	Key	Example	Key	Example
Cumulative depreciation 125% declining balance method		5,255		5,255
Cumulative depreciation straight-line method	[−]	4,312	[ENTER]	4,312
Recaptured depreciation	[=]	943*	[−]	943*
Tax rate	[x]	0.40		0.40
Tax on recaptured depreciation	[=]	377*	[x]	377*

(b)

Term	Algebraic		RPN	
	Key	Example	Key	Example
Cumulative depreciation 125% declining balance method		7,687		7,687
Cumulative depreciation straight-line method	[−]	6,468	[ENTER]	6,468
Recaptured depreciation	[=]	1,219*	[−]	1,219*
Tax rate	[x]	0.40		0.40
Tax on recaptured depreciation	[=]	488*	[x]	488*

(c)

Note: For personal property, *all* gain attributable to previous depreciation deductions is subject to recapture tax. For real property, as above, only the excess depreciation over that which would have been allowed under the straight-line method is subject to the tax.

Figure 9-18. (a) Recapture Tax, First Year. (b) Recapture Tax, Second Year. (c) Recapture Tax. Third Year.

(including land) (a) *plus* initial investment costs and additions for capital improvements, (b) *minus* deductions for depreciation and such items as uninsured casualty losses. In the routine in Figure 9–19, the only capital improvement to the townhouse in the previous examples is assumed to be the finishing of a roughed-in bathroom at a cost of $2,000; the only reduction in the original basis other than by depreciation is through an uninsured casualty loss of $200 when the bathroom was being finished.

One part of total gain is recaptured depreciation, if an accelerated depreciation method has been used and the asset is sold before fully depreciated. The other part of total gain is *capital gain,* found by subtracting recaptured depreciation from *total gain.*

In computing tax on the capital gain, under the *Revenue Act of 1978,* the amount of the gain is first reduced by 60 percent (only 50 percent under the previous law). The result is then multiplied by the investor's ordinary tax rate to determine the capital gain tax.

16. NET PRESENT VALUE

A *cash flow* is an amount of money paid, payable, received, or receivable at the beginning or end of a given period. To discount a cash flow is to reduce it by reversing the operation of a compounding (or "interest") rate over a

Term	Algebraic		RPN	
	Key	Example	Key	Example
Purchase price		58,000		58,000
Capital improvements	[+]	2,000	[ENTER]	2,000
Cost	[=]	60,000*	[+]	60,000*
Cumulative depreciation deductions	[−]	7,687		7,687
	[=]	52,313*	[−]	52,313*
Uninsured casualty loss	[−]	200		200
Adjusted basis	[=]	52,113*	[−]	52,113*
Sale price (appreciated at 15% per year)	[STO] [1]	88,200	[STO] [1]	88,200
Constant for disposition costs	[−]	8	[ENTER]	8
Disposition costs	[%]	7,056*	[%]	7,056*
Amount realized	[=]	81,144*	[−]	81,144*
Adjusted basis	[−][RCL][1]	52,113*	[RCL] [1]	52,113*
Total gain	[=]	29,031*	[−]	29,031*
Recaptured depreciation	[−]	1,219		1,219
Capital gain	[=]	27,812*	[−]	27,812*
Percentage of capital gain exempt from tax	[−]	60		60
Amount of capital gain exempt from tax	[%]	16,687*	[%]	16,687*
Taxable capital gain	[=]	11,125*	[−]	11,125*
Investor's tax rate	[x]	0.4		0.4
Capital gain tax	[=]	4,450*	[x]	4,450*

Figure 9-19. Capital Gain Tax, Third-Year Sale.

given number of periods in the future. A *present value constant* is the reciprocal of such a compounding rate. One way to find the present value constant for a specific compounding rate, as well as the number of compounding periods, is to divide the base amount at time zero (that is, now) by the amount to which the base increases through compounding by the applied rate. The routines in Figure 9–20 show the development of such constants for the 15-percent compounding rate for 3 periods (that is, years).

For example, let's say that these constants are used to determine the total value at time zero, which is the net present value, of $300, which is to be received in increments of $100 each year. Let's also say that the value of

Term	Algebraic		RPN	
	Key	Example	Key	Example
Number of compounding periods		1		1
	[n]	1.00*	[n]	1.00*
Compounding rate		15		15
	[i]	15.00*	[i]	15.00*
Present value 0		100		100
	[STO] [1]	100.00*	[CHS] [STO] [1]	−100.00*
Future value 1	[PV] [FV]	115.00*	[PV] [FV]	115.00*
Present value 0	[RCL] [1]	100.00*	[RCL] [1]	−100.00*
Future value 1	[X⇌Y] [÷]	115.00*	[X⇌Y]	115.00*
Present value constant 1	[=]	0.869565*	[÷]	0.869565*
Number of compounding periods		2		2
	[n]	2.00*	[n]	2.00*
Future value 2	[FV]	132.25*	[FV]	132.25*
Present value 0	[RCL] [1]	100.00*	[RCL] [1]	−100.00*
Future value 2	[X⇌Y] [÷]	132.25*	[X⇌Y]	132.25*
Present value constant 2	[=]	0.756144*	[÷]	0.756144*
Number of compounding periods		3		3
	[n]	3.00*	[n]	3.00*
Future value 3	[FV]	152.0875*	[FV]	152.0875*
Present value 0	[RCL] [1]	100.00*	[RCL] [1]	−100.00*
Future value 3	[X⇌Y] [÷]	152.0875*	[X⇌Y]	152.0875*
Present value constant 3	[=]	0.657516*	[÷]	0.657516*

Note: This and the following routine are presented primarily for illustration or for use in checking results in other routines. The present value and future value constants above are built into all financial calculators, most of which also have a built-in net present value program operated via an [NPV] key.

Figure 9-20. Present Value Constants.

Term	Algebraic		RPN	
	Key	Example	Key	Example
Present value 0		100		100
Present value constant 1	[STO] [1] [x]	0.869565	[STO] [1] [ENTER]	0.869565
Present value 1	[=][STO][2]	86.96*	[x][STO][2]	86.96*
Present value 0	[RCL] [1]	100*	[RCL] [1]	100*
Present value constant 2	[x]	0.756144		0.756144
Present value 2	[=][STO][3]	75.61*	[x][STO][3]	75.61*
Present value 0	[RCL] [1]	100*	[RCL] [1]	100*
Present value constant 3	[x]	0.657516		0.657516
Present value 3	[=]	65.75*	[x]	65.75*
Present value 1	[+][RCL][2]	86.96*	[RCL] [2]	86.96*
	[=]	152.71*	[+]	152.71*
Present value 2	[+][RCL][3]	75.61*	[RCL] [3]	75.61*
Net present value	[=]	228.32*	[+]	228.32*

Figure 9-21. Net Present Value.

the $300 is being reduced, or discounted, at a rate of 15 percent per year. The routines in Figure 9-21 may be worked without the use of financial keys or on a calculator not having them.

17. RATE OF RETURN FROM INCOME

The rate of return from income is an analytical criterion that is used to compare properties with each other, in terms of their respective income streams, without considering the final cash flow resulting from the disposition of the investment. The income rate of return is the net present value of the after-tax income stream at a given discount rate, divided by the present value (time zero) of the investment outlay.

In the routines in Figure 9-22, the after tax (or net spendable) income for 3 years are separately computed. The interest and depreciation calculations are carried over from previous examples, and a 15-percent annual rate of increase in net operating income is applied. Annual payments on the first and second loans remain a constant $6,203. The resulting cash flows from net spendable income for years 1, 2 and 3, respectively, are: −$123, $193, and $669. The initial investment outlay consists of the $5,800 down payment plus settlement costs of $1,690 plus $2,000 for capital improvement, a total of $9,490.

In these routines, use of an NPV program is added to the financial calculator's repertoire of functions. This program works in conjunction with built-in constants for various interest rates and compounding periods. If the three cash flows in our example are simply added up (−123 + 193 + 669 = 739), the result is their undiscounted net present value. Dividing that result by the initial investment outlay (739 ÷ 7,490 = 9.87%) provides a rate of return on the investment, from income, for the 3 years covered.

But to derive a more meaningful rate of return, you might want to

Term	Year		
	1	2	3
Cash flow	−123	193	669
x Present value constant	0.869565	0.756144	0.657516
= Present value	−106.96*	145.94*	439.88*
Net present value (cumulative sum of present values)	−106.96*	38.98*	478.86*
÷ Initial investment	9,490	9,490	9,490
= Rate of return from income	−0.0113*	0.0041*	0.5046*

(a)

Term	Algebraic		RPN	
	Key	Example	Key	Example
Discount rate		15		15
	[%i]	15.00*	[i]	15.00*
First cash flow	[1] [X⇌Y]	−123.00		−123.00
Net present value, cash flow 1[1]	[2nd] [NPV]	−106.96*		
Second cash flow	[2] [X⇌Y]	193	[g] [CFj]	193
Net present value, cash flow 1 and 2	[2nd] [NPV]	38.98*		
Third cash flow	[3] [X⇌Y]	699	[g] [CFj]	669
Net present value, cash flow 1, 2, and 3	[2nd] [NPV]	478.86*	[g] [CFj] [f] [NPV]	478.86*
Initial investment	[÷]	9,490		9,490
Rate of return	[=]	0.5046*	[÷]	0.5046*

(b)

[1]The RPN routine does not require solving for intermediate NPVs, although that can be done. Intermediate NPVs can also be checked by a three-stroke routine after NPV for the desired period is found. The routine presented here for the algebraic method of entry is only one of several variations.

Figure 9-22. (a) Rate of Return from Income. (b) Rate of Return.

weigh the effects of inflation on the cash flows. It might also make sense to reduce the cash flows by the interest rate that could be earned on money by depositing it in a passbook savings account. Assuming an inflation rate of 9.5 percent and a passbook savings interest rate of 5.5 percent, the overall discount rate would be 15 percent.

Deriving a rate of return "by hand" to accommodate such assumptions involves developing the PV constants (as demonstrated) or looking them up on a table. You then apply them to each cash flow, add up the results to arrive at net present value, and divide that figure by the initial investment, in a manner shown in Figure 9-22.

Older methods such as the rate of return from income gradually are being replaced by more advanced techniques (for example, the discounted annual rate of return; see discussion and example in Chapter 5), which are possible to do routinely on evermore widely available computer terminals.

18. NET SALE PROCEED

The most comprehensive rate of return on an investment in real estate is one that considers returns not only from income, but also from gain or loss upon sale. Due to the effects of interest and depreciation deductions on real estate investments, the overall rate of return is ordinarily computed on an after-tax basis. In our hypothetical townhouse investment, the third-year before-tax sale proceed is $30,378. The third-year tax on recaptured depreciation is $488, and, finally, the capital gain tax for a third-year sale is $3,878. Given these figures, you can use the procedure in Figure 9-23 to find the net sale proceed, upon which an after-tax rate of return can be computed.

Term	Algebraic		RPN	
	Key	Example	Key	Example
Gross sale proceed		30,378		30,378
Tax on recaptured depreciation	[−]	488	[ENTER]	488
	[=]	29,890*	[−]	29,890*
Capital gain tax	[−]	5,108		5,108
Net sale proceed	[=]	24,782*	[−]	24,782*

Figure 9-23. Net Sale Proceed (Third-Year Sale).

19. INTERNAL RATE OF RETURN

The internal rate of return (IRR) is more and more widely used to measure the return on real estate as well as on other kinds of investments. Mathematically, it is the compounding (or "interest") rate that makes the net present value of the cash flows for all periods equal to the investment outlay. In IRR, the cash flow for the last period consists of both income for the period and the proceed from disposition.

The IRR can be computed on either a before-tax or an after-tax basis. On a before-tax basis, gross spendable income (net annual cash flow) and gross (before-tax) sale proceeds are the input cash flows. On a post-tax basis, net spendable income and net sale proceed are used.

IRR is computed by an "iterative" procedure. First you select an estimated rate, and then you check back to see if the net present value it produces makes the cash flows that it is applied to equal to the investment outlay. If it does not, the difference is noted and another rate is selected and checked back. These steps are continued until the correct rate is found. With two or more trial rates, you can also use a graph to find the correct rate, if you are doing the procedure by hand (for, say, educational purposes).

You can determine the IRR with any financial calculator having the NPV function. However, if the calculator does not have a program to perform the iterative procedure, you have to reenter the cash flows and/or the compounding rate repeatedly until the correct rate is found. Since calculators in the $100 and substantially lower range have programs for the whole iterative procedure, the routines in Figure 9-24 assume the

Term	Algebraic		RPN	
	Key	Example	Key	Example
Initial investment		9,490		−9,490
First cash flow	[STO] [0]	−123	[CHS] [g] [CFo]	−123
Second cash flow	[+/−] [STO] [1]	193	[CHS] [g] [CFj]	193
Third cash flow	[STO] [2]	669	[g] [CFj]	669
Net sale proceed	[+]	26,012	[ENTER]	26,012
Last cash flow entry	[=]	26,681*	+	26,681*
IRR (as a percentage)	[STO] [3] [2nd] [IRR]	41.19*	[g] [CFj] [f] [IRR]	41.19*

Figure 9-24. Internal Rate of Return (Third-Year Sale).

availability of such a program. Keep in mind that the IRR computed for disposition of an investment in a given year reflects an annual (or other periodic) rate of return for the number of years or periods covered.

20. FINANCIAL MANAGEMENT RATE OF RETURN

Although the IRR has become widely accepted as an accurate measure of returns on investment, its use without modification is not completely free of problems or limitations. (They are not, however, nearly as great as those involved in measures that are not based on the IRR.)

The first basic mathematical limitation is with a long string of uneven cash flows, which might, in effect, go up and down cumulatively to zero more than once. This circumstance presents the possibility of there being more than one IRR, which renders the method of dubious value as a tool of analysis.

Secondly, should negative cash flows, other than the capital outlay, be treated separately from that outlay? For instance, the investor who goes into a deal with "nothing down" and manages to have settlement costs covered has an initial capital outlay of zero. You can't even compute a return on such an "investment." As a practical matter, such cash-free investments are ordinarily entered at the cost of increased subsequent negative cash flows. Those cash flows can then be regarded as part of the investment outlay.

Still another question arises about the initial investment outlay. Since the money invested in the property under consideration would be placed elsewhere if not in that investment, shouldn't the alternative return be weighed in?

A fourth concern, for investment projects of any size, is what should be done with positive cash flows, which have to go somewhere when they are generated by the project.

The routines in Figure 9-25 address these basic questions. To avoid the general possibility of more than one IRR, the projected negative cash flows are combined in a net present value routine to constitute the investment outlay. In this case, such cash flows consist only of the initial investment of $9,490 and the first-year negative cash flow of −$123, which would not present the actual possibility of multiple IRRs, of course.

On the assumption that the moneys needed to cover these two negative cash flows are in a passbook savings account earning a "safe rate" of interest at 5.5 percent per year, you account for the loss of that yield by using the rate of 5.5 percent to discount the investment outlay in a net

Term	Algebraic		RPN	
	Key	Example	Key	Example
Discount rate		5.5		5.5
Initial investment	[%i][0][X⇌Y]	9,490	[i]	−9,490
Net present value, initial investment	[2nd] [NPV]	9,490	[CHS] [g] [CFo]	
First cash flow	[I] [X⇌Y]	−123		−123
Net present value, initial investment + first cash flow	[+/−] [2nd] [NPV]	9,606.59	[CHS] [g] [CFj][f][NPV]	−9,606.59
First cash flow (IRR routine)	[STO] [0]	0	[g] [CFo]	0
Second cash flow (IRR routine)	[STO] [1]	193	[g] [CFj]	193
Third cash flow (IRR routine)	[STO] [2]	669	[g] [CFj]	669
Net sale proceed	[+]	26,012	[ENTER]	26,012
Last cash flow entry	[=]	26,681	[+]	26,681
FMRR (as a percentage)	[STO] [3] [2nd] [IRR]	41.04	[g] [CFj] [f] [IRR]	41.04

Figure 9-25. Modified IRR (FMRR).

present value routine before entering the outlay as the initial cash flow. Then you follow the regular IRR routine, entering zero for any period (in this case only the first year) in which a negative cash occurs. The result is one version of the financial management rate of return (FMRR).

In large projects, other versions of the FMRR are used to account for positive cash flows by such mechanisms as placing them in passbook accounts incrementally—at 5.5 percent or at another safe rate—then moving them to time deposits bearing larger interest rates as the required minimum deposit levels are reached. In some routines, all positive cash flows are (dubiously) assumed to be reinvested automatically at the IRR. In others, the analyst selects a separate rate (such as the expected yields from a money market fund) and "folds" it into the IRR or FMRR routine.

INDEX